Luca Rodolfi

Photorealism with Twinmotion
RASTER – PATH TRACER – LUMEN

2023 edition

Legal Note 4

The Author 5

Acknowledgements 6

Introduction 7

What is Twinmotion? 10

   Description 10

The importance of photorealism 15

   The "three engines" of Twinmotion 16

Photorealism with RASTER Engine 24

   Pronounced lack of global illumination and ambient occlusion. 25

   Absence of reflection in glassy and reflective materials 28

   Lack of shadows created by indirect light. 31

   Absence of colored shadows caused by translucent materials like colored glass. 33

   Flat glassy material without light reflections. 34

Photorealism with PATH TRACER 40

   Light and Camera Settings for Photorealism with Path Tracer 45

   How to Create "Water" with the Path Tracer 60

   How to Create Clouds with the Path Tracer 62

Photorealism with LUMEN 64

   Best Practices for Using Lumen in Twinmotion 69

   Light and Camera Settings for Photorealism with Lumen 73

Mastering Urban Environments 85

   Architectural Excellence: Rendering Cities and Buildings 85

   On the Move: Crafting Realistic Cars in Urban Spaces 95

Mastering Archviz: Interior Rendering 100

   The Role of Lighting: Natural vs. Artificial Sources 100

   Material Matters: How to Choose and Apply Textures 107

   Camera Placement: Finding the Best Angles 109

Unlocking the Beauty of Natural Environments 110

   Lush and Alive: Rendering Rocks and Vegetation 111

   The Power of Water: Simulating Oceans and Rivers 121

   Peaks and Valleys: Capturing Mountains 125

Exploring Fantasy Environments 129

   Sci-fi Realms: Crafting Futuristic Landscapes 129

   Stepping Back in Time: Creating Historical and Fantasy Scenes 138

   Enter the Matrix: A Look at Cyberpunk Environments 149

Manipulating Environmental Conditions 154
The Dark Side: Night-time Rendering 154
A New Day: Cloudy Daylight Rendering 157
Sun-Kissed: Rendering in Bright Summer Sunlight 158
Conclusions 160

Legal Note

This project is a private initiative and has no direct affiliation with Epic Games or Twinmotion.

It is fueled solely by passion and a commitment to sharing the outcomes of various experiments. Special thanks go to Adam Gil for sharing ideas, conducting tests, and providing cross-checks.

Copyright 2023 - Luca Rodolfi

All rights reserved. No part of this book may be reproduced, stored or transmitted in any form or by any means, without the prior written consent of the author, except in the case of short quotations incorporated in articles or reviews.
Every effort has been made in the preparation of this book to ensure the accuracy of the information presented. However, the information contained in this book is sold without warranty, express or implied. Neither the author nor his resellers and distributors will be held liable for any damage caused or allegedly caused directly or indirectly by this book, the author has endeavored to provide information on all quotations, references, and assets.

Please forgive my approximate grasp of the language, if you are a native English speaker, you will surely find some sentences weird or just wrong.

The Author

With over 20 years of experience in 3D graphics, I've had the opportunity to contribute to the community in various ways. My website, which offers a range of fantasy and sci-fi models, has been visited by hundreds of thousands of people worldwide, and a significant amount of 3D models have been downloaded. I've also been involved in the beta-testing of Twinmotion, giving me a close look at how the software has evolved. Additionally, I moderate the Twinmotion Facebook group, which has a growing membership of over 70,000 as of mid-2023. Through these activities, I aim to provide valuable insights and resources to both professionals and hobbyists in the field of 3D rendering with Twinmotion.

Some of my renderings made with Twinmotion - https://www.artstation.com/lucarodolfi

Acknowledgements

Writing a book is a collective endeavor, even if one person's name appears on the cover. Though I wish I could delve into the unique contributions of each person who has supported this project, such a detailed account would be exhaustive and perhaps deserving of a book itself. That said, I want to extend my deepest appreciation to some key figures who've made this journey possible.

First and foremost, I owe an enormous debt of gratitude to my family for their unconditional support. A special mention must be made of my wife, Michela, whose patience has been unwavering, even during the long hours spent rendering and writing. Your understanding and encouragement have been the emotional bedrock upon which this work was built.

I am humbled and grateful for each contribution, whether direct or indirect, that has shaped this book. To every person who has played a part in this endeavor: your influence has not gone unnoticed or unappreciated.

Thank you all for being a part of this incredible journey.

Lucas Ammann, Pierr-André Biron, Vincent Boutaud, Roberto De Angelis, Atakan Demirkiran, Anett Mózes Fehér, Adam Gil, James Hannigan, Piotr Ignatowicz, John Klm, Martin Krasemann, Blessing Mukome, Anh Pham, Ken Pimentel, Fabrice Picou, Raphael Pierrat, Rod Recker, Pawel Rymza, Gabriel Sellam, Day Sena, Colin Smith, Joep van der Steen, Tamàs Roth, Sebastien Miglio, Tianxsiao Wang, Janick Valois, Laurent Vidal, Ziggy Ziegler.

If I have inadvertently left anyone out, I sincerely apologize and want to express my gratitude for every contribution, big or small, that has helped make this book possible.

Introduction

3D rendering has long become an enabling factor for many industries, from cinema to video games, from the emerging metaverse to architecture. Whether one accesses 3D rendering platforms for work or as a hobby, today's dedicated hardware technology and increasingly sophisticated software allow for ever-faster and more effective development pipelines. This translates into high productivity when, for whatever reason, one needs to develop images and videos in virtual environments.

Approaching this world can be an exhilarating experience. One can discover their artistic side and give free rein to their imagination, just as a painter creates a canvas from scratch, someone proficient with a 3D rendering platform can create any "world" seemingly without boundaries.

The goal of this book is to guide you in acquiring the skills needed to produce photorealistic images and videos using the various rendering engines that Twinmotion offers. You should already be a user of Twinmotion to fully appreciate my suggestions for achieving perfect photorealism.
While I do provide a brief introduction to Twinmotion, you won't find exercises or tips for creating your scenes, importing objects, or leveraging standard features here. Instead, the focus will specifically be on acquiring the knowledge needed to generate photorealistic images.

If you are approaching Twinmotion for the first time, I recommend practicing using the knowledge available online, both in documentation and tutorials. A good starting point is this (updated to version 2023):

https://www.twinmotion.com/en-US/docs/2023.1

Here you will find all the necessary information and all the steps to go through to learn how to use Twinmotion.
In this volume, you'll find guidance and examples to create realistic images using the various rendering engines that Twinmotion inherits from Unreal 5. I'll use two versions of Twinmotion to show you the path to photorealism, both related to the Windows environment (if you use a Mac, you can still reap great benefits from my book, even if one of the engines I'll describe is not supported by Mac. Thus, there won't be any need to delve into it; you can skip that chapter without any problems).

The versions I've used are:

- Twinmotion 2023.1.2, which is the latest official release, to describe functionalities and photorealism techniques for the RASTER and PATH TRACER rendering engines.
- Twinmotion 2023.2Beta4, which is a build of Twinmotion that also implements the LUMEN engine.

This book will only be released when the Preview or final version is available. If there are significant changes in the final version, you can find any corrections at this address: **www.rodluc.com**.

Note: The Twinmotion GUI is black in color. To make the rendering settings more readable, you will often find images with inverted colors; the original black-magenta will become a unique white-green.

Now, let's get started!

Twinmotion 2023 (Luca Rodolfi)

The image above shows the final result of a project I created with Twinmotion. Later on, it will be explained step by step how to set up a scene, choose objects, set up the light, and the camera that "frames" the environment, and finally how to "take" the final photograph.

But what is 3D rendering, essentially?

3D rendering is the 3D computer graphics process of converting 3D models into 2D images on a computer. 3D renderings can include photorealistic effects or non-photorealistic styles.

Rendering is the final process of creating the actual 2D image or animation from the prepared scene. This can be compared to taking a photo or filming the scene after the setup is finished in real life.
Several different, and often specialized, rendering methods have been developed. These range from the distinctly non-realistic wireframe rendering through polygon-based rendering, to more advanced techniques such as: scanline rendering, ray tracing, or radiosity. Rendering may take from fractions of a second to days for a single image/frame. In general, different methods are better suited for either photorealistic rendering, or real-time rendering[1]

Rendering for interactive media, such as games and simulations, is calculated and displayed in real time, at rates of approximately 20 to 120 frames per second. In real-time rendering, the goal is to show as much information as possible as the eye can process in a fraction of a second (a.k.a. "in one frame": In the case of a 30 frame-per-second animation, a frame encompasses one 30th of a second).

---

[1] Wikipedia

The primary goal is to achieve an as high as possible degree of photorealism at an acceptable minimum rendering speed (usually 24 frames per second, as that is the minimum the human eye needs to see to successfully create the illusion of movement). In fact, exploitations can be applied in the way the eye 'perceives' the world, and as a result, the final image presented is not necessarily that of the real world, but one close enough for the human eye to tolerate.

Rendering software may simulate such visual effects as lens flares, depth of field or motion blur. These are attempts to simulate visual phenomena resulting from the optical characteristics of cameras and of the human eye. These effects can lend an element of realism to a scene, even if the effect is merely a simulated artifact of a camera. This is the basic method employed in games, interactive worlds and VRML.

The rapid increase in computer processing power has allowed a progressively higher degree of realism even for real-time rendering, including techniques such as HDR rendering. Real-time rendering is often polygonal and aided by the computer's GPU.

Animations for non-interactive media, such as feature films and video, can take much more time to render.
Non real-time rendering enables the leveraging of limited processing power in order to obtain higher image quality. Rendering times for individual frames may vary from a few seconds to several days for complex scenes. Rendered frames are stored on a hard disk, then transferred to other media such as motion picture film or optical disk. These frames are then displayed sequentially at high frame rates, typically 24, 25, or 30 frames per second (fps), to achieve the illusion of movement.

When the goal is photo-realism, techniques such as ray tracing, path tracing, photon mapping or radiosity are employed. This is the basic method employed in digital media and artistic works.

Techniques have been developed for the purpose of simulating other naturally occurring effects, such as the interaction of light with various forms of matter.
Examples of such techniques include particle systems (which can simulate rain, smoke, or fire), volumetric sampling (to simulate fog, dust and other spatial atmospheric effects), caustics (to simulate light focusing by uneven light-refracting surfaces, such as the light ripples seen on the bottom of a swimming pool), and subsurface scattering (to simulate light reflecting inside the volumes of solid objects, such as human skin).

The rendering process is computationally expensive, given the complex variety of physical processes being simulated. Computer processing power has increased rapidly over the years, allowing for a progressively higher degree of realistic rendering. Film studios that produce computer-generated animations typically make use of a render farm to generate images in a timely manner. However, falling hardware costs mean that it is entirely possible to create small amounts of 3D animation on a home computer system given the costs involved when using render farms.
The output of the renderer is often used as only one small part of a completed motion-picture scene. Many layers of material may be rendered separately and integrated into the final shot using compositing software.

As you've probably understood by now, Twinmotion (henceforth referred to also as TM) is a software that enables real-time 3D rendering, using three of the rendering engines made available by Epic Unreal Engine (currently at the state-of-the-art Unreal 5.3).

What is Twinmotion?

Description

Twinmotion is a realtime 3D rendering software acquired by Epic Games in 2019. It allows for the creation of images and videos of 3D environments, enabling users to compose scenes with 3D models that are either natively available and usable within Twinmotion (such as trees, cars, common objects, etc.) or by importing them from external sources.

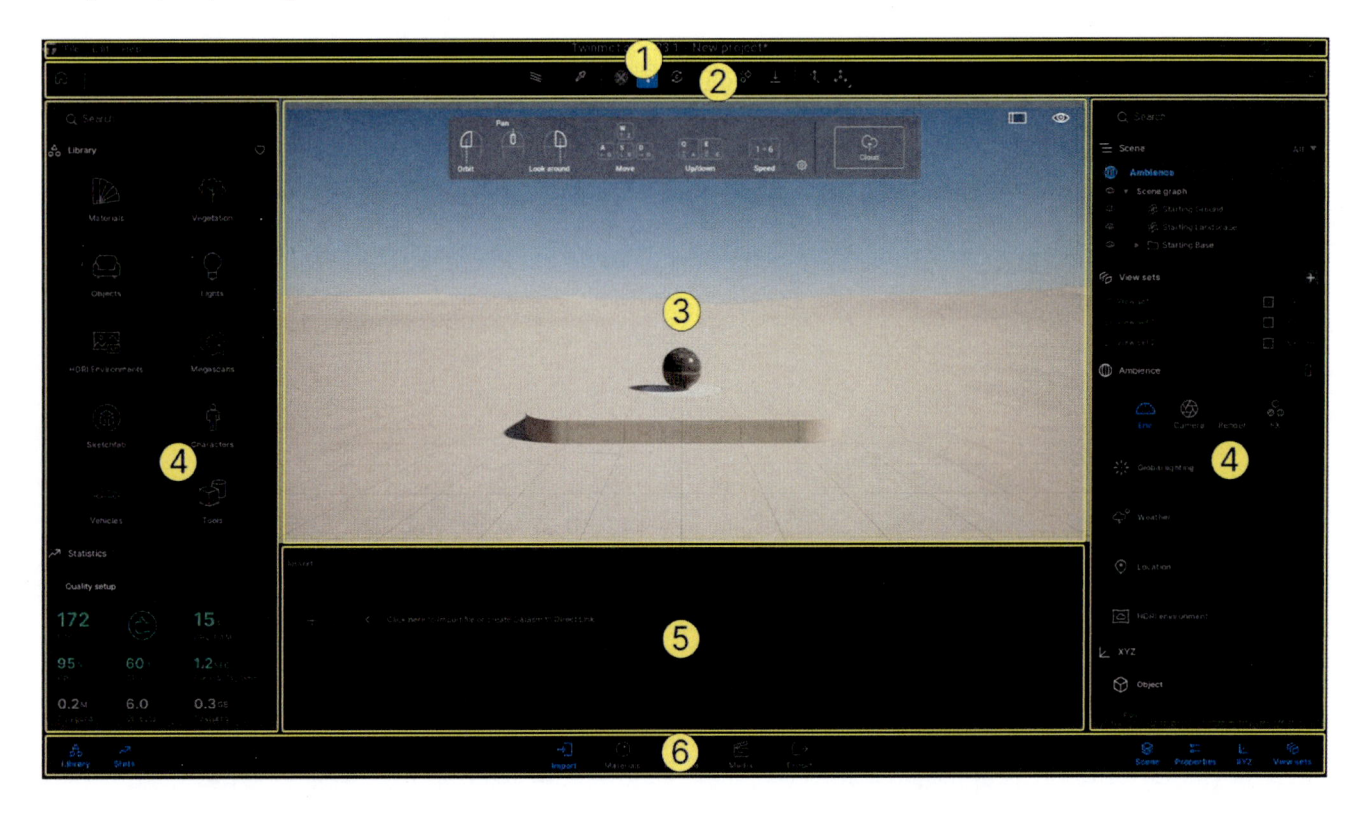

Twinmotion GUI (Official docs)

Even though the purpose of this guide is to provide directions for achieving photorealistic results and assumes you are already familiar with Twinmotion's standard features, in these introductory chapters, I will provide a general description of the interface so that users can navigate Twinmotion more easily.

Please refer to the official Twinmotion documentation for more information and guidance on features.

If you're not familiar with Twinmotion at all, these chapters might offer some insights. However, for a comprehensive overview of how to use Twinmotion, I refer to the numerous free resources available online mentioned earlier.

On the other hand, if you're already comfortable with Twinmotion's interface, you can entirely skip this chapter and jump to the next where we dive deep into achieving photorealism with Twinmotion!

The image above shows the interface of Twinmotion, in which we can identify 6 areas[2]:

1. The Top bar
2. The Header
3. The Viewport
4. The Panels
5. The Docks
6. The Footer

For your convenience, I'm providing you with the description directly from Twinmotion's official documentation. If you want more details, please refer directly to that documentation.

1- Top Bar
Within the upper section lies the Top Bar, which hosts the Menu Bar, showcases the current Twinmotion version and file designation, and offers a pathway to initiate Twinmotion in Full Screen mode. Positioned at the upper-left corner, the Menu Bar encompasses the File, Edit, and Help sections.

Engaging Full Screen mode amplifies the dimensions of the Twinmotion interface, seamlessly enveloping your entire computer display, thus granting you an expanse of creative room.

2- Header
The Header encompasses a shortcut leading to the Home panel, the Toolbar, and a prompt for accessing your Epic Account and Twinmotion Cloud services.

The Home panel icon, positioned in the upper-left corner, offers a swift route back to the Home panel.

Housed within the Toolbar, you have the capability to activate or deactivate the Path Tracer feature, along with gaining entry to a diverse array of tools designed for manipulating assets within the Viewport. Such tools encompass the Material Picker and the Translate Tool. Upon selecting the Open icon, a broader spectrum of the Toolbar is revealed, granting access to tools like Rotate, Scale, Move with Collision (Early Access), Gravity (Early Access), Toggle Local / World Axis, and Pivot Editing.

Upon logging into your Epic Account, a realm of possibilities opens up. This includes downloading and utilizing cloud-based assets from the Library, harnessing the capabilities of Twinmotion Cloud, and joining the Twinmotion Support Community. For an in-depth exploration of Twinmotion Cloud and the Twinmotion Support Community, delve into the sections dedicated to "Twinmotion Cloud" and "Twinmotion Support Community." Directly accessible from the official online documentation.

3 - The Panels
On both sides of the Viewport, you'll find several panels that make up the user interface.

Library Panel: This is where you access a wide range of 3D assets for your scenes, including Twinmotion's own as well as those from Quixel Megascans and Sketchfab. The panel also contains various tools like Section Cubes and Reflection Probes to improve your scene with raster engine.

---

[2] Twinmotion Epic documentation

The Library isn't just for storing assets; it's also a place where you can save your custom and imported items. You can easily share these with other Twinmotion users.
Statistics Panel: This dashboard gives you quick insights into your computer's performance and various aspects of your scene, like frame rate and CPU usage.

Scene Panel: This features the Scene Graph, which shows the structure of all the elements in your scene. It's useful for organizing these elements and making quick adjustments. The Scene Panel also gives you access to the Ambience panel, where you can tweak the atmosphere of your scene.

The XYZ Panel: This is where you can precisely adjust the position, rotation, scale, and size of objects in your scene. It's also useful for adjusting your camera's view.

View Sets Panel: Formerly known as Scene States, this panel allows you to create different versions of a single scene, each with its own settings and assets.

Properties Panel: This panel is a central hub for a variety of settings and features, such as:

- Adjusting materials
- Export settings for images, videos, and panoramas
- Modifying objects, landscapes, lighting, vehicles, and characters
- Replacing assets in your scene
- Accessing asset metadata

The panel layout is straightforward, highlighting essential settings for easy access.

In the Ambience panel, you'll find a range of settings organized under these tabs:

- Env (Environment): This section allows you to fine-tune global illumination, select weather conditions, set geographical coordinates, and add HDRI environments or backgrounds like oceans and rivers.
- Camera: Here, you can control camera settings such as field of view, focal length, and depth of field.
- Render (Renderer): This area lets you choose your rendering mode, be it Real-time Raster, Path Tracer or Lumen. Screen Space Reflections (SSR) can also be enabled here.
- FX (Effects): Use this section to adjust visual aspects like contrast and saturation. You also have options to add gradients, filters, or even apply a clay rendering style.

Navigate through the Ambience panel to make the most out of these settings, each offering specific controls to enhance your project.

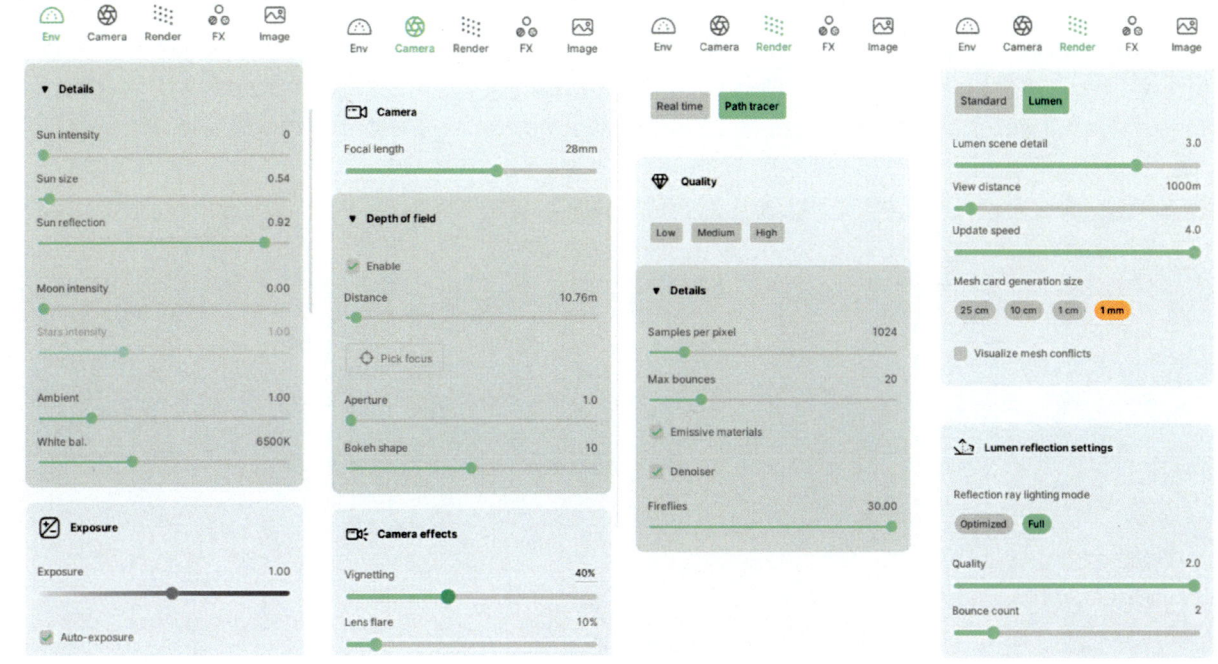

Ambience panel

In the Populate panel, you can find the following three sections:

- In Foliage, you can paint and scatter vegetation.
- In Paths, you can create animated Character, Bicycle, Vehicle, and Custom paths.
- In Urban, you can search for and download areas on a map to add context to your scene.

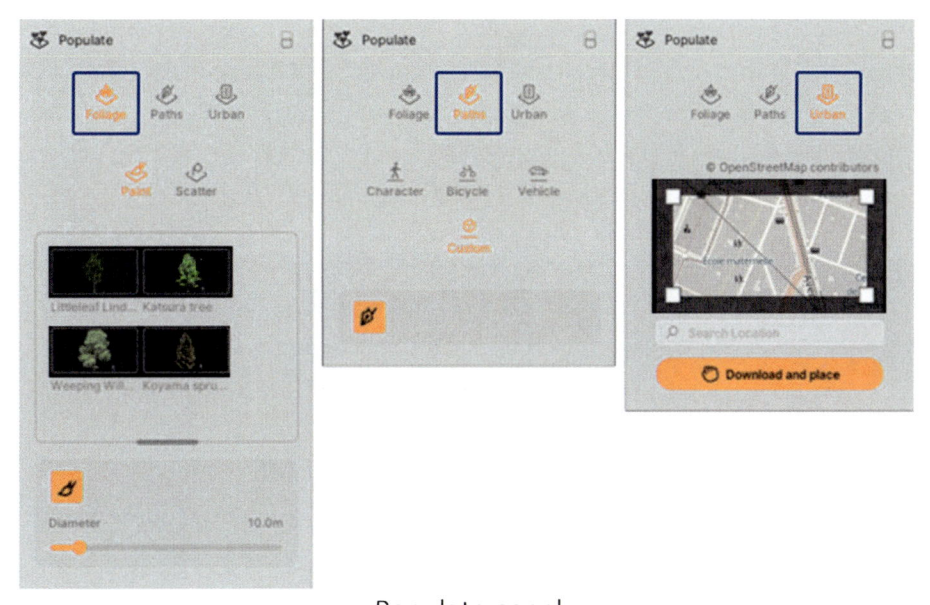

Populate panel

The Export panel is where you export images, videos, panoramas, Panorama Sets, and Presentations either locally on your computer or to Twinmotion Cloud. You can also view and modify the global export parameters for each type of media.

4 – Viewport

The Viewport serves as the canvas for your 3D scenes, appearing as you import or open them. By default, it features components like the Starting Ground, Landscape, and Base. Additionally, you'll find the Navigation panel here, along with links to employ Twinmotion in Presenter mode and access the View menu.

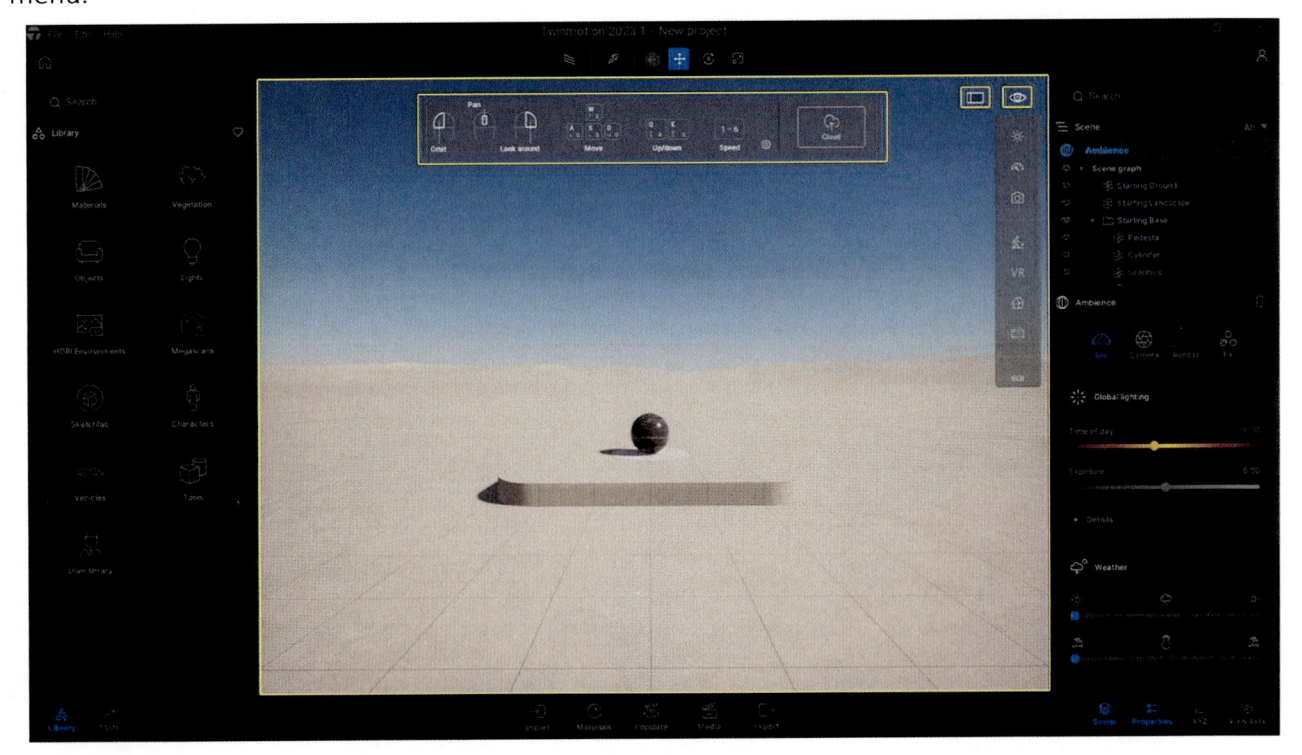

Viewport

5 - The Docks

Below the Viewport, you'll find three main areas: the Import Dock, the Materials Dock, and the Media Dock.

- Import Dock: This is where you can link your Datasmith files and upload 3D geometry, landscapes, and point cloud files.
- Materials Dock: Use this area to create new materials and manage existing ones in your scene.
- Media Dock: This section is your go-to for managing images, videos, panoramas, and presentations.

6 - Footer

The Footer contains the shortcuts to show or hide the panels and docks in the user interface.

The importance of photorealism

In the vast universe of digital visual representation, there's a specific kind of magic that has held our collective imagination captive for decades: photorealism. As the name suggests, photorealistic rendering is the art and science of creating images that are almost indistinguishable from a real photograph or, by extension, reality itself.
Now, one might wonder, with so many rendering styles available, from the deliberately abstract to the cartoonishly exaggerated, why has photorealism gained such prominence? The answer lies in the innate human attraction to realism. We are intrigued by our ability to replicate reality to such an intricate degree, as it serves both an aesthetic and functional purpose.

In fields such as architectural visualization, the impact of photorealism is undeniable. For architects, developers, and stakeholders, a photorealistic rendering can paint a picture of a future building or space in its intended environment. It provides clarity on how sunlight might cascade through a window or how raindrops would bead up on a freshly paved path. Such detailed visualizations can be instrumental in decision-making processes, reassuring investors or even helping designers spot potential design flaws.

Similarly, in the video game industry, the march towards photorealism has been relentless. While many games thrive on stylistic artistry, there's a vast market segment that yearns for hyper-realistic gaming experiences. For these gamers, the thrill is in experiencing virtual worlds that feel as tangible and immersive as our own, blurring the lines between reality and simulation.
Yet, it's not just about creating a 'mirror image' of the real world. Photorealistic rendering offers artists and developers a tool to hyper-focus on details that might otherwise go unnoticed. It can heighten the senses, eliciting emotions and feelings based on the sheer authenticity of the scene.
That said, photorealism, while significant, is just one mode of expression. There are projects where abstraction or stylization might better serve the intended message or purpose. But in instances where the aim is to recreate, represent, or even enhance reality, photorealistic rendering stands as a powerful testament to human creativity and our ever-evolving technological prowess.

In an era marked by rapid technological advancements, our pursuit of photorealism reflects a deeper, intrinsic desire. It's not just about mimicking the world around us, but understanding, appreciating, and at times, reimagining it with a clarity and precision that only photorealism can offer.

The realm of architectural visualization, known commonly as "archviz", has witnessed a surge in technologies and tools that enable professionals to render their visions into lifelike depictions. These tools not only aid architects and designers in refining their creations but also help stakeholders visualize and understand projects in their near-complete glory. Among these powerful tools stands Twinmotion, a solution that has been carving its distinct niche, thanks largely to its foundation on the Unreal Engine platform.
Unreal Engine, primarily renowned for its contributions to the video game industry, brings with it a rich legacy of real-time rendering capabilities, robustness, and scalability. When Twinmotion decided to leverage this platform, it was tapping into a reservoir of cutting-edge visual potential. This collaboration effectively bridged the gap between the gaming world's technological advancements and the nuanced needs of architectural visualization.

While many tools in the archviz space employ varied rendering engines, what makes Twinmotion stand out is its ability to harness multiple rendering technologies. The software's capability to employ raster-based rendering ensures rapid feedback, which is paramount during initial design phases when changes are frequent and iterative. On the other hand, its utilization of the Path Tracer engine elevates the quality of renders, allowing for more realistic light interactions, reflections, and detailed representations.

However, Twinmotion's real game-changer came with its 2023.2 version, which integrated the Lumen real-time global illumination technology. Lumen, hailed by many as the zenith of real-time 3D rendering, has revolutionized how scenes are illuminated, shadows are cast, and reflections are captured. With Lumen, architectural scenes come alive with a dynamic range of light and shadow interplay that was previously unattainable in real-time visualizations.

So, where does Twinmotion fit in the grand tapestry of archviz tools? It is a bridge between the speed and efficiency of real-time game rendering and the precision and detail-oriented needs of architectural visualization. It marries the best of both worlds, making it an indispensable asset for professionals who demand both speed and unmatched visual quality. By building on the strengths of Unreal Engine and continuously integrating advancements like Lumen, Twinmotion asserts its place at the forefront of architectural visualization technologies.

In essence, Twinmotion epitomizes how the future of architectural visualization is not just about static, photorealistic images but dynamic, interactive, and deeply immersive visual experiences.

The "three engines" of Twinmotion

The first question you might be asking yourself is, "Why three engines and not just one?" and I can confirm that it's a valid question.

The presence of three engines has historical reasons, as each additional engine is a result of the evolution of Unreal Engine. In fact, the first available engine (used as a real-time 3D engine in video games) is the Raster engine.

Later on, the Path Tracer was released, which has characteristics entirely different from raster. And finally, in this version of Twinmotion, we have Lumen, an engine similar to Raster but significantly enhanced and packed with features aimed at photorealism.

Each engine has distinct characteristics, and depending on your rendering needs, one might be more suitable than another.

In reality, the Raster engine could be phased out and no longer used because Lumen is its natural evolution. However, it's worthwhile to understand how to create photorealistic images with the Raster engine. This engine has one advantage that the other two don't: it requires fewer computational resources to create renderings. Think of it as a "Plan B" for when the scene you've created in Twinmotion becomes too large and demanding for your computer's specifications, preventing you from using the other two more resource-intensive engines.

Unless you're considering a hardware upgrade in these cases, the Raster engine can address various challenging situations. That's why I'll also dedicate space to the Raster engine.

Speaking of computational resources, let's remember the recommended configurations for both Windows PCs and Macs.

Windows (RASTER + PATH TRACER + LUMEN)

- Operating System:Windows 10 64-bit version 1909 revision .1350 or higher, or versions 2004 and 20H2 revision .789 or higher.
- Processor: Quad-core Intel or AMD 2.5 GHz or faster.
- Memory: 8GB VRAM / 16GB RAM
- Graphic Card: DirectX 11 or 12 compatible graphics card
- RHI Versions: DirectX 11: Latest drivers, DirectX 12: Latest drivers,
- Vulkan: AMD (21.11.3+) and NVIDIA (496.76+)

Mac (RASTER + LUMEN)

- Operating System:Latest Monterey.
- Processor: Quad-core Intel, 2.5 GHz or faster.
- Memory: 8GB VRAM / 32GB RAM
- Video Card: Metal 1.2 Compatible Graphics Card

If you're a Mac user, you might wonder why the Path Tracer is not supported. The answer doesn't lie, as you might assume, in Twinmotion and Epic Games' willingness to release a Path Tracer version for Mac. The reason Mac users can't use the Path Tracer in Unreal Engine is that Apple does not yet support hardware-accelerated ray-tracing, and thus, the Path Tracer doesn't support it either.

I want to highlight that to fully leverage Twinmotion and all three engines on a Windows environment for reasonably complex scenes, you'll need a fairly modern PC. I will teach you some tricks to best handle situations that risk creating scenes too large to be rendered effectively.

All the images you'll see in this book have been rendered by me using a relatively old PC (which only had one upgrade with a recent graphics card). The specifications of my PC are:

- Windows 10 64-bit
- Processore Intel(R) Core(TM) i7-4790K CPU @ 4.00GHz
- Memory 32 GB
- Graphic card : RTX3070 8G VRAM

Since this book isn't a thriller and aims to be a practical guide without unnecessary embellishments, I'll reveal right away when it makes sense to use one rendering engine over the others. Later in the book, I will demonstrate for each engine how to transform your renderings into photorealistic images, describing the limitations and capabilities of the different engines. In a dedicated section, I'll show you some tricks to enhance photorealism that apply across all the engines.

- **RASTER**: As I mentioned earlier, you'll resort to using Raster when you can't use Lumen, typically due to limitations of your workstation. There's no other reason you might prefer Raster over the other two engines.
- **PATH TRACER**: For any static image rendering, nothing can beat the photorealistic capabilities of the Path Tracer. You'll see later why this engine is so extraordinary. However, you'll quickly discover its shortcomings when transitioning from static images to creating videos.
- **LUMEN**: For any video content, Lumen is the definitive solution. The quality of rendering is in some aspects comparable to the Path Tracer, but its rendering speed is remarkably faster. Hence, it's always preferable over the Path Tracer when creating animations and videos.

In the upcoming images, I'll show you, for the same scene, how the three engines generate the render. For each rendering, I'll highlight some typical "issues" associated with the engines.

In these static images, as previously mentioned, the Path Tracer outperforms in quality and capability compared to the other two engines. The images are not optimized for photorealism; they are three versions of the same scene without specific enhancement efforts. Later on, you'll see how to address some of the issues I point out.

RASTER ENGINE

1 - Pronounced lack of global illumination and ambient occlusion.

2 - Absence of reflection in glassy and reflective materials (such as mirrors).

3 - Lack of shadows created by indirect light.

4 - Absence of colored shadows caused by translucent materials like colored glass.

5 - Flat glassy material without light reflections.

PATH TRACER ENGINE

1 – Lack of caustics; light passes through colored glass but does not generate reflective caustics.

LUMEN ENGINE

1 - Lack of colored shadows; translucent materials like colored glass are not rendered in a physically accurate manner.

2 - Reflection quality is superior compared to Raster, but it reveals some artifacts.

Now I suggest you the same test but with an image of an outdoor environment. Please note that these are renderings made by setting up the scene and generating the render with the three different engines. They are not scenes optimized for the best photorealism. Later on, we'll revisit these scenes to see which parameters and tricks to use to improve them (especially Raster and Lumen).

RASTER ENGINE

1 - Pronounced lack of global illumination and ambient occlusion.

2 - Absence of reflection in glassy and reflective materials (such as mirrors).

3 - Lack of shadows created by indirect light.

4 - flat image with no depth

5 - Flat glassy material without light reflections.

PATH TRACER ENGINE

1 – The image in terms of colour and contrast lacks those features that could make it look like a real photograph

LUMEN ENGINE

1 - Glass does not seem to be there and does not show any reflectivity at all

These first two comparisons immediately highlight how Path Tracer can best achieve photorealism right from the start. Once the light is set correctly, the Path Tracer quickly generates quality renderings. Lumen produces excellent results, though, as you will see later, its configuration is a bit more complicated. Raster remains (as I have written several times) the least convincing, but even with this engine, more than acceptable results can be achieved if one manages to configure the theme of reflections and light most convincingly. Some small tricks will help us improve the areas where the raster engine shows several limitations.

Before delving into the secrets of Twinmotion's photorealism, I offer you a brief insight into the three engines. It's useful to know how they work because it helps us better understand how they might behave according to our instructions.

We will see in detail how, with the three engines, it is possible to manage and make photorealistic:

- Urban environments (cities, buildings, cars)
- Natural environments (vegetation, oceans, mountains)
- Fantasy environments (sci-fi, historical, cyberpunk)

In different environmental conditions (using both Twinmotion's native sky and Skydomes based on HDRI):

- At night
- During the day
- With rain and snow
- With a beautiful summer sun.

Numerous examples will lead you to the perfect recipe for photorealism, as I walk you through concrete examples, I'll also take the opportunity to include observations and best practices that can help you optimize your workflow. This way, you can better understand the concepts and directly apply them to enhance your 3D rendering skills.

Some information on the raster engine

Within the vast realm of game development, the Unreal Engine has been a beacon for many creators. A fundamental component of this powerful tool is its raster engine. At its core, rasterization is the process of converting geometric representations of objects into a format suitable for rendering on a screen, pixel by pixel. In the Unreal Engine, this process has been refined and optimized to deliver breathtaking visuals in real-time.

The principles upon which Unreal's raster engine is based draw from the foundational concepts of computer graphics. Every scene is broken down into geometric shapes which are then mapped onto a grid of pixels – the raster. Each pixel is colored based on textures, lighting, and other effects, giving us the final image that the player sees.

Lighting and shadows are critical aspects of realism in games, and the Unreal Engine handles them with a sophisticated approach. The raster engine computes how light interacts with different objects, determining the brightness and color of each pixel. Shadows are produced by analyzing the relationship between light sources and objects, ensuring that occluded areas are darkened appropriately. This is particularly challenging in real-time scenarios, but Unreal's engine employs several techniques to speed up this process.

Reflections, too, play a pivotal role in immersion. The raster engine calculates reflections by assessing the angle of incoming light and determining how it bounces off surfaces. It's a complex process that involves both the properties of the light and the attributes of the material.

Speaking of materials, Unreal Engine's raster engine boasts an advanced material system. Each material is defined by its characteristics – such as its roughness, reflectivity, and texture. These properties determine how light interacts with the surface, whether it's the shiny gloss of a car or the matte finish of a stone wall.

There are undeniable advantages to using Unreal's raster engine. It's fast, efficient, and capable of producing high-quality visuals with less computational overhead compared to ray tracing methods. However, like all technology, it has its limitations. The inherent challenge with rasterization is that it doesn't always handle global illumination or complex light interactions as accurately as ray tracing.

In today's evolving landscape, some consider Unreal's raster engine to be surpassed by other engines that prioritize ray tracing for its superior realism. But why is it still in use? Legacy, optimization, and ease of use make it a preferred choice for many developers. While newer technologies emerge, Unreal's raster engine remains a testament to the balance between performance and visual quality, making it a valuable tool in the game developer's arsenal.

Path Tracer: The Pursuit of Photorealism

In the intricate dance of light and shadow, path tracing stands out as a method that captures the mesmerizing play of illumination with near-photorealistic accuracy. Unlike the quicker but less precise rasterization technique, path tracing seeks to simulate the way light travels and interacts with objects, delivering visuals that can often be indistinguishable from reality.

Path tracing, at its heart, is a type of ray tracing. It involves casting rays from the camera (or viewer's perspective) into a scene. Instead of terminating these rays upon their first contact with an object, as done in some simpler ray tracing techniques, path tracing allows these rays to bounce multiple times, simulating the scattering of light. This recursive nature mimics how light photons travel in the real world, bouncing off surfaces until they lose energy or are absorbed.

The method in which path tracing handles illumination is both its strength and its computational challenge. Every time a ray strikes a surface, it can spawn multiple secondary rays in random directions, accounting for reflections, refractions, and diffuse scattering. By averaging the results of numerous rays per pixel, path tracing creates an image rich in detail and free of the noise often associated with simpler ray-casting techniques.

The technique's treatment of materials is remarkable. As rays interact with different surfaces, they consider the physical properties of materials, such as their albedo, refractive index, and surface roughness. This ensures that a polished marble floor will reflect light distinctly from a soft velvet curtain.

But with great detail comes great computational demand. Path tracing's main challenge is its intensive resource requirements. Each ray's journey and subsequent bounces demand calculations, and for a single frame, millions of rays might be cast. This can lead to longer render times, making it more suitable for offline rendering like in movies, rather than real-time scenarios such as video games.
However, advancements in hardware and optimized algorithms are narrowing this gap, making real-time path tracing a foreseeable reality. While some contemporary graphics engines lean towards hybrid approaches, integrating both rasterization and ray tracing techniques, the allure of path tracing's fidelity remains compelling for those chasing the ultimate in visual realism.

Lumen: Lighting the Way in Unreal Engine

In the endless quest for heightened realism and immediacy in computer graphics, Lumen emerges in Unreal Engine as a beacon of innovation. It stands not just as a lighting technology, but as a testament to the continuous evolution in the world of game development and visualization.

Lumen is a fully dynamic global illumination solution that immediately reacts to scene and light changes, providing the ability to craft more dynamic and reactive worlds. Historically, achieving global illumination in real-time was a substantial challenge. The computational demands of calculating how light interacts with every object in a scene, and how that light then affects other objects, were immense.

What sets Lumen apart is its adaptability and its ability to scale. Instead of relying solely on ray tracing, which, while precise, can be computationally expensive, Lumen utilizes a combination of techniques. It harnesses the power of both traditional screen space techniques and traces rays in a more limited capacity, balancing between performance and visual accuracy.

The way Lumen handles different scenes is noteworthy. Be it vast landscapes with changing sunlight or intricate interiors with multiple light sources, Lumen adapts, offering nuanced shadows, reflections, and illuminations. It's especially adept at handling indirect lighting – the soft glow you might see on a wall opposite a brightly lit window, or the subtle reflections in a room filled with shiny objects.

In terms of materials, Lumen shines (pun intended). Its integration within Unreal Engine means it works seamlessly with the engine's established material system. Whether depicting the rough surface of a brick wall or the gleaming exterior of a car, Lumen ensures that materials respond to light in a realistic manner.

However, as with any technology, Lumen is not without its challenges. While it bridges the gap between the need for speed and visual fidelity, it's not always the go-to for all scenarios. Extremely detailed scenes with countless light interactions might still push its limits.

Yet, Lumen's arrival signals a shift in real-time rendering capabilities. As graphics hardware continues to advance, solutions like Lumen pave the way for developers to craft experiences that blur the line between the virtual and the real, without having to wrestle with lengthy bake times or rigid lighting setups.

Delving into Lumen's Implementation for Twinmotion, Lumen stands as a real-time global illumination and reflection tool within Twinmotion, reshaping how scenes in the software are illuminated.

At the heart of Lumen's magic is its precise simulation of how light behaves with objects and materials. This interaction gives your scenes a depth and realism that previously required advanced techniques and heavy computing.
Twinmotion's real-time rendering Lumen takes it a step further with ray tracing, simulating indirect lighting with stunning accuracy. This includes diffuse interreflections, where light bounces from non-reflective surfaces to illuminate surrounding objects, taking on their color hues.

Specular reflections, on the other hand, arise when light beams bounce off shiny surfaces, akin to what you'd see with a mirror. Lumen's technical prowess extends beyond this. It gathers material properties from meshes at different angles to create a 'Surface Cache'. This cache is a treasure trove of direct and indirect lighting information that Lumen taps into during rendering. The cards within this cache are prepared offline for each mesh, streamlining the rendering process.
A cornerstone of Lumen's capability is ray tracing. While software ray tracing is versatile across various hardware, hardware ray tracing, which Twinmotion currently supports only on Windows, offers more extensive capabilities but demands robust system specs.

Lumen doesn't just stop at revolutionizing global illumination. It brings vibrancy to ambient lighting, even in intricate scenarios where indoor spaces are in stark contrast to outdoor brightness. Its prowess extends to simulating global illumination for translucent materials and height fog, albeit at a slightly diminished quality.

Emissive materials, when used with Lumen, can radiate and bounce both specular and diffused light, lighting up surrounding objects. But caution is advised: using excessively bright and small emissive objects can introduce noise. For optimal results, Twinmotion's native light sources should be leveraged.

Reflections get a significant boost with Lumen, offering dynamic interplay across a spectrum of roughness values in materials. The software ensures skylight shadows are in place, allows glossy reflections on translucency, and supports multiple specular reflections, creating scenes that are vividly lifelike.

But like every technology in its evolution, Lumen has its constraints. It currently doesn't support Dynamic Meshes like Cycloramas and LED walls, nor scattered and painted vegetation for light bounces. While it can function in Virtual Reality mode, it isn't optimized due to the high demands of VR. There are also limitations with how reflections are handled, especially when objects are outside the viewport or when working with translucent materials.
To harness the full power of Lumen and to stay updated on its advancements, always refer to the official documentation provided by the Twinmotion team.

Later in the book, I'll delve deeper into the limitations of Lumen in Twinmotion and discuss strategies to navigate or bypass some of these constraints.

Photorealism with RASTER Engine

Let's begin our journey with the most complex engine for creating photorealistic renderings, the engine that requires the most configurations and tricks to achieve acceptable results, the engine that perhaps you may never use, but that could "save your life" when you find yourself managing a scene that has become too large for the other two engines.

The Raster engine is equipped with a range of parameters tailored to shape the rendering's visual outcome. By fine-tuning these settings, one can significantly enhance the overall rendering quality.

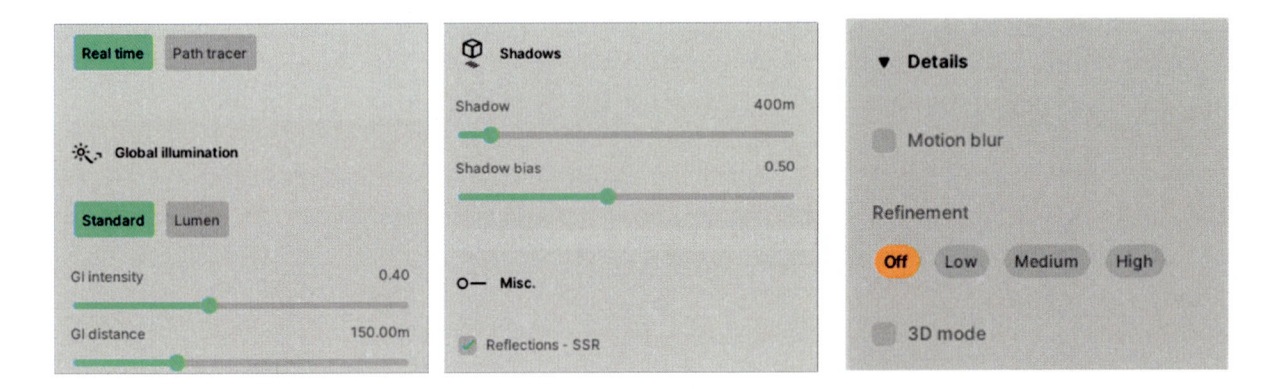

Raster engine settings and export Raster Refinement

Gi intensity: this setting sets the intensity of global illumination.

GI distance: this setting controls the distance from the camera within which global illumination is applied. For example, if the value is set to 400 meters, global illumination is applied only to the first 400 meters from the camera

Shadow: Sets the distance from the camera up to which shadows on objects are cast; for example, if the value is set to 500 meters, shadows on objects are cast for 500 meters only beginning at the camera; smaller values provide a shorter range for cast shadows, but produce shadows that are more detailed (higher-resolution). Inversely, higher values provide a longer range, but result in less detailed shadows.

Shadow bias: increasing this value reduces self-shadowing artifacts on object, but can also reduce the quality of the shadow

Reflection – SSR: add local reflection to opaque reflective surface, local surface are created using items in the scene that are visible in the scene.

The "Export Definite Refinement" option allows you to increase the reflection area beyond the visible field of the viewport, thereby improving the quality of the rendering.

Let's start with the first example I showed you earlier and see how we can best address the significant photorealism issues.

RASTER ENGINE

1 - Pronounced lack of global illumination and ambient occlusion.

2 - Absence of reflection in glassy and reflective materials (such as mirrors).

3 - Lack of shadows created by indirect light.

4 - Absence of colored shadows caused by translucent materials like colored glass.

5 - Flat glassy material without light reflections.

Pronounced lack of global illumination and ambient occlusion.

You should be familiar with what global illumination and ambient occlusion are, but in case you aren't, I provide a brief description here, so there's no doubt about what is meant when discussing these two topics that are crucial in the realm of photorealism.

Global Illumination (GI):
Within the realm of rendering, particularly in tools like Twinmotion and Unreal Engine, Global Illumination stands as a cornerstone technique. At its core, Global Illumination refers to the simulation of how light interacts not just with a singular surface, but how it reflects, refracts, and diffuses across multiple surfaces within a scene. Unlike direct lighting, which illuminates objects based solely on a direct light source, GI calculates the indirect light that bounces between surfaces, ensuring a more realistic and holistic lighting model. This attention to indirect light is crucial for achieving the depth and vibrancy that mirrors the complexities of real-world lighting.

Ambient Occlusion (AO):
Another pivotal concept in the world of rendering in tools like Twinmotion and Unreal Engine is Ambient Occlusion. AO provides a method to simulate the soft shadows that occur in the nooks, corners, and crevices of objects, where ambient light is less likely to reach. It's not so much about the direct play of light but about the absence of it. By darkening areas where two surfaces meet, or where there are folds and recesses, Ambient Occlusion adds a layer of depth and realism, emphasizing spatial relationships within a scene. While it's a subtle effect, its contribution to the perception of realism and depth in a render is significant.

Remember, while both Global Illumination and Ambient Occlusion contribute immensely to the realism of a scene, the nuances of their application and fine-tuning can vary based on the specific rendering engine being used. In the context of Twinmotion and Unreal, both techniques are harnessed and optimized for architectural visualization and beyond.

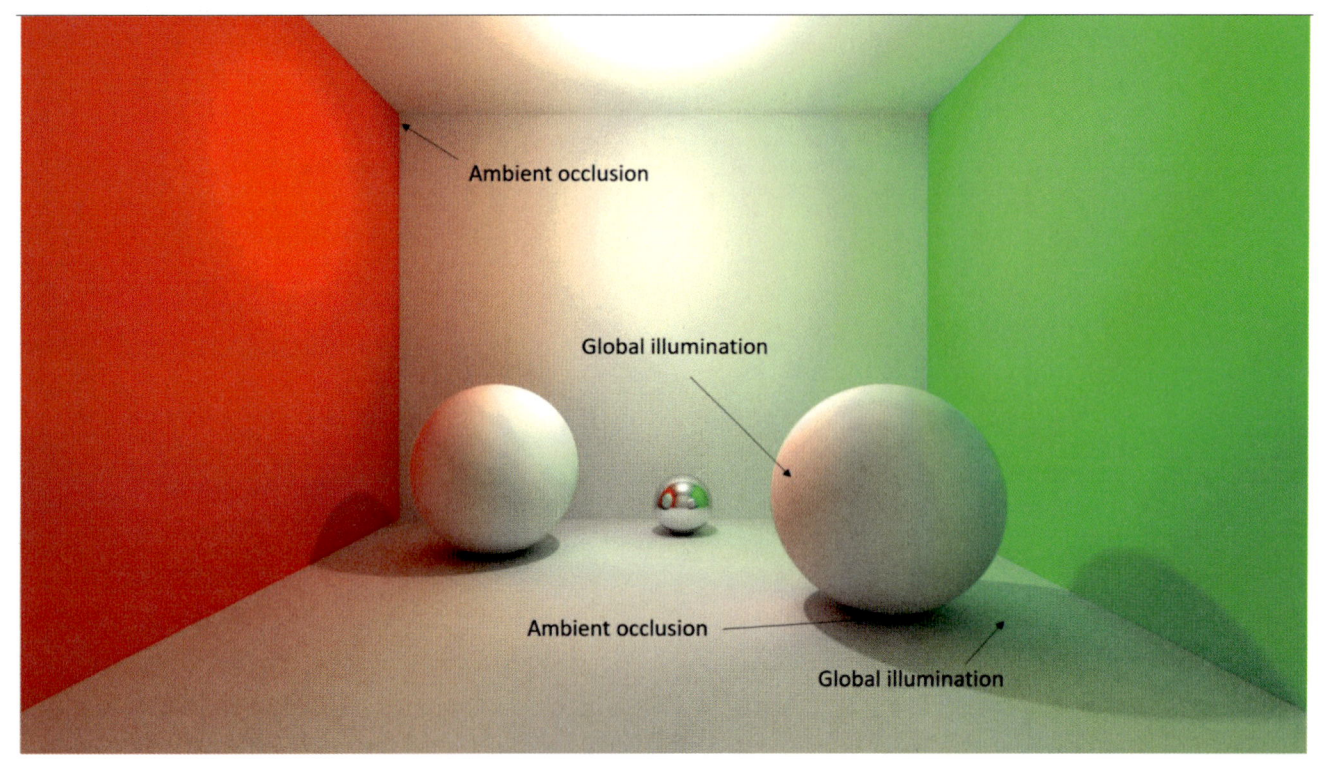

Image from web

The possibilities to improve these parameters in the raster engine are really few and often relate to the careful use of light and intensity. If you look at the previous images, you'll notice that with the same parameters, the rendering done with the raster engine has much less contrast and the light coming in from the window is less "strong" compared to the renderings made with Path Tracer and Lumen. A starting point for intervention is precisely to act on brightness, contrast, exposure, and saturation of the image.

So, we work on the contrast and exposure to have a more vivid light from the window. You can adjust the parameters and see the results of your actions in real-time.

Original raw Raster engine

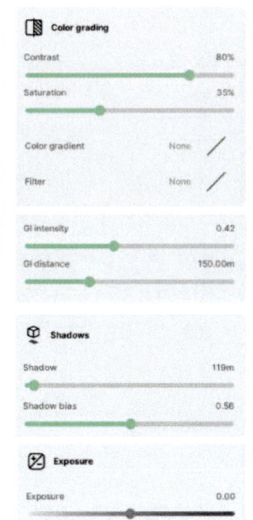

Working on light Raster engine

As you can see, with just a few parameters, the Raster engine improves the light rendering, though it doesn't fully address the issue of global illumination. If you have the capability to use an external tool like Photoshop, Twinmotion offers an intriguing rendering feature that allows, with some composition work, to further enhance the global illumination and ambient occlusion aspects with the raster engine. This process is relatively straightforward for static images, but it becomes more complex if you want to create videos.

Let's see what can be done: in the Twinmotion effects tab (FX), you can select the Clay render:

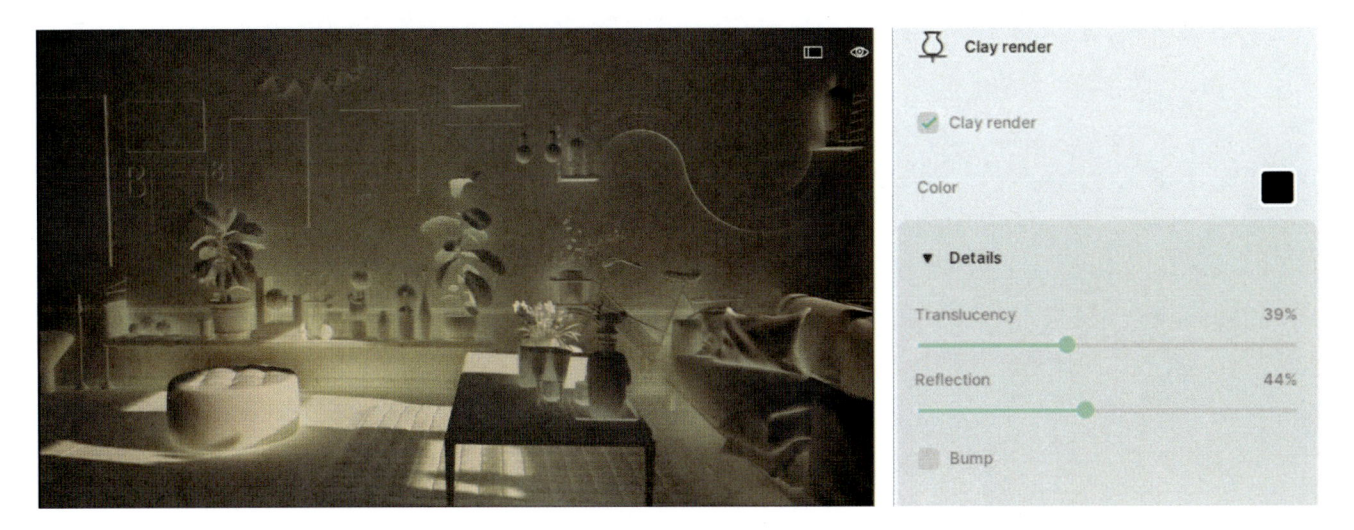

The rendered image can be used to enhance the performance of the Raster engine in terms of ambient occlusion and global illumination.

It's enough to create two renderings: one in Raster with the appropriate parameters (as shown above) and a monochromatic Clay rendering. Then, open both images in a graphic software (I use an older version of Photoshop) and blend them together using opacity functions.

90-95% of the composition will be based on the color rendering, while 5-10% will be derived from the Clay rendering. This method will provide more depth to the shadows and create a better global illumination effect.

See the quality of the result for yourself!
The wall with the paintings and the mirror, which previously appeared so flat and lacking in depth, now displays much greater depth in the various details. To achieve this result in Photoshop, I used two layers and blended the two images, setting the clay render layer to 83% in "Overlay" mode.

Absence of reflection in glassy and reflective materials

Reflections with the Raster engine will give you numerous headaches, simply because this type of engine is not capable of "reflecting" objects in the scene the way ray tracing-based engines do.

The Raster engine, primarily designed for real-time rendering, grapples with several challenges when tasked with depicting reflections accurately.

Approximations Over Accuracy: The Raster engine tends to prioritize speed over physical accuracy. It often employs approximations and shortcuts in its rendering processes. This approach, while beneficial for rendering speed, can compromise the detail and accuracy of reflections.

Static Environment Maps: To handle reflections, the Raster engine frequently uses pre-computed environment maps. These static maps provide a snapshot of the scene from a particular point. However, their static nature means they can't adjust to real-time changes or dynamic objects within a scene, leading to reflections that might not represent the current state of the environment.

Probe Limitations: Reflection probes, or "probes," act as localized tools for capturing the environment and generating reflection data for the Raster engine. While they offer an enhancement in reflection quality, they come with their own set of challenges. Their placement needs to be strategic, and even then, they might not capture every nuance or dynamic change in a scene.

Inherent Limitations with Ray Handling: The fundamental methodology of the Raster engine does not involve tracing rays through the scene as they bounce between surfaces. Without this ability to trace rays, achieving realistic, detailed reflections becomes inherently challenging. Objects like mirrors or highly reflective surfaces can reveal these limitations, as the Raster engine might not be able to depict their reflections with true-to-life accuracy.

Tutti questi punti rendono complicato gestire le riflessioni con il motore raster.
Tuttavia esiste uno strumento che può mitigare questo limite e creare approssimazioni di riflessioni (fai attenzione che la riflessione piana tipo specchio è sempre problematica e spesso impone compromessi)

Lo strumento è il probe di riflessione:

Sphere Reflection Probes and Box Reflection Probes are both tools used in rendering engines to help approximate reflections in real-time graphics. They capture the surrounding environment to generate reflection maps, which objects in the scene can then use to reflect the environment. Here's a breakdown of the differences and when you might opt for one over the other:

Sphere Reflection Probe:

- Shape and Capture: As the name implies, it captures the environment in a spherical manner around its center point.
- Use Cases: It's best suited for open spaces or larger areas where reflections don't need strict adherence to room boundaries, such as outdoor settings or rounded interiors.
- Reflection Behavior: Objects reflect the environment as if it's being seen from the center of the sphere. This means it's crucial to place the probe's center where reflections will look most accurate.

Box Reflection Probe:

- Shape and Capture: This probe captures reflections within a defined cubic volume. It respects the boundaries of the cube, which means it can better account for the shape and confines of a room or enclosed space.
- Use Cases: It's ideal for interiors or spaces with more defined edges and boundaries, such as rooms with flat walls or hallways. The cube shape allows it to provide more accurate reflections in such environments.

- Reflection Behavior: Within the defined cube volume, reflections are more localized, ensuring that walls and other boundaries are considered, leading to more accurate reflections within that space.

When to use each:

- Use a Sphere Reflection Probe when dealing with open spaces or rounded interiors where the reflection doesn't need to adhere closely to strict boundaries.
- Opt for a Box Reflection Probe in enclosed spaces with defined edges, such as building interiors or corridors, where reflections should respect room boundaries.

In our image, we will use a Box Reflection Probe (simply dragging it into the scene will activate it).

A series of parameters will allow you to position and size the Box Reflection Probe in the best way for the image's needs. Always remember that this type of reflection is just an approximation.

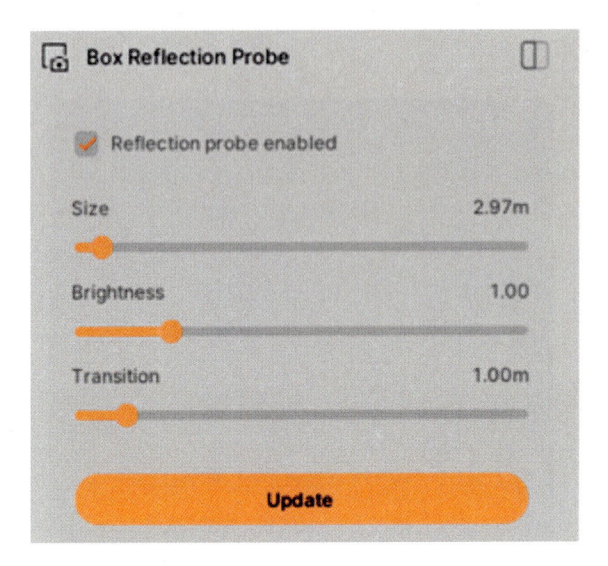

At this point, we can carry out the rendering with the fixed reflection, repeat the Clay, and regenerate the composition with the overlay set to 83%.

Lack of shadows created by indirect light.

Shadows created by indirect light and various phenomena related to global illumination are practically "impossible" to create in Twinmotion with the Raster engine. Fortunately, you can use decals to simulate parts that have an indirect shadow.

Let's see in our image the substantial difference between having this type of shadow and not having it, as is the case with the Raster engine.

Raster engine — Flat image, no indirect shadow

Path Tracer — Indirect shadow

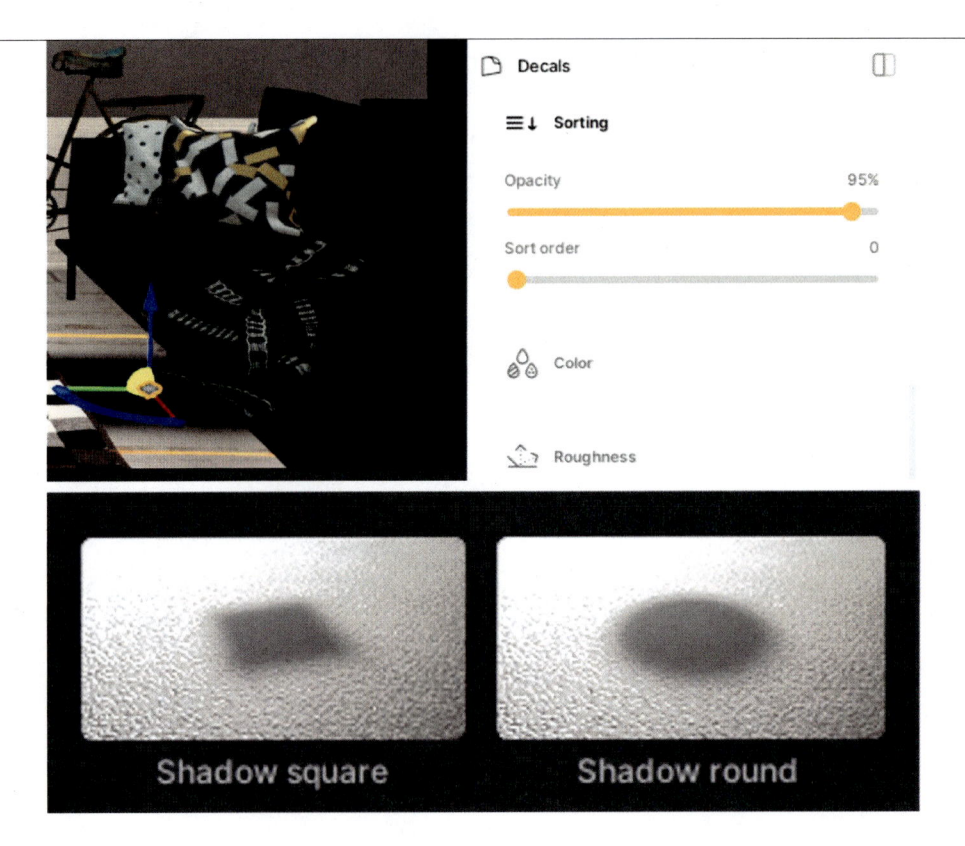

We use a Shadow Square decal and drag it into the scene, positioning it under the sofa. We will need to resize it appropriately, reduce its opacity, until we obtain an image that shows a faded shadow under the sofa, just like in the rendering done with the Path Tracer.

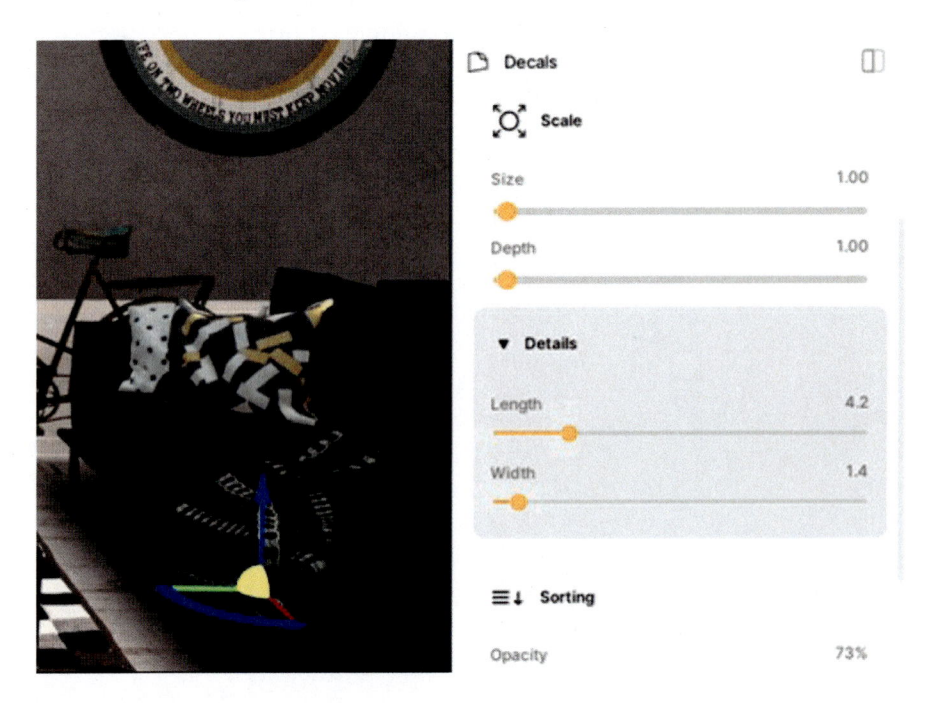

By adjusting the opacity, you can achieve a convincing result.

Now, let's repeat the operation with the clay render and further improve the rendering.

Absence of colored shadows caused by translucent materials like colored glass.

This is probably the most challenging point to correct; even Lumen cannot handle translucent materials, and only the Path Tracer engine (which, as we have seen, has a completely different nature) can create convincing colored shadows.

The only possible way to simulate something similar is to skillfully use some additional lighting. Naturally, you have to be very careful because a light isn't easily manageable and can cause problems in other parts of the rendering.

Very weak colored lights can enhance the rendered scene, but remember well that it must be worth it: ask yourself if it's essential in your rendering to have a colored shadow or not. If it isn't, move on, below is how the Path Tracer manages to render the colored shadow of the glass.

Create two lights of the glass color with the shadow turned off and position them accurately in the direction of the sunlight near the base of the glass object (in our case, the vase of flowers). Modify the parameters to make the lights long and narrow as in the image below:

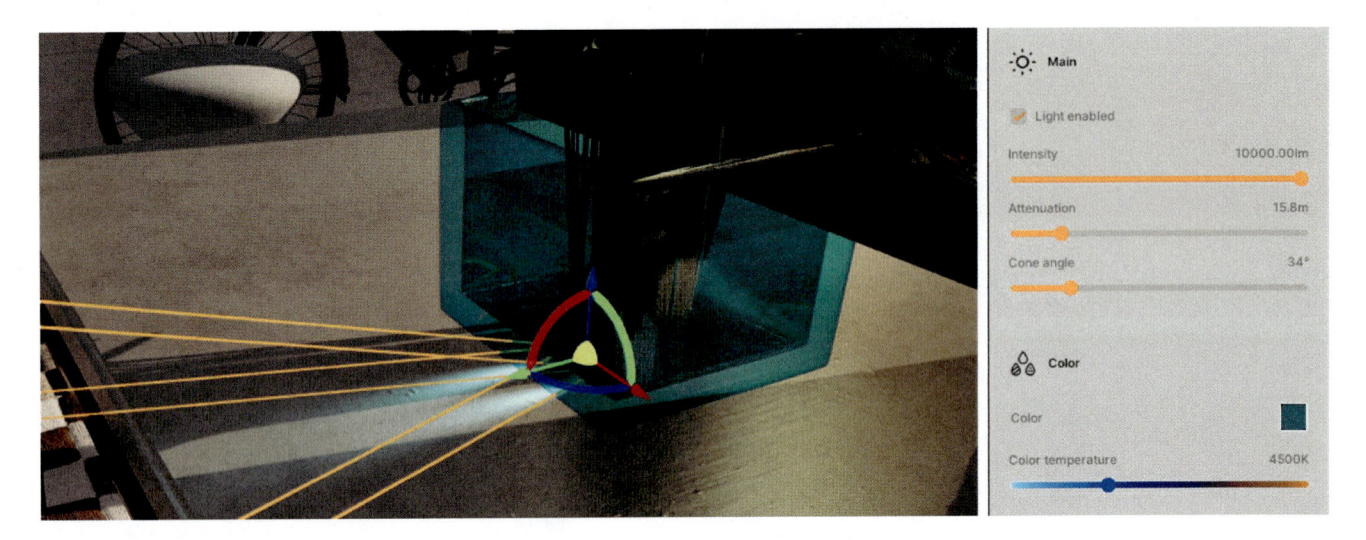

The rendering will create a fake colored shadow due to the positioning of the lights.
Here's the result after merging with the Clay rendering:

Flat glassy material without light reflections.

The final major challenge is adjusting the appearance of the glass. Here, I've learned that the only true option is to use a glassy material that has a refractive index, because all others will undeniably appear "inconsistent", with an unnatural transparency and devoid of any reflection.
The quintessential material to use is "item glass."

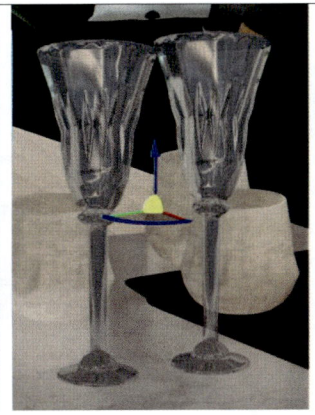

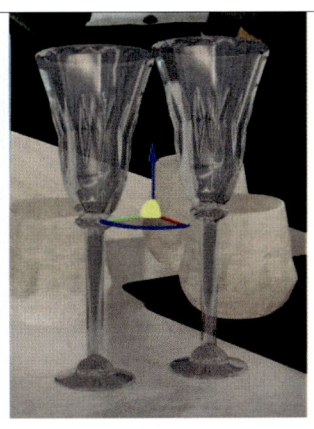

Above are various types of glass, the first one on the left is the 'item glass'. In the Raster engine (in my opinion), it's the glassy material that best represents the characteristics of transparency, refraction, and reflection of the glass. I recommend using this material in most cases, especially if dealing with glasses or bottles.

After also adjusting the glass, we can redo the rendering and with the overlay of the Clay rendering, we get the final image. Below, you can notice the difference in photorealism between the very first version and the last one after all the applied fixes.

The difference between the version rendered with Lumen is also reduced, and the quality of the raster seems to come very close to Lumen. Obviously, the work that needs to be done is no small feat.

Before tackling the second example, take the time you need to experiment with Twinmotion using the techniques I just described. It won't always be easy to transform a "flat" Raster rendering without photorealism into something more convincing. Practice and tests are needed, only in this way will you find the right balance in Twinmotion to push it to its maximum potential.

The second example is distinctly different; it's an outdoor scene on a rainy day, with a strong DOF (Depth of Field) from the camera that blurs out non-relevant objects for the scene. The careful use of DOF can create extremely photorealistic images.

RASTER ENGINE

1 - Pronounced lack of global illumination and ambient occlusion.

2 - Absence of reflection in glassy and reflective materials (such as mirrors).

3 - Lack of shadows created by indirect light.

4 - flat image with no depth

5 - Flat glassy material without light reflections.

What immediately stands out, as in the previous example, is how the Raster engine essentially produces flat images by default. This takes us back to retracing the steps from the previous example. However, this time, to make the outcome more straightforward and to show you how to act, I'll use more images and fewer words.

Let's start by fixing points 1 and 3 using decals as in the previous example and placing a shadow square under the white car in front, adjusting the parameters to ensure the shadow is convincing.

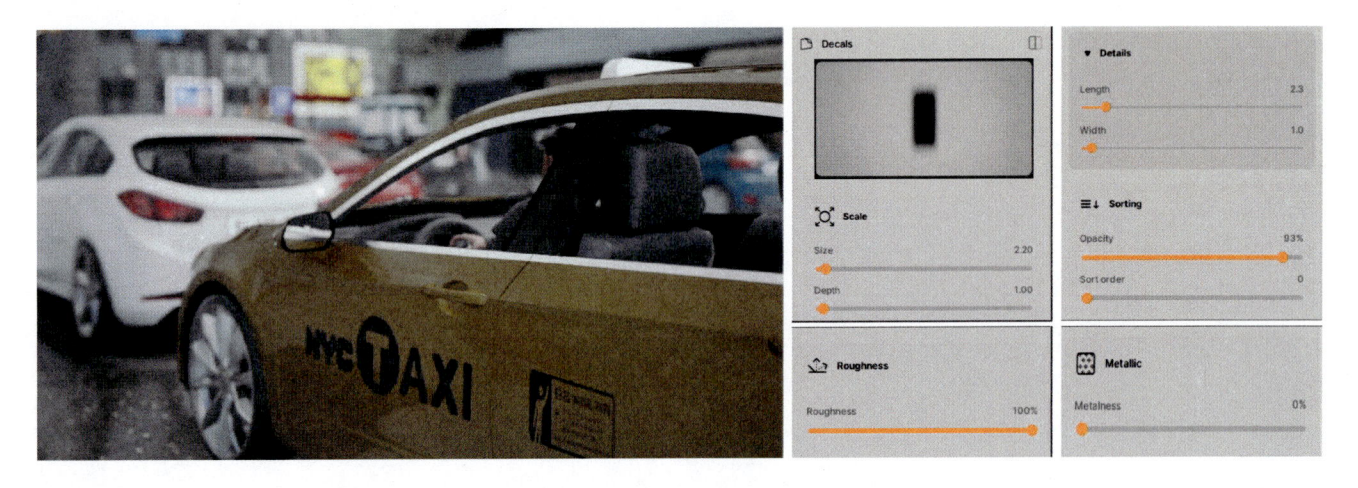

Now, you can address point 2, which makes all the difference between having a photorealistic image and not. As it involves reflection, you now clearly understand that a reflection probe is needed. In this case, the box reflection probe is the most appropriate because it allows for an approximate reflection of the environment, and we can expect to see the car reflected as clearly evident in the renders made with Path Tracer and Lumen.

If you drag the box reflection probe trying to achieve a good reflection for both the taxi and the white car in front, you'll notice that you'll be forced to significantly enlarge the box reflection probe. This will cause a distortion in the reflection, making it oversized and unrealistic. Lastly, to address point 4, it's essential to work on contrast, saturation, and exposure to achieve more convincing lighting, even in the blurred parts of the image.

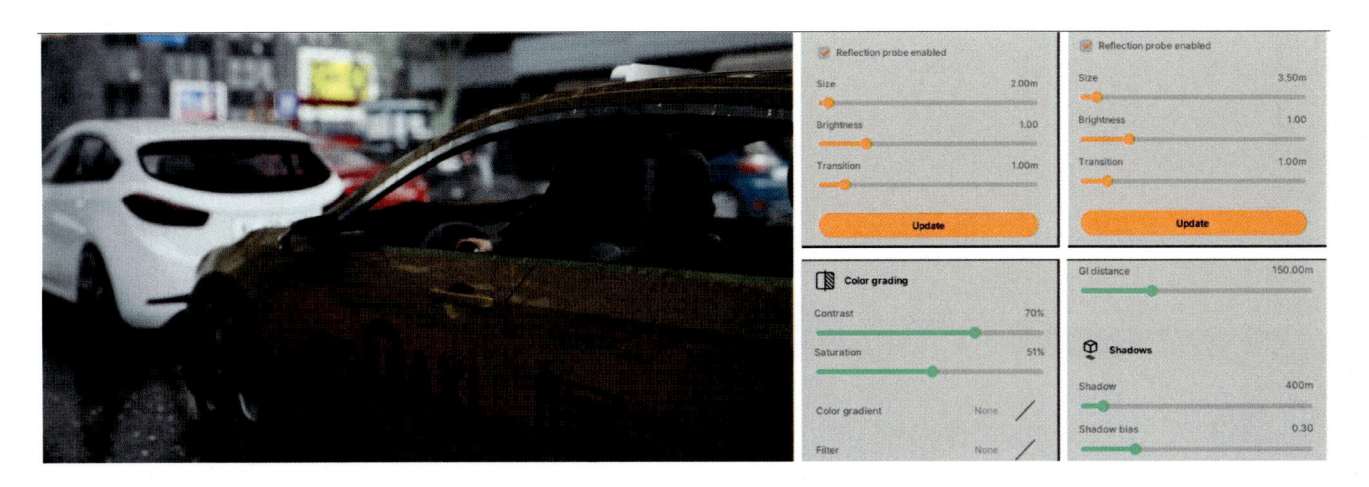

And point 5? Well, actually, given the light and the angle of the camera, it's correct that there's no reflection even after activating the reflection probe. In fact, it's enough to change the angle to see the reflection on the glass.

At this point, for a final test, we can do a clay render and use the Overlay option to see the final result to further improve photorealism.

For ambient light and the camera, these parameters were used:

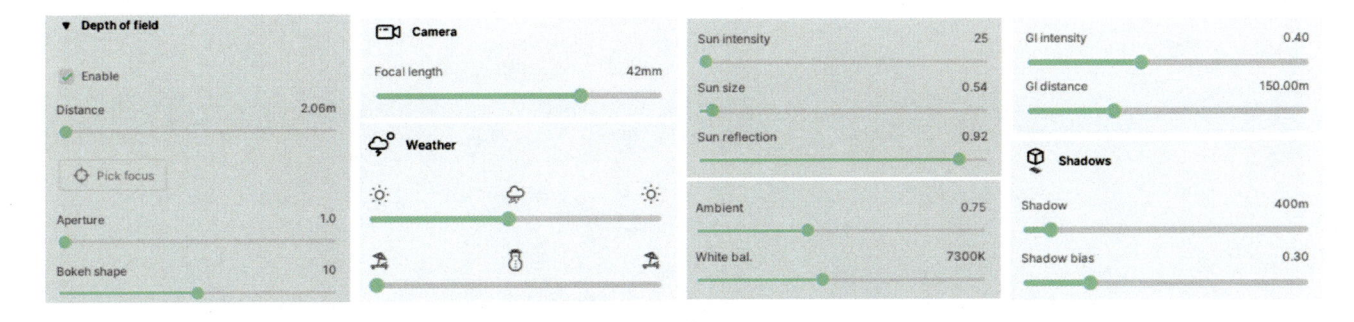

Always keep in mind that Twinmotion also has post-production features with the possibility to apply filters to images. Some of these allow defining particular moods with photorealistic results, similar to analog and digital photography. Below, I provide a couple of examples.

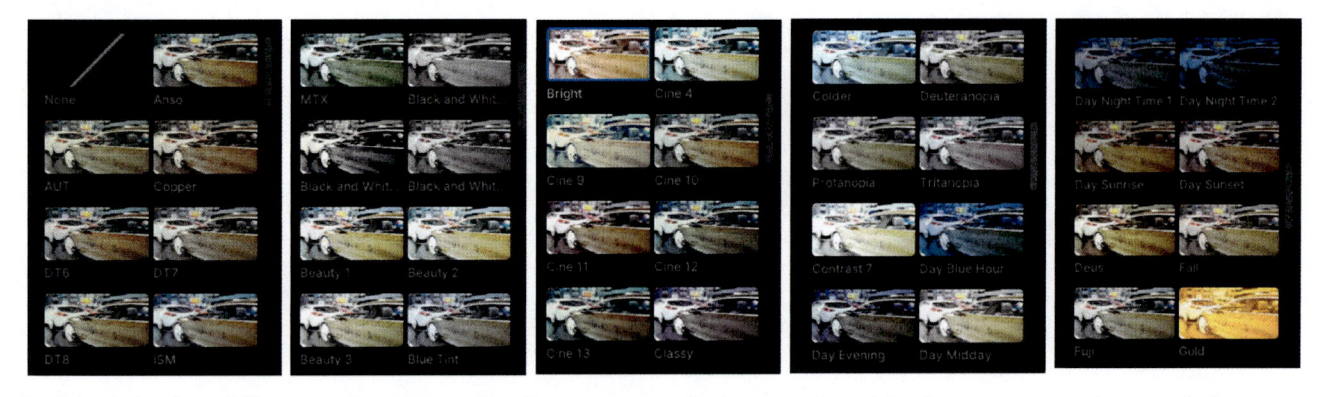

And here's the difference between the first raw rendering made with the raster engine and the one obtained by applying my guidelines.

Now let's move on to analyze how Path Tracer and Lumen can be optimized to generate photorealistic images. Later, we will revisit specific topics related to different types of assets and environments to render.

Photorealism with PATH TRACER

You will discover that working with the Path Tracer is often quite straightforward. A basic setup with good ambient lighting can yield captivating results simply by activating the Path Tracer, without the need for intricate configurations.

The Path Tracer has a distinct set of parameters compared to the Raster Engine for defining rendering quality. It's crucial for you to understand these settings to achieve the highest quality renders. Unlike real-time engines, the Path Tracer allows you to configure rendering quality at the expense of longer image generation times. Keep in mind that rendering a complex scene at high quality could take several minutes, in contrast to the few seconds needed by the Raster Engine and Lumen.

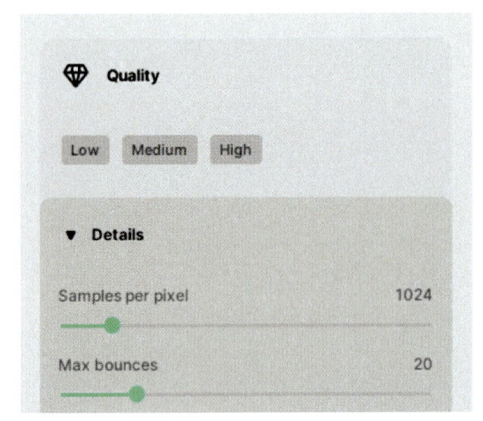

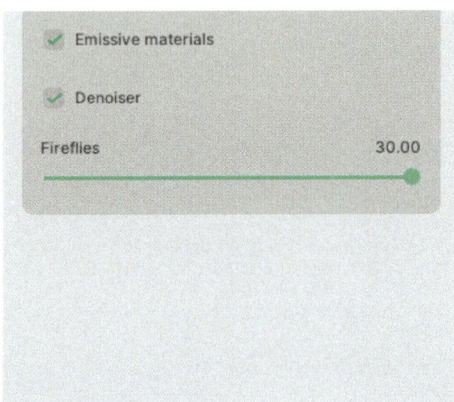

Path Tracer settings

The Path Tracer offers three default settings: Low, Medium, and High. These are convenient for quick test renders to swiftly evaluate the expected output. However, for your final render, you'll need to manually adjust the parameters, as even the High setting may not provide impeccable quality.

Samples per pixel: number of samples per pixel to use, higher values decrease image noise from rendered media, but increase rendering time. Generally, a value of 1024 ensures high-quality rendering.

Max bounces: maximum number of light bounces, higher values increase rendering time. Depending on the presence of transparencies and reflections (e.g., mirrors and glass), the value can be increased from 10 (for simple reflections) to 20 or 30 (for complex reflections between multiple reflective objects). In the next image, you'll see how the reflection bouncing between two mirrors becomes more accurate as the number of bounces increases. Note that the scene's color also changes dramatically, as the bounces directly affect the ambient light.

6 bounces   8 bounces   30 bounces

Emissive materials: add bounce lighting to emissive material, This parameter allows for enhanced brightness benefits, especially when using emissive materials.

Denoiser: remove image noise after the rendering

Fireflies: control the visibility and exposure of fireflies artifact.

In Twinmotion the Path Tracer is unique for its capability to manage translucent materials, like casting colored shadows. However, it has limitations affecting the use of some native Twinmotion materials. For example, the 'water' material doesn't display transparency or caustics as you'd expect. This makes it tricky to create scenes with water using the Path Tracer. But there are workarounds, which I'll discuss in this chapter.

If you recall, at the beginning of the book, I pointed out that while the Path Tracer is optimal for still images, it isn't the best choice for animations, especially when compared to Lumen. Here are the primary reasons why it might not be advisable to use the Path Tracer for crafting animations in Twinmotion:

- **Rendering Time for Each Frame**: The Path Tracer isn't a real-time 3D rendering engine. Instead, it's an "off-line" engine that leverages the GPU's capability for high-quality rendering. This means that a frame, which the raster engine or Lumen might produce in mere seconds, could take minutes with the Path Tracer. Consequently, an animation that takes minutes to render with the raster engine or Lumen could require hours with the Path Tracer.
- **Artifacts and Background Noise**: The Path Tracer introduces artifacts and noise into animations. This stems from various reasons:

  - Frame Independence: In most rendering engines that utilize path tracing, each frame is computed independently from the others. This means that even if two frames depict moments very close in time within an animated sequence, the engine does not account for the information from the previous frame when computing the next.
  - Stochastic Noise: Path tracing is a stochastic technique, meaning it relies on random sampling to simulate light behavior. In each frame, rays are sampled slightly differently. This can lead to visible differences (often manifested as noise) between consecutive frames.
  - Flickering: Due to the stochastic nature of path tracing and the absence of temporal coherence, a phenomenon known as "flickering" can occur. This manifests as rapid variations in light intensity or color from one frame to the next.

Creating animations with the Path Tracer not only demands a significant amount of time (often spanning hours or even days), but in most cases, it also necessitates the use of "denoising" algorithms to eliminate flickering. While many of these algorithms are found in paid software, Twinmotion does offer its own denoising solution. However, as of current advancements, it's not particularly effective compared to the state of the art.

The Path Tracer is the engine that requires the least amount of adjustments overall. To enhance photorealism, your main focus will mostly be on light settings, unless you're using materials or assets known to have limitations with the Path Tracer.

The main limitations of Twinmotion's Path Tracer are:

- Inability to correctly handle the "water" material, resulting in a lack of transparency and caustics.

- The native sky of Twinmotion isn't rendered in Path Tracer, so you can't have clouds in your sky if you're using Path Tracer.
- Vegetation swayed by the wind will be static in an animation made with the Path Tracer.
- Rain and snow particles aren't rendered with Path Tracer.

These are the primary limitations; if you need these features in your scene, you'll have to use certain approaches and tricks that I'll unveil later on.

Let's start with the previous examples used for the Raster engine, and you'll see that there are very few limitations of the Path Tracer in terms of photorealism and physical accuracy

PATH TRACER ENGINE

1 – Lack of caustics; light passes through colored glass but does not generate reflective caustics.

If you look at the image above, it's hard to find any weak points in terms of photorealism. Ambient occlusion and global illumination work flawlessly, reflections are physically accurate, and colored translucent materials transmit color (as in the case of the blue vase). Images like these usually require a setup of the ambient light and the camera to achieve convincing results.

When you think of classic offline rendering engines like Vray and Corona render, one thing that might challenge the Path Tracer are the "usual" glassy materials: reflection, refraction, transparency, etc. These are attributes that can be a challenge for the Path Tracer. In particular, a physical phenomenon like refractive caustics is not handled by the Path Tracer. In fact, the Unreal Engine 5 environment allows for the calculation of caustics, but this requires enormous computational power. This specific configuration, however, is not available in Twinmotion. Below is an image that shows the difference between having and not having caustics (credit: hoc3dmax.com)

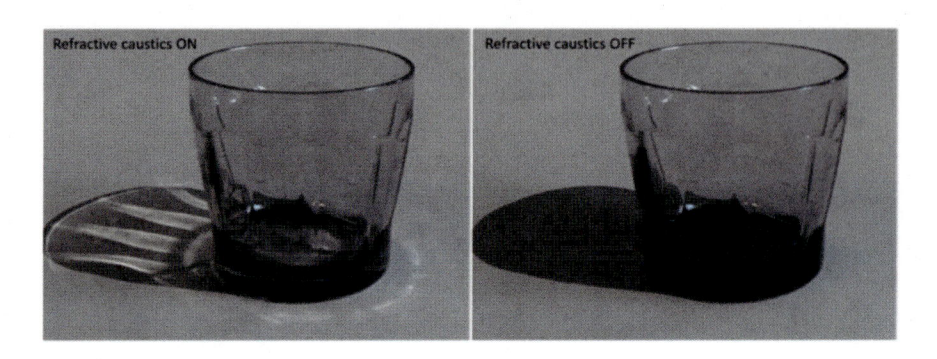

This effect cannot be natively produced by Twinmotion's Path Tracer. If you need your scene to display something of the sort, then follow my instructions.

Set up a scene by importing a glass model. Inside this, you can insert another model that simulates water or another beverage, and perhaps some ice cubes. In the example I'm showing you, I used a glass downloaded from the Sketchfab library. Remember, the entire library, which consists of thousands of models, is natively linked to Twinmotion, allowing you to search for and download assets simply by conducting a search:

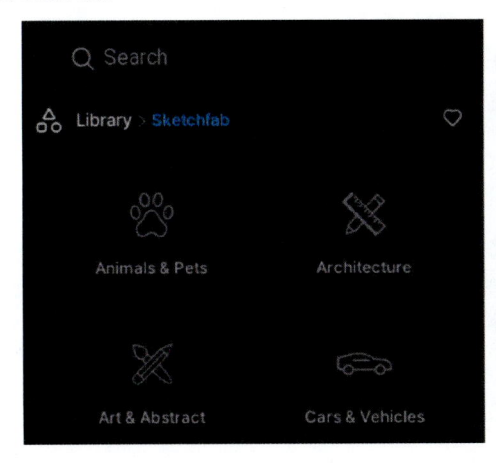

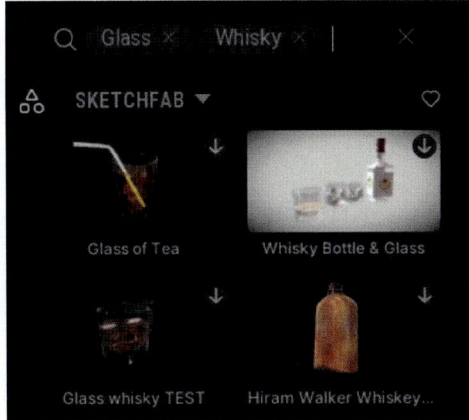

The images you see below were created by downloading a whiskey glass model and inserting a model that uses colored glass material. Using an orange hue, I created the liquid part of the scene. The scene does not use any artificial lighting, only sunlight positioned at 10:45 AM.

Using the parameters shown below, I rendered the glass with the active Path Tracer.

The rendering result shows an image of good quality (remember, glass is the most challenging material for photorealistic rendering). The colored shadow from the whiskey, when hit by light, projects onto the surface, highlighting some internal artifacts resulting from the color map and the shape of the glass. This makes the final result quite accurate.

However, if you look at the previous image with the two glasses – one with caustics on and the other off – you'll notice that there's no visible light distortion. If we deem this light distortion essential for our scene, we can artificially create it using Twinmotion's powerful opacity maps.

The first thing you need to do is find suitable maps. You can find various types online. With a quick search, I found these, which can be used effectively.

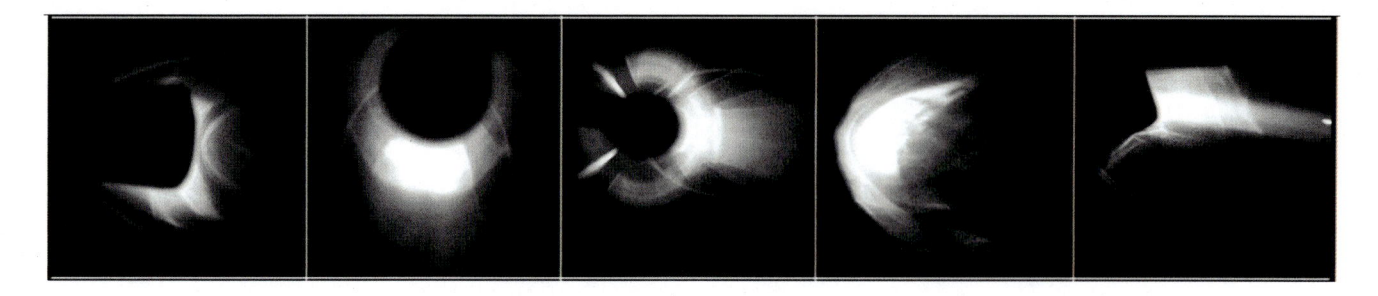

Once you've identified a map, all you need to do is assign it to a 2D plane in Twinmotion, adjust the size, and then work on opacity and brightness. Here, you can read step-by-step how to do it:

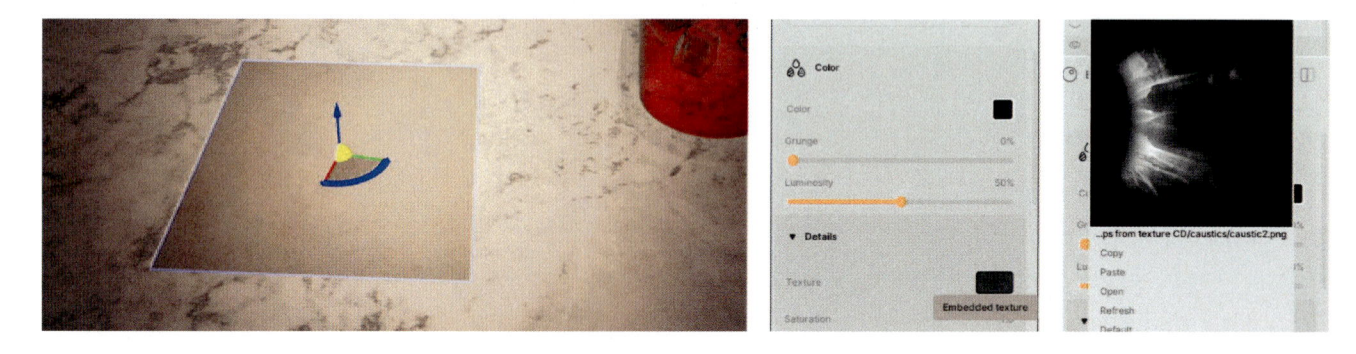

Import a 2D plane into the scene and assign the caustic image as the color map. You might need to resize and rotate the map to achieve the best representation for your scene. Once you've done this, activate the "opacity" shader.

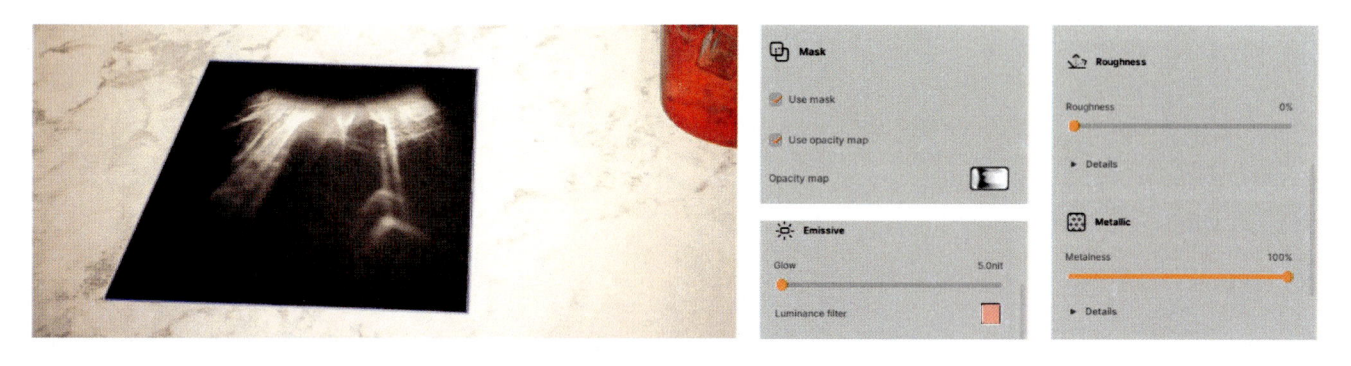

Once the "opacity map" is activated, you'll need to add some brightness using the "emissive" shader. This will give the characteristic luminous shine of caustics generated by light passing through glass. You can then position the 2D plane close to the glass, rotate it in the direction of the light, and activate the Path Tracer to see the result.

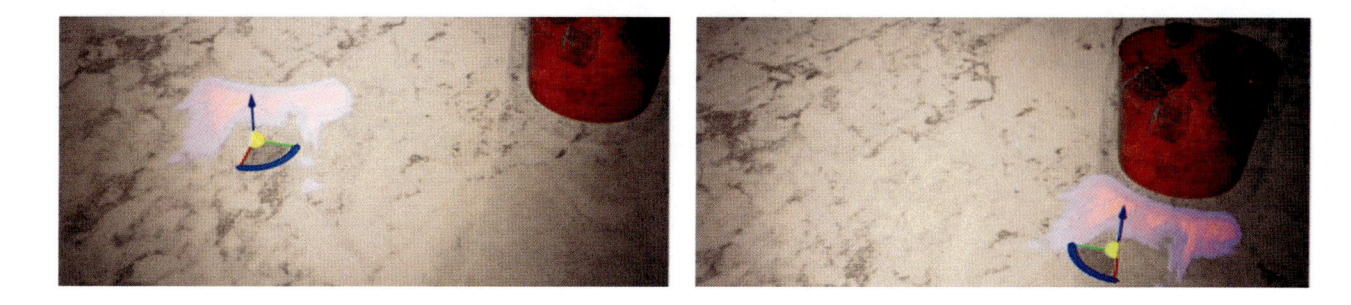

Once you can see the result of the Path Tracer, it will be easy to increase the light strength of the map or its size to achieve a quality result. You can add as many maps as you want. In the image below, I used two maps for a better outcome.

Light and Camera Settings for Photorealism with Path Tracer

In the following pages, I'll show you some specific settings that can help you craft very convincing renderings using the Path Tracer. You'll discover how certain settings can drastically change the quality of photorealism: specific lighting angles, the presence of artificial lights, shadowed scene portions, contrast, exposure, and saturation can substantially alter the rendering quality.

Let's see how to create a scene that's convincingly photorealistic depicting a city corner: firstly, it's vital to understand what contributes to photorealism. Beyond light and camera settings, the objects in the scene make a significant difference. Using high-quality detailed models with realistic textures is the first thing to consider. If you resort to inferior models or unconvincing textures, achieving a high-quality result becomes nearly impossible.

In this scene, I created a city corner using a mix of commercial models and free ones available online: the buildings in the background are models available on the Kitbash3D website, while the street and sidewalk are models available in Twinmotion through the Quixel bridge. I downloaded and arranged them to form a sort of curve in the road and on the sidewalk. The small restaurant on the right is a free model from Sketchfab, also available in Twinmotion.

Beyond the models, you need a clear concept of what you want to achieve. You can draw inspiration from specific references (for instance, I often use Pinterest for inspiration), or you might already have a clear vision of what you want to produce. Generally, having a firm grasp of your end goal and sourcing the necessary models and materials is the best way to set up a scene.

If you examine the scene, you'll notice the presence of many additional objects, especially decals. These are crucial for realism as they can introduce the typical imperfections found in the real world, such as cracks, inaccuracies, mold, mud, graffiti, and so on.

In the image above, you can see some graffiti on the light pole. These are all decals available from the native bridge in Twinmotion Quixel. Adding all these decals makes the image appear more natural and, thus, realistic.

The pedestrian crossings above are also a decal placed on the road, as are the cracks on the left. Below, the same object (the road) without the decal, the difference is substantial.

Decals are, therefore, essential if you're aiming for realism and photorealism.

I realize that many architects using Twinmotion professionally might be hesitant about incorporating imperfections into their renderings. This is because if an architect needs to render a new building (presumably to be sold to a client), it's natural they'd want a flawless rendering in terms of camera and lighting. However, they might want to avoid showcasing a crack on the building's wall. Here, I can only provide guidance on achieving photorealism. In the real world, buildings aren't devoid of signs of wear, dirt, or imperfections. If you're aiming for a photorealistic effect, these are considerations to be aware of, but the final decision is yours.

Let's identify a point in the scene and try to create a photorealistic rendering using the Path Tracer. We'll adjust the framing, light direction, ambient light, and camera features like DOF (Depth of Field) and FOV (Field of View).

First, run the Path Tracer with the scene "as is" to immediately see the result that the default setup produces:

While the image isn't entirely photorealistic, it already demonstrates its potential. Indeed, the many models used, the decals, and all the scene details are promising for a positive outcome.

The first thing to do is find a better light angle. Remember that global illumination in shadowed areas can create profoundly photorealistic effects. So, let's rotate the horizon, cast part of the scene in shadow, and adjust the exposure, weather, and global lighting.

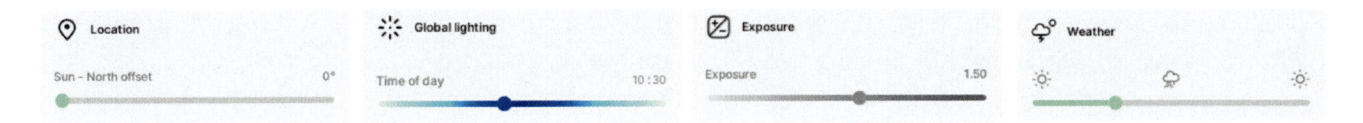

You'll find that often when the weather is overcast, some outdoor scenes become particularly photorealistic. This is because direct sunlight tends to create a strong contrast, which in many cases results in beautiful renderings but not perfectly photorealistic ones. You'll discover that one of the most challenging tasks is achieving photorealism in scenes on sunny days.

You can enhance the ambient light by adding an skydome directly from Twinmotion. The skydome creates a simulated sky, allowing the scene to inherit the light from the HDRI image that defines the sky.

In the rendering, let's add the skydome "Noon Overcast 007".

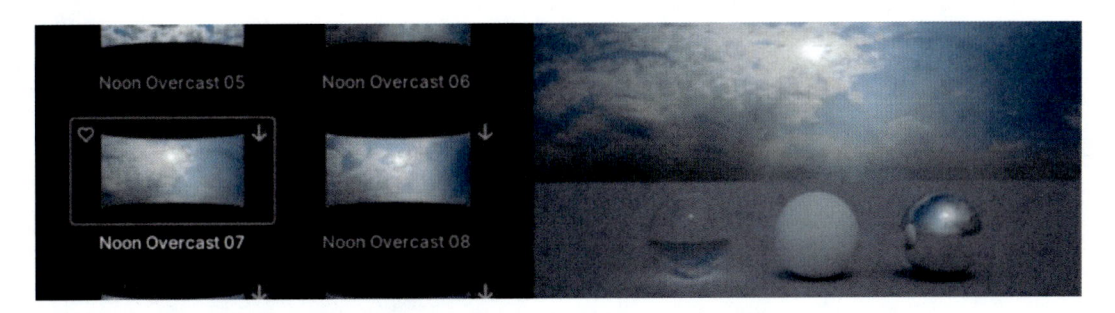

The next step you'll need to take is to focus on a specific area. Imagine being a photographer wanting to capture a detail, such as the sign seen in the center of the image above.
With Twinmotion, you have two ways to zoom in on the sign:

1. Move within the scene and get closer.
2. Perform an optical zoom using your camera's FOV.

You'll find that the second option offers a much broader range of possibilities for photorealism. Observe the difference between moving closer to the sign and zooming in using the FOV.

approaching the point of interest

using the zoom (FOV) of the camera

As you can see, the image using the FOV (with a focal length set to 115mm) displays more details and a different perspective. Look at the right side that features a sign and part of the electrical pylon. Also, notice the building in the background; everything appears more harmonious and isn't distorted like in the other image.

Now, by enabling the DOF (focusing on the billboards) and adjusting the contrast and saturation values slightly, we can achieve this rendering that showcases its full photorealistic quality.

In general, photorealistic rendering is closely tied to the camera settings. The use of DOF (Depth of Field) and FOV (Field of View) will allow you to create very "natural" shots, increasing the likelihood of producing convincing renderings that resemble real photographs.

Here are the parameters used for the final rendering:

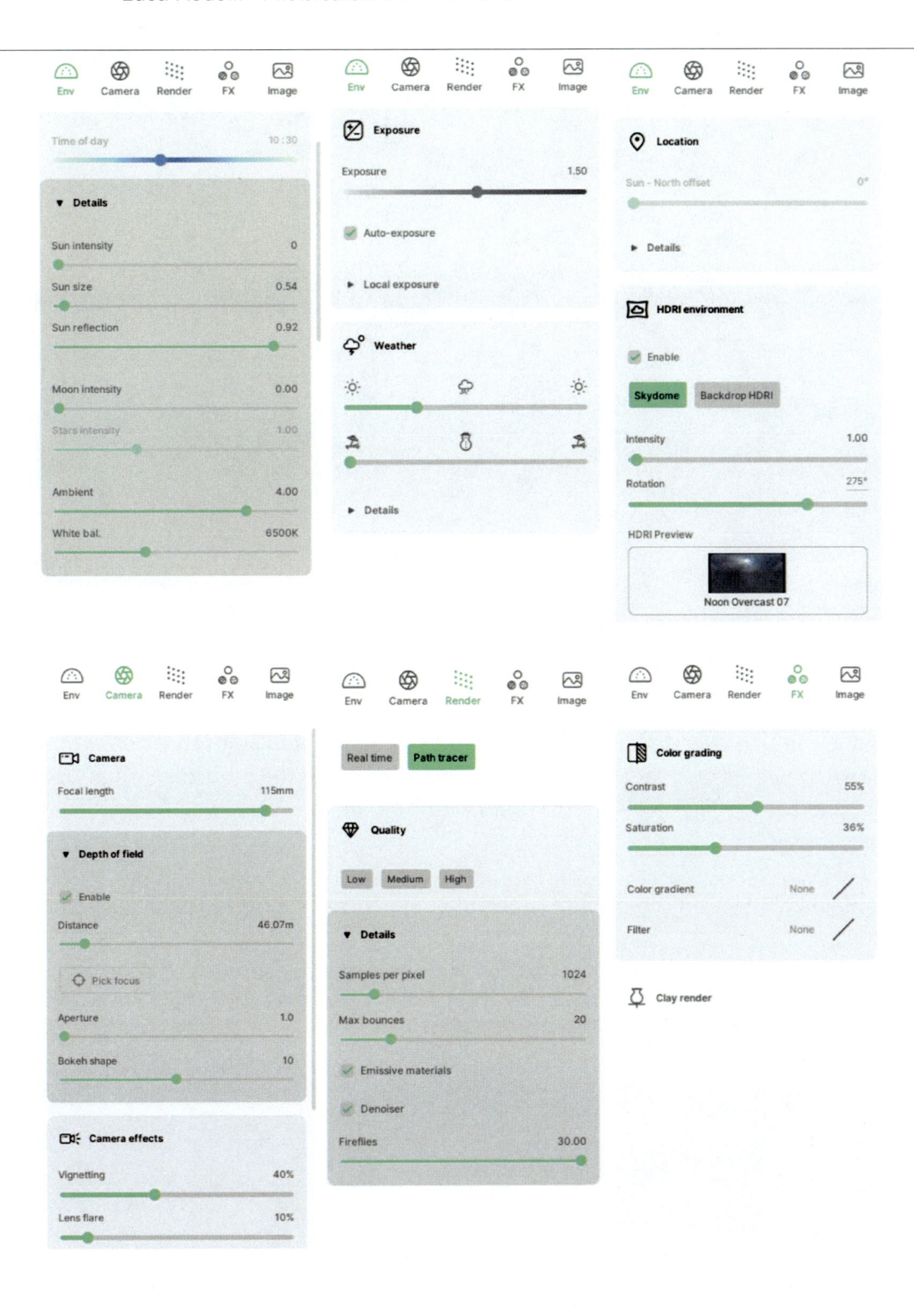

In the same scene, with the same settings, it becomes easy to take other high-quality shots like this one:

Always remember that realism is intrinsically linked to the quality of the models. I know I've mentioned it before, but it can't be overstated. If you scrutinize the image, you'll observe numerous details: the inside of the shop with lights meticulously positioned to emulate the ambiance of an "old store," the out-of-focus puddles adding a layer of drama to the image, and walls adorned with decals, imperfections, and graffiti.

All these elements of the scene contribute to the high-quality rendering you're striving to achieve.

Let's wrap up by showcasing the key shot that fully captures this city corner's detail.

Before moving on to another test, I want you to focus on the left side of the image above. You'll notice some trash bags. I aimed for a highly convincing effect by creating a "yellow" bag that contains paper and plastic waste and is partially transparent. The material I used is a colored glass with a roughness set to 20%, opacity at 0%, and metallic at 0%.

This kind of approach (using FOV and DOF) is crucial for photorealistic close-up shots or when emphasizing specific details. Even when you're aiming for a cinematic atmosphere, this method will allow you to achieve outstanding results.

Below are some of my renderings created using the technique described in this chapter:

- High-quality models with rich details, the use of decals, and high-quality PBR materials.
- Light setup with shadowed areas and diffused sunlight that's not too intense.
- Using DOF and FOV to create a cinematic shot effect.
-

Assets from: Sketchfab, Quixel, Kitbash3D

Assets from: Sketchfab, Quixel, Kitbash3D

Assets from: Sketchfab and Quixel

Assets from: Sketchfab, Quixel, Kitbash3D

Assets from: Quixel

In the upcoming section, you'll discover how to achieve photorealistic renderings using a Path Tracer in low-light settings like nighttime. You'll learn to optimize artificial lighting options in Twinmotion.

It's crucial to note that the Path Tracer is highly sensitive to light scarcity, often producing nearly 'black' images. This is unlike raster engines and Lumen, which benefit more from ambient light sources, such as moonlight found under the 'Env' tab.

Therefore, properly configuring ambient and artificial lights is key to achieving photorealistic results
Let's start by analyzing this rendering of mine set at a particularly dark time of day (like early morning).

In the image above, you can see the final result of a rather complex scene. There are numerous artificial lights, there's a typical haze of adverse weather mornings (there's a light rain in the picture), and there's a bluish hue that very much characterizes this rendering. I immediately point out that this image is very suitable for various types of photorealistic shots, just imagine the same version in black and white and with a thicker grain.

The scene setup mainly focuses on the placement of various models, including the tracks, trains, people, and the station. Decals are added to introduce as much detail as possible, complemented by select buildings that offer a distinct backdrop. The train, station, and railway models are sourced from Evermotion, while the decals and certain materials are provided by Quixel. Some additional assets come from Sketchfab. Furthermore, some of the human figures are courtesy of the 3Dpeople library.

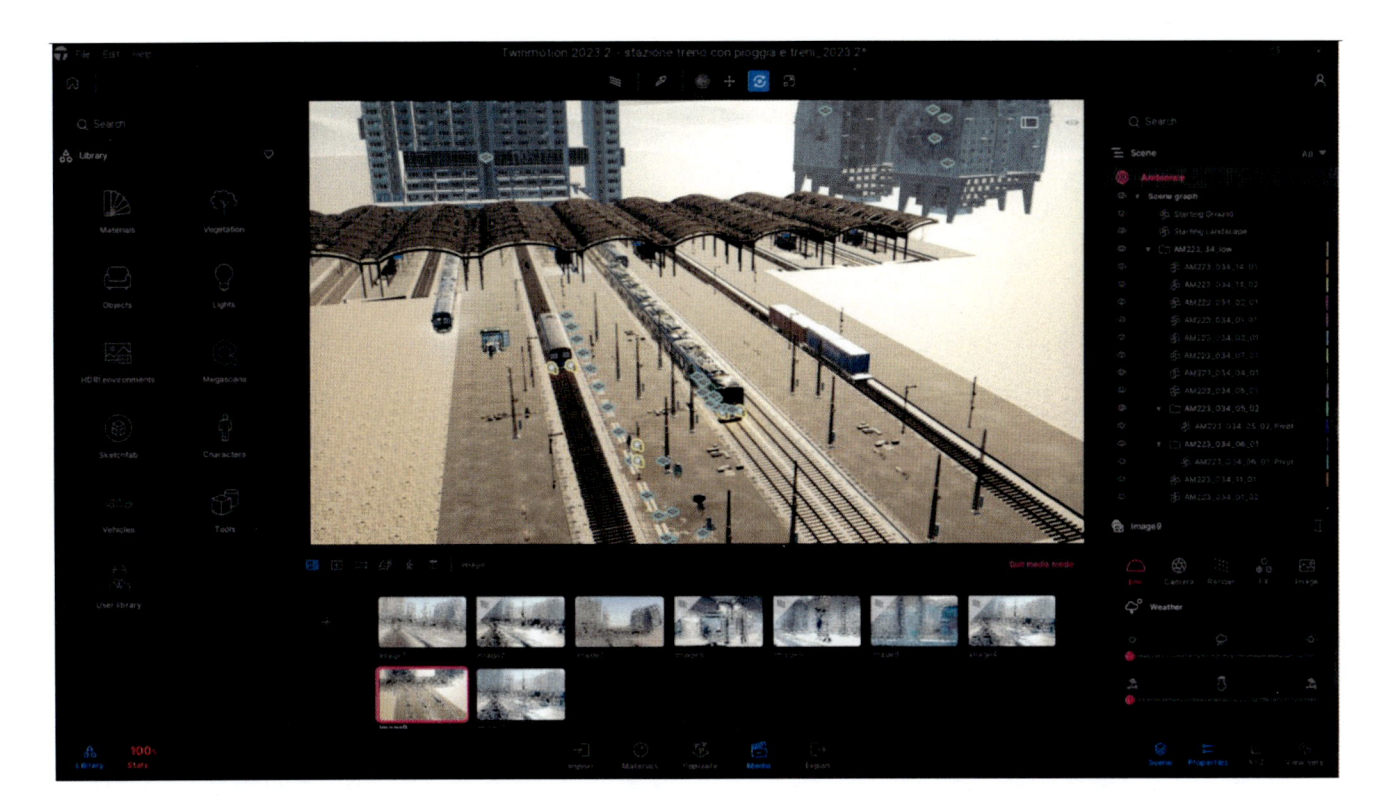

One of the distinct features of this scene is its sheer size: it encompasses a multitude of models totaling almost 40 million polygons. On my computer, this leads to a significant slowdown, making it challenging to work at a satisfactory FPS (Frames Per Second). When Twinmotion begins to falter due to excessive resource usage, one must tread carefully. The GPU on your graphics card could unexpectedly crash, leading to an abrupt closure of Twinmotion

The majority of Twinmotion crashes result from the exhaustion of the graphics card's resources. In these circumstances, it's essential to optimize the scene resources meticulously to prevent it from becoming overly extensive. When constructing a scene, I usually adopt the following two strategies:

1. When I need to integrate numerous models, I try to decimate the polygons of models situated in the distant parts of the scene (using tools like Blender or 3D Studio Max). If these models are remotely placed, they don't require extreme detailing, allowing for a reduction in the polygon count.

2. Just as with the above point, the same principle applies to material textures. If I possess exquisite materials with 4K or 8K textures but the models using these materials aren't foregrounded, it's more efficient to downscale the resolution to 1024x1024. For swift and bulk image downsizing, I employ the 'image converter' tool.

In this scene, I use 26 artificial lights of two different types: omnidirectional light and neon light. I generally prefer using omnidirectional lights for greater control over light distribution. However, in this case, neon lights were particularly useful. The lights inside the train cars are generated by long neon lights, allowing me to illuminate the interiors with fewer, appropriately-sized lights.

In the example above, I used a single neon light repeated across each train car to generate interior lighting. This method reduced the number of lights needed and ensured uniform illumination, unlike using multiple omnidirectional lights in each car.

Above is a detail of the rendering with the lights turned off. As you can see, even without lights, the image retains a convincing level of photorealism. This is largely due to the skydome I used, which generates a compelling rainy-day ambient light. Additionally, the Field of View (FOV) and Depth of Field (DOF) settings of the camera also contribute to the realism.

I want to highlight the quality of the umbrella material, which adds significantly to the photorealism. The upper part of the umbrella is wet from the rain, yet, like most canvas umbrellas, its surface is matte, resulting in a uniform and satin-like light reflection.

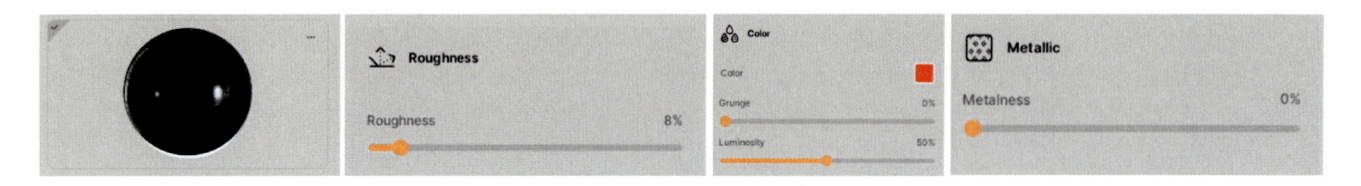

Below, you can find the parameters used for the rendering.

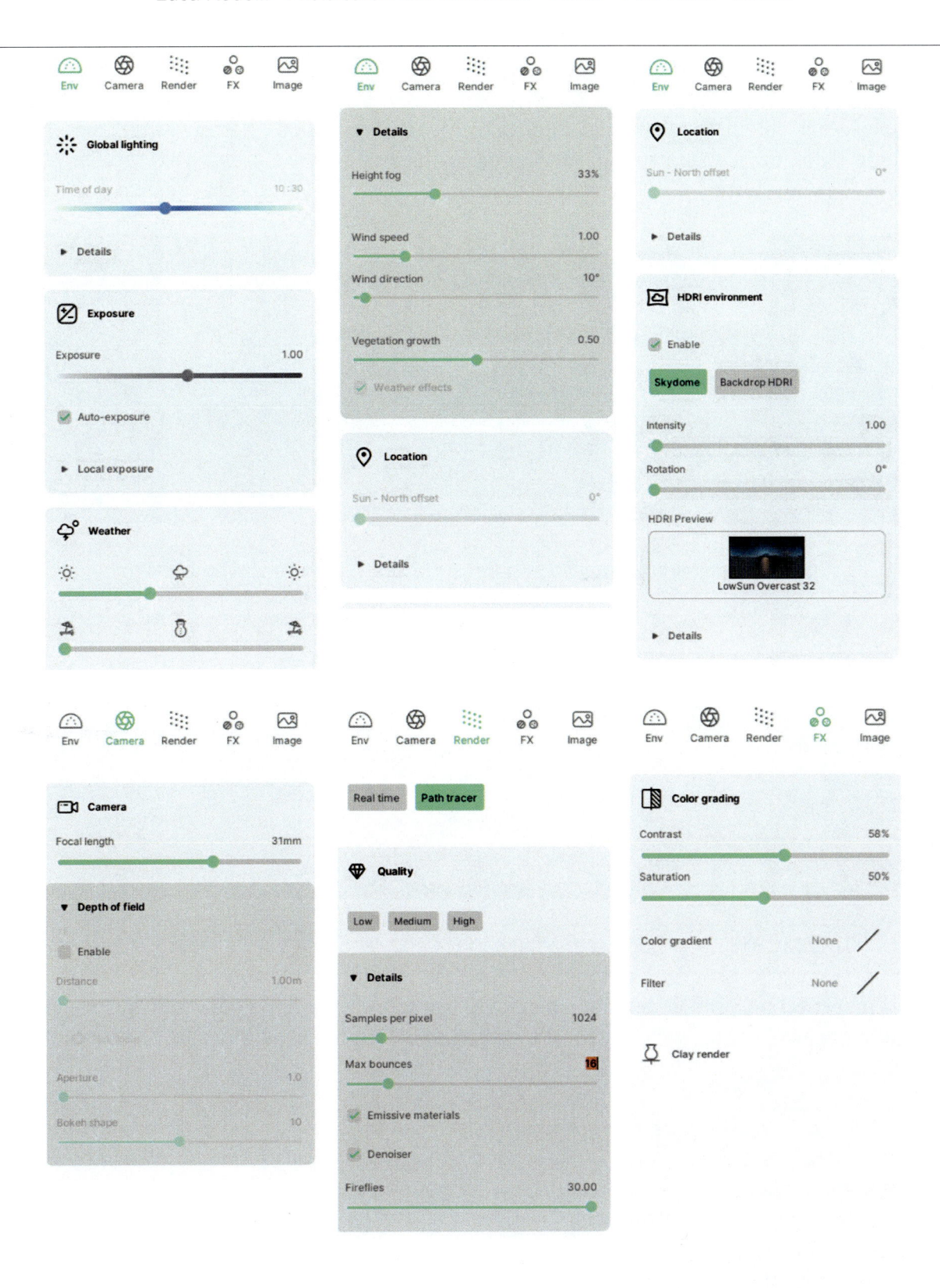

Luca Rodolfi - Photorealism with Twinmotion – Raster – Path Tracer - Lumen

Env panel

Global lighting
Time of day — 10:30
▶ Details

Exposure
Exposure — 1.00
☑ Auto-exposure
▶ Local exposure

Weather

Env panel (Details)

▼ Details
Height fog — 33%
Wind speed — 1.00
Wind direction — 10°
Vegetation growth — 0.50
☐ Weather effects

Location
Sun - North offset — 0°
▶ Details

Env panel (Location / HDRI)

Location
Sun - North offset — 0°
▶ Details

HDRI environment
☑ Enable
[Skydome] [Backdrop HDRI]
Intensity — 1.00
Rotation — 0°
HDRI Preview
LowSun Overcast 32
▶ Details

Camera panel

Camera
Focal length — 31mm

▼ Depth of field
☐ Enable
Distance — 1.00m
Aperture — 1.0
Bokeh shape — 10

Render panel

[Real time] [**Path tracer**]

Quality
[Low] [Medium] [High]

▼ Details
Samples per pixel — 1024
Max bounces — 16
☑ Emissive materials
☑ Denoiser
Fireflies — 30.00

FX panel

Color grading
Contrast — 58%
Saturation — 50%
Color gradient — None
Filter — None

Clay render

How to Create "Water" with the Path Tracer

As previously highlighted, the Path Tracer doesn't support Twinmotion's native "water" material. As of the current Twinmotion roadmap, improvements to this material are in progress. If you attempt to render a scene with "water" using the Path Tracer, you'll encounter unexpected results.

The water material applied to a flat surface and rendered with Lumen.

The water material applied to a flat surface and rendered with the Path Tracer.

If surface reflection seems to work (to some extent), transparency is completely lacking. Imagine having to render a pool where you want clear and transparent water; this type of water is unusable with the Path Tracer.

The best solution is to use a different type of material: colored glass. This works particularly well for still images, providing nearly all the physical characteristics needed to simulate water convincingly. However, if you require additional features like caustics, you'll need to use the technique I taught you in earlier pages when we analyzed the whiskey glass scene.
For videos, things can get more complex. Animation of texture maps in the material is only possible in the X and Y directions. This limits the type of animation, making it less suitable for simulating more complex water turbulence.

By applying colored glass (I used turquoise-tinted glass, slightly modifying the color to make it less turquoise), the results are immediately noticeable.

If you revisit the section on creating caustics for the whiskey glass, you'll find a reference on how to achieve the same effect for caustics in this scene. The key difference is that in the whiskey glass case, we used a 2D plane, whereas here we'll modify a Twinmotion decal using an opacity map (like the one shown below) in the color, mask, and emissive channels.

Above is the rendering done with the Path Tracer, using glass material for the water and decals for the caustics.

In the case of the whiskey glass, we could have also used a decal instead of a 2D plane. There's no specific reason to prefer one over the other; it depends on the particular needs of your scene.

The image above shows an example of photorealistic rendering with the Path Tracer for water, using the technique I've described earlier. The colored glass allows you to use images in the "color" shader that can directly reference water surfaces. In this case, I've defined crystal-clear water using a reference map found on the web. The ripples are created using a normal map, also sourced from the web.

Above, you can see the same scene, but here I've used a "color" map texture featuring foam and less clarity than the previous one. By adjusting the material's opacity, it becomes possible to make the water murkier. On the left, you can see the two maps used: the top one for color (in PNG format with 10% transparency) and the bottom one used for wave ripples in the "normal" shader.

How to Create Clouds with the Path Tracer

Twinmotion features a Weather Control System that allows you to set the conditions in a scene. You can choose the time of day to create a typical noon lighting environment, or opt for a sunset or sunrise.

Alongside these settings, you can also decide to create a scene with cloudy weather, rain, snow, or bright sunshine—it's all up to you.
However, you'll have limited control over the appearance of the sky and clouds, especially when using the Path Tracer, which cannot render the native clouds in Twinmotion.

Don't confuse Twinmotion's native sky and weather conditions with HDRI environments, which offer a range of high-definition sky images under various conditions. The latter are always correctly rendered by the Path Tracer and are often the go-to option when setting up a scene.

However, there are instances where you'll need to use Twinmotion's native sky—think of situations where you need to display renderings at different times of the day or under varying weather conditions.

In such cases, if you need to render clouds, you'll be required to use custom models. If you don't want to go through the hassle of finding cloud examples and creating models for Twinmotion, don't worry—I've already done that for you. You can download the ZIP file from this link:

https://drive.google.com/file/d/154nrwDb_9q5D8fLM4DcfMzH70aS5qs0r

To make the "Clouds" package available for your projects, you'll need to place the downloaded content in the path designated for your custom library. This will ensure that the cloud models are readily accessible from your Twinmotion library.

With this package, you can transition from a Twinmotion-native sky without clouds to one where you have complete control over cloud placement.

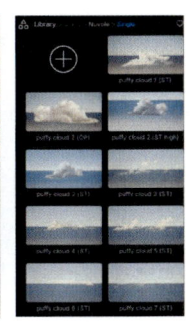

Photorealism with LUMEN

Please note: Everything I write related to Lumen in Twinmotion stems from early access I had due to my role as a beta tester. It's possible that some details may change in the final versions. Always refer to the official documentation that the Twinmotion team will provide on the official website.

Lumen is the standout feature in this version of Twinmotion, eagerly awaited by all Twinmotion users since its integration in Unreal Engine 5. Essentially, it's a raster engine with high-quality global illumination and reflection systems, offering photorealistic quality that approaches the level of a Path Tracer, albeit with some limitations.

As I've already mentioned, it's perfect for rendering animations due to its incredible rendering speed. Below is a frame from a 21-second animation, rendered using both Path Tracer and Lumen on the same workstation:

As you can see, rendering with the Path Tracer took 3 hours and 30 minutes, while Lumen completed the task in 14 minutes. That means Lumen is (for this specific scene) about 15 times faster than the Path Tracer. Keep in mind that "15 times" isn't a universal multiplier; some scenes may render more quickly or slowly in either engine. However, the speed difference between Lumen and the Path Tracer is significant.

If Lumen is a game-changer for animations, it also holds its own for static images, delivering quality very similar to the Path Tracer. Despite this, I'd still recommend using the Path Tracer for still images.

It's important to note that the tests I've conducted are based on Twinmotion 2023.2 beta 4. The final version released to the public should not differ significantly. Should there be unfortunate discrepancies, I will publish a correction on my website www.rodluc.com.

Lumen doesn't offer many configuration parameters. Those available primarily focus on rendering quality and real-time reflection modes.

Please note that the current version I'm using (beta 4) doesn't always provide an accurate estimate of the rendering times with Lumen. Sometimes it indicates an exceptionally high time, only to complete the rendering in much less time. I speculate that the final version will address this anomaly.

The image below outlines the available parameters.

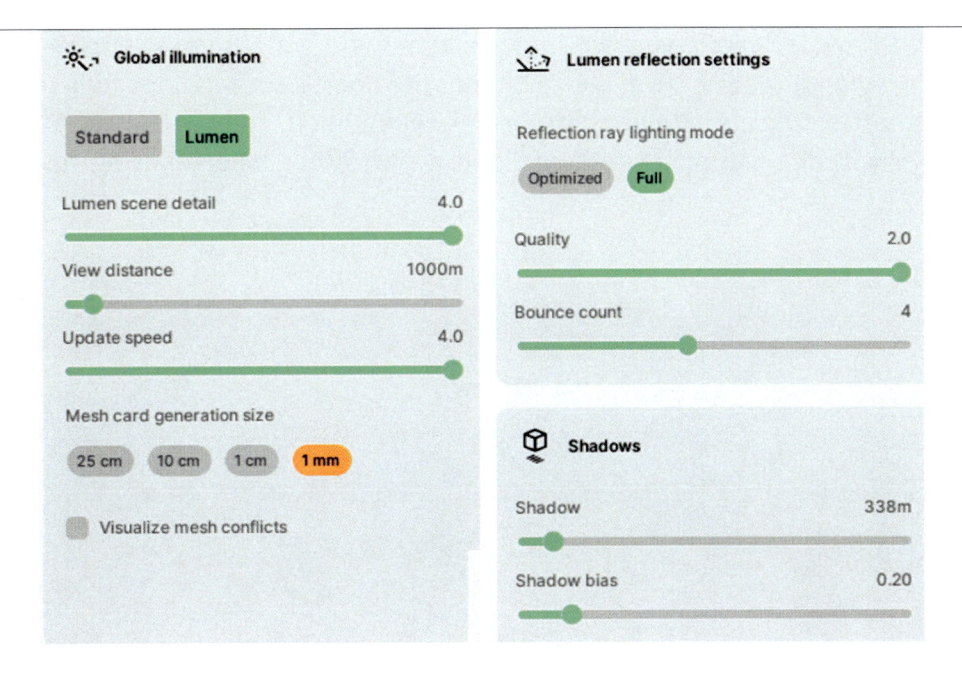

Global illumination

Standard | **Lumen**

Lumen scene detail — 4.0
View distance — 1000m
Update speed — 4.0

Mesh card generation size: 25 cm | 10 cm | 1 cm | **1 mm**

☐ Visualize mesh conflicts

Lumen reflection settings

Reflection ray lighting mode: Optimized | **Full**

Quality — 2.0
Bounce count — 4

Shadows

Shadow — 338m
Shadow bias — 0.20

Scene Detail: set the size at which objects are culled by Lumen, higher value include more objects but increase VRAM usage.

View Distance: set the view distance from the camera in which Lumen has an effect.

Update Speed: the speed at which Lumen updates real-time global illumination.

Mesh card generation size: The minimum size for the generation of card mesh. Note: This option may not be available in the final release. Early tests from the beta 4 version indicate that using larger cards does not yield any benefits in terms of FPS. As such, it is likely that this feature will be removed, and the optimal card size will be used by default.

Visualize mesh conflicts: show surfaces culled by Lumen, magenta areas are too complex, yellow areas are too small, big or far away.

Reflection Optimized – Full: Optimized use cached data to calculate reflections, Full use realtime data to calculate reflections.

Quality (reflection): set the quality of the reflections, higher values give sharper results.

Bounce Count: the number of light bounces between reflective surfaces

Shadow: Sets the distance from the camera up to which shadows on objects are cast; for example, if the value is set to 500 meters, shadows on objects are cast for 500 meters only beginning at the camera; smaller values provide a shorter range for cast shadows, but produce shadows that are more detailed (higher-resolution). Inversely, higher values provide a longer range, but result in less detailed shadows.

Shadow bias: increasing this value reduces self-shadowing artifacts on object, but can also reduce the quality of the shadow.

The first thing you need to learn if you want to use Lumen as your rendering engine is how to import models and their required specifications. Certain types of imports, such as importing models "collapsed by material," are not compatible with accurate rendering in Lumen. It becomes crucial to follow specific guidelines to avoid having too many magenta and yellow areas when clicking on "Visualize Mesh Conflict."

- Encountering yellow suggests that the mesh areas might be too small, overly large, or situated too far from the central viewpoint. But don't be misled into thinking these areas are automatically incompatible with Lumen. Their influence and appearance can be effectively managed using the Scene detail and View distance settings. For a comprehensive understanding of how to tweak these settings, I recommend referring to the Render Settings section.
- On the other side of the spectrum is magenta, which indicates areas with a high level of complexity. Such areas challenge the capabilities of mesh cards, making them unable to completely cover the highlighted region. The result? These magenta-marked areas won't contribute to light bounces, and when it comes to reflections, they will be rendered as dark or black spots.

One of the critical terms you'll frequently encounter when working with Unreal Engine's Lumen in Twinmotion is "card mesh." A card mesh is essentially a simple, flat polygon—often a quad—that serves as a placeholder or a simplified representation for more complex geometry or effects, such as foliage, fabrics, or intricate detailing.

Card mesh becomes particularly crucial in the context of Lumen's real-time global illumination and reflection calculations. Since Lumen aims for rapid rendering speeds without compromising much on quality, simplifying complex scenes using card mesh can greatly optimize the rendering process. This is especially beneficial in environments where resources are limited or where real-time rendering is essential.

The use of card mesh allows you to create visually stunning environments without taxing the engine excessively. For instance, in the case of dense foliage in a natural scene, rather than rendering each leaf or plant individually, you can use a card mesh with a texture applied. This maintains the illusion of complexity while allowing Lumen to compute global illumination more efficiently.

Understanding the optimal size and implementation of card mesh in your 3D scenes can make a significant difference in both the quality and efficiency of your Lumen renders.

Twinmotion (Beta4) allows you to specify the dimensions of the card mesh so that they can be tailored to fit the size of your scene and the models you are using.

Mesh card size: 25 cm

Mesh card size: 1 cm

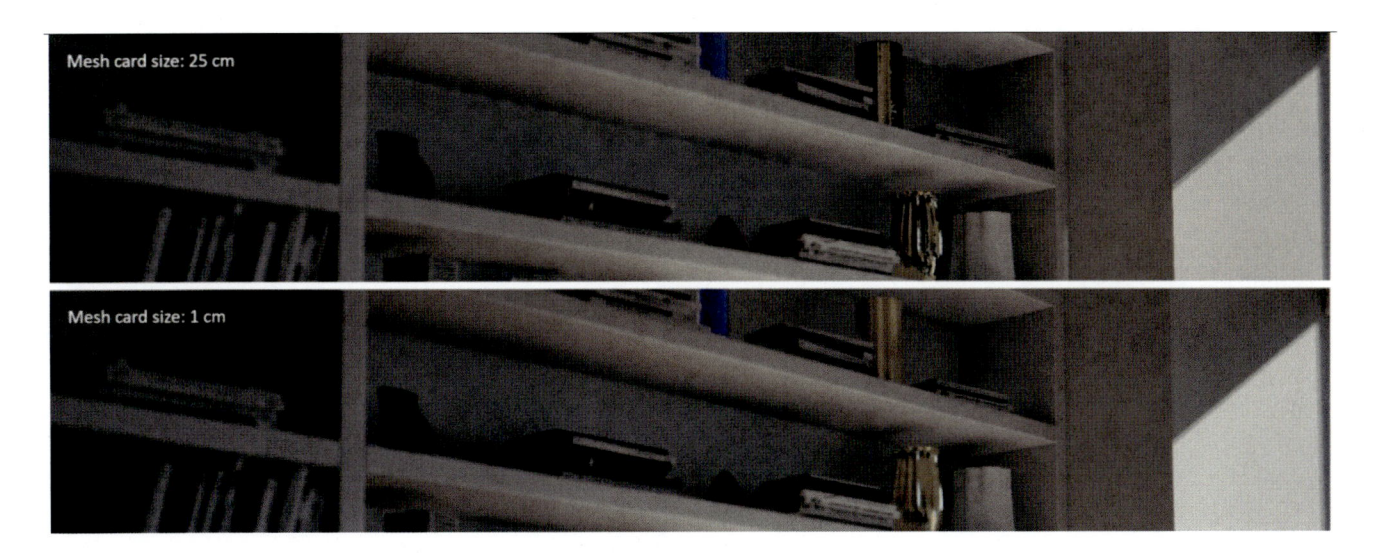

Let's circle back to our initial example and see what insights I can offer regarding Lumen.

LUMEN ENGINE

1 - Lack of colored shadows; translucent materials like colored glass are not rendered in a physically accurate manner.

2 - Reflection quality is superior compared to Raster, but it reveals some artifacts.

If you consider that this image was generated in just a few seconds and can be navigated in real-time within the viewport, you'd likely agree that the quality is astonishing. However, there are a couple of points worth diving into for a better understanding:

1 – Lack of Colored Shadows: Similar to the raster engine, Lumen does not handle translucent materials, so achieving effects like colored shadows is not possible. If colored shadows are essential for your scene, you'll need to follow the guidelines I provided in the chapter on the raster engine.

2 – Reflection Quality and Limitations: While Lumen offers high-quality reflections for glass and mirrors—especially when set to 'Full' mode and maximum quality —it does come with some limitations compared to the Path Tracer. These limitations will be detailed further in subsequent pages. For video production, Lumen is often the preferred choice due to its speed. However, for static images, the Path Tracer remains the superior option for achieving the most realistic reflections. It's crucial to be aware of these nuances when selecting your rendering engine

Next, I'll detail how reflections behave in Lumen. This should help you understand how to best structure your scenes to avoid any potential artifacts or distortions in the reflections.

As you can see in the image below, Lumen's reflection system struggles to accurately reflect transparent and translucent elements. Additionally, some meshes appear completely black depending on the viewing angle.

Before assuming that this behavior is a bug or a limitation of Lumen's implementation, one must consider the origin of the scene's meshes. Indeed, the current version of Twinmotion that enables Lumen may encounter some issues when loading scenes created with a previous version of Twinmotion:

- As previously mentioned, there's a specific approach to follow when importing models. These models should not be "collapsed" into a single mesh or have 3D structures "fused" together. For example, if you have two walls at a 90-degree angle, they should be two separate meshes, not one single mesh. This allows Lumen to accurately calculate global illumination.
- Opening a scene created in an older version could result in performance issues. I've noticed this firsthand: the difference between opening an old scene filled with models and importing the same models into an empty scene can be significant. This is an annoying limitation, but it's important to keep it in mind.
- When opening an older version, you might encounter "flaws" in some models. For instance, Lumen may fail to render them correctly, as seen in the example below where the reflection isn't functioning properly, and some portions of the meshes seem devoid of indirect lighting, appearing almost black.

In such cases, you can make specific adjustments, perhaps by removing the "non-functioning" models and either replacing them or reimporting them as FBX or Datasmith files.

While it's possible that the final release version of Twinmotion could improve upon these issues, they are clearly present in the beta 4 version.

Therefore, keep in mind that for still images, you can bypass this limitation by using the Path Tracer. However, for animations, you'll need to be very cautious with your scene setup to ensure that highly reflective flat surfaces (like mirrors, for example) do not play a central role in the scene and are not the focus of close-up shots or main frames.

It's essential to understand the existing limitations in Lumen's reflection technology, especially if you're aiming for photorealistic outcomes. While Lumen does a commendable job at generating screen-space reflections—that is, reflections of pixels that are visible to the camera—there are challenges when these pixels are not within the screen space. In such cases, Lumen defaults to using the Surface Cache for reflections. The downside? If your Surface Cache is dark or black, any parts of your model not visible to the camera will reflect as black in mirrors.

Moreover, the reflected part not visible directly in the scene will also appear black in mirror reflections, adding another layer of complexity to achieving realistic outcomes. The Unreal Engine team is actively working on Lumen's capabilities, including the addition of multiple reflection bounces, and it's anticipated that future versions will offer more accurate mirror reflections.

If you have to use Lumen, for instance because you're working on a video, and you want to be sure that the model is compatible with the engine., your only option is to identify the non-functional models. Try re-importing them, ensuring the model isn't collapsed into a single mesh, and experiment with card mesh of different dimensions. For example, let's see how the plant from the above image appears in a 3D modeling software like 3D Studio Max:

The image on the left shows the mesh with the leaves selected. As you can see, all the leaves make up a single mesh, which can pose challenges for Lumen during rendering.

You can optimize the model by separating each individual leaf into its own distinct mesh. This can enhance Lumen's ability to accurately calculate global illumination.

Keep in mind that this type of operation can be quite resource-intensive in terms of model optimization and does not guarantee a perfect solution. However, guidelines for accurate model representation in scenes rendered with Lumen should definitely take this kind of model structure into account.

Now you've uncovered one of the pain points of using Lumen in Twinmotion, along with the tools to manage it effectively.

Best Practices for Using Lumen in Twinmotion

Drawing from the documentation released with the Beta 4 of Twinmotion 2023.2, I highlight some best practices that can allow you to set up a scene with all the ideal characteristics to ensure it runs smoothly with the Lumen engine.

Mesh Structure and Lumen's Compatibility in Twinmotion

When importing a 3D model into Twinmotion, such as an entire room complete with a floor and multiple walls, it's important to note that Lumen may struggle with a single, contiguous mesh. It's advisable to separate the geometry into distinct meshes within your design software before bringing it into Twinmotion.

To illustrate this point, consider how Lumen interacts with global illumination on a structure that consists of either a single mesh or multiple meshes. For instance, when the floor and walls of a room are combined into a single mesh, Lumen's global illumination capabilities are compromised. On the other hand, when the floor and walls are separated into different meshes, Lumen can more accurately calculate global illumination across all surfaces.

In some instances, when working with a single-mesh structure, you'll find that Lumen does not account for certain surfaces, appearing as magenta-colored areas. Conversely, this issue is not present when working with a structure comprised of multiple meshes. You can verify this in Twinmotion by navigating to Ambience > Render > Global Illumination > Lumen and selecting the 'Visualize mesh conflicts' checkbox.

When Lumen is enabled, the global illumination on the structure built from multiple meshes is more accurate and thorough than it is on the single mesh structure. Therefore, optimizing your 3D models by separating them into multiple meshes can make a significant difference in achieving realistic global illumination with Lumen.

Surface Size and Emissive Properties in Lumen-Enabled Scenes

With Lumen enabled in Twinmotion, emissive materials gain the ability to influence indirect lighting, as well as generate specular and diffuse bounces. This offers you the flexibility to apply an emissive material to objects, such as cubes, and use them as light sources to illuminate your scenes.

However, it's essential to note that this approach has its limitations. When an object has a surface that is too bright in relation to its size—think of extremely luminous neon signs or light bulbs—the resulting emissive surfaces can produce noise artifacts in the scene. This can compromise the visual fidelity of your render.

To mitigate these issues, it's recommended to utilize the pre-configured lights available in the Twinmotion Library as your primary sources of illumination. You can find these under Library > Lights.

For example, consider a scene where a small object with an emissive material has been included. This scenario is generally not advised, as it can introduce noise artifacts that detract from the scene's overall quality. When the same scene is rendered without the small, overly bright emissive object, the global illumination is calculated correctly, resulting in a more visually pleasing outcome.

By understanding these nuances, you can make more informed choices about how to use emissive materials and lighting in your Lumen-enabled Twinmotion projects.

The Importance of Material Roughness in Lumen-Enabled Scenes

In scenes where Lumen is enabled, the roughness value of materials plays a significant role in both performance and visual accuracy. Lumen performs optimally when the Roughness value of the materials is set at 40% or higher. Materials with lower Roughness values demand more computational resources because additional rays have to be traced to generate accurate reflections.

For instance, consider a scene featuring a floor with an excessively glossy surface. In such a situation, you'll likely encounter various reflection artifacts, disrupting the visual integrity of the render. These artifacts can manifest as aberrations or inconsistencies in the reflections on the floor.

However, when the floor's surface roughness is adjusted to a value that is more compatible with Lumen, these reflection artifacts become significantly less noticeable. The surface not only looks more natural but also allows Lumen to calculate reflections more efficiently.

Understanding how material roughness affects Lumen's performance can help you make more educated decisions in your rendering workflow. This knowledge will enable you to fine-tune your scenes for both visual quality and computational efficiency.

Importing Files: Best Practices for Optimal Lumen Performance

Working with SketchUp Pro Files

When you import native SketchUp Pro (.skp) files into Twinmotion, you'll notice some inherent limitations. These files have two-sided geometry that does not work well in Lumen-enabled scenes. The outcome is often a darker scene with noisy and incorrect global illumination. For improved rendering, it's advisable to convert your SketchUp Pro files to Datasmith (.udatasmith) format before bringing them into Twinmotion. You can use the Datasmith Exporter plugin for SketchUp Pro for this purpose. Converting your files to Datasmith format ensures that the geometry is better understood by Lumen, resulting in proper lighting.

Importance of Collapse Mode

Another key aspect to consider while importing files into Twinmotion is the collapse mode you choose. Twinmotion offers different collapse modes, each affecting how Lumen interprets the scene.

- Keep Hierarchy: This mode retains the original 3D model's hierarchical structure, allowing Lumen to generate 'Cards' effectively for accurate global illumination. It is the recommended setting to avoid any light bleeding or other unwanted artifacts.
- Collapse by Material: While this mode might look acceptable for simpler scenes, it can create issues with global illumination and can lead to darker scenes. It also restricts the number of Cards Lumen can generate, thus compromising the accuracy of the render.
- Collapse All: This mode flattens the entire hierarchical structure, which can lead to severe issues such as light bleeding artifacts. Virtually no Cards are generated for Lumen to function properly, leading to inaccurate and unrealistic renders.

To ensure that your Lumen renders are as accurate as possible, we highly recommend using the 'Keep Hierarchy' collapse mode during import. Understanding how your choice of file format and collapse mode impacts Lumen's performance will enable you to make better decisions for more accurate and efficient rendering.

Known Limitations

Specular Reflections
As of the current version, Lumen does not support specular, or mirror-like, reflections. This is a known limitation and something to be aware of when aiming for hyper-realistic scenes.

Dynamic Meshes: Cycloramas and LED Walls
While Lumen handles Static Meshes well, it lacks support for Dynamic Meshes. This means that elements like Cycloramas and LED walls are not compatible with Lumen. Although they might look similar to Static Meshes, their functionality differs. However, it's worth noting that support for Dynamic Meshes is in the pipeline and should be integrated in future releases.

Limitations in Mirror Reflections
As I've shown you previously, mirror reflections are another area where Lumen falls short. Direct specular reflections, specifically those not visible in the camera's screen space, are rendered as low-resolution approximations. This can be a significant limitation when high fidelity is required.

Double and Multiple Reflections
Lumen's current build only partially supports the complex interplay of light between two or more reflective surfaces—known as double reflections. These appear black when the reflecting surface is not visible to the camera. Like other features, improvements in this area are in development.

Scattered and Painted Vegetation
In scenes that include scattered or painted vegetation, Lumen's global illumination does not account for light bounces from these elements.

By understanding these known limitations, you'll be better equipped to work around them or wait for future updates that address these issues. Keep an eye out for ongoing developments as the Unreal Engine team continues to enhance Lumen's capabilities.

Light and Camera Settings for Photorealism with Lumen

In the coming pages, you'll discover how Lumen closely resembles Path Tracer in setting up scenes ideal for photorealism. Often, simply activating Lumen yields an immediately convincing image in the Twinmotion viewport. For those who have been working in Twinmotion for a while and have struggled with the raster engine—especially Mac users, for whom Path Tracer isn't an option—this can seem nothing short of miraculous.

For our first example, let's consider a typical archviz interior scene. I'll be using a scene from Evermotion's Archinteriors 51, designed for 3D Studio Max.

The scene was first opened in 3D Studio Max and exported using the Datasmith format. It was then imported into Twinmotion . Upon import, some manual adjustments were necessary to fix the materials. This included selecting the two-sided option and loading some missing texture maps—a tedious but essential step for achieving photorealism. Always remember that flat materials, created using only the "color" shader, negatively affect the quality of photorealism.

Important Note: When importing a Datasmith scene into Twinmotion with the intent of using it with Lumen, it's crucial to import it using the "collapse" function set to "keep hierarchy."

Once loaded into Twinmotion, the scene initially appears flat and far from photorealistic with the raster engine active. However, this is hardly a concern if your models and textures are detailed and of high quality. The scene will dramatically improve when Lumen and other advanced rendering techniques are applied.

Above the image of the loaded scene, you'll notice improvements after adjusting some materials using Twinmotion's available shaders. For instance, I've fine-tuned some reflective materials to make them a bit more opaque, like the vases on the foreground table.

In the next image, Lumen is activated with no special tweaks. Notice the immediate shift from flat to photorealistic, showcasing Lumen's effectiveness in 3D enhancement.

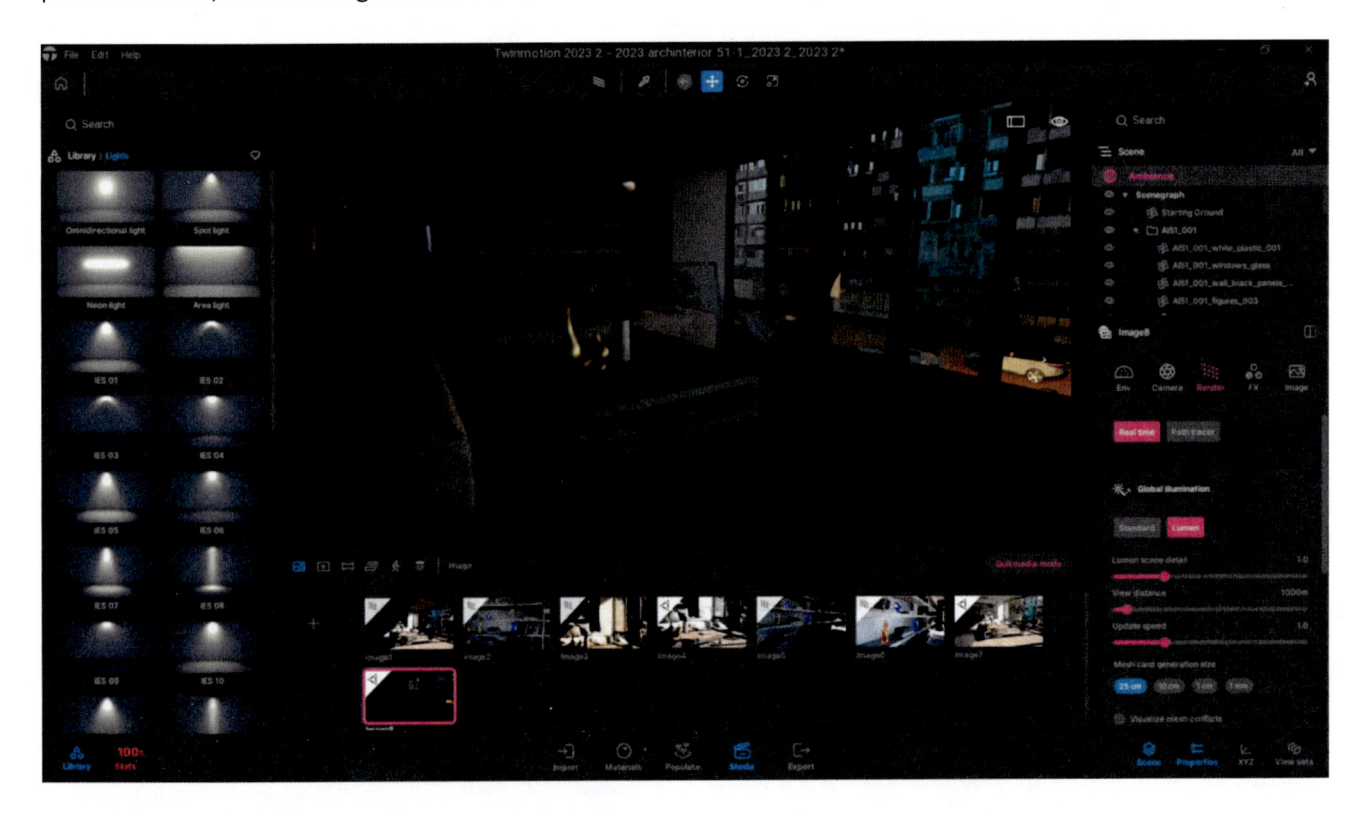

The image may start off dark, but the immediate realism comes from global illumination and indirect shadows. We'll fine-tune lighting and more in upcoming sections.

First, set the right lighting for realism with global illumination and ambient occlusion. Adjust the "time of the day" to 18:45 and rotate the horizon 200 degrees. No special settings yet, just observe the changes.

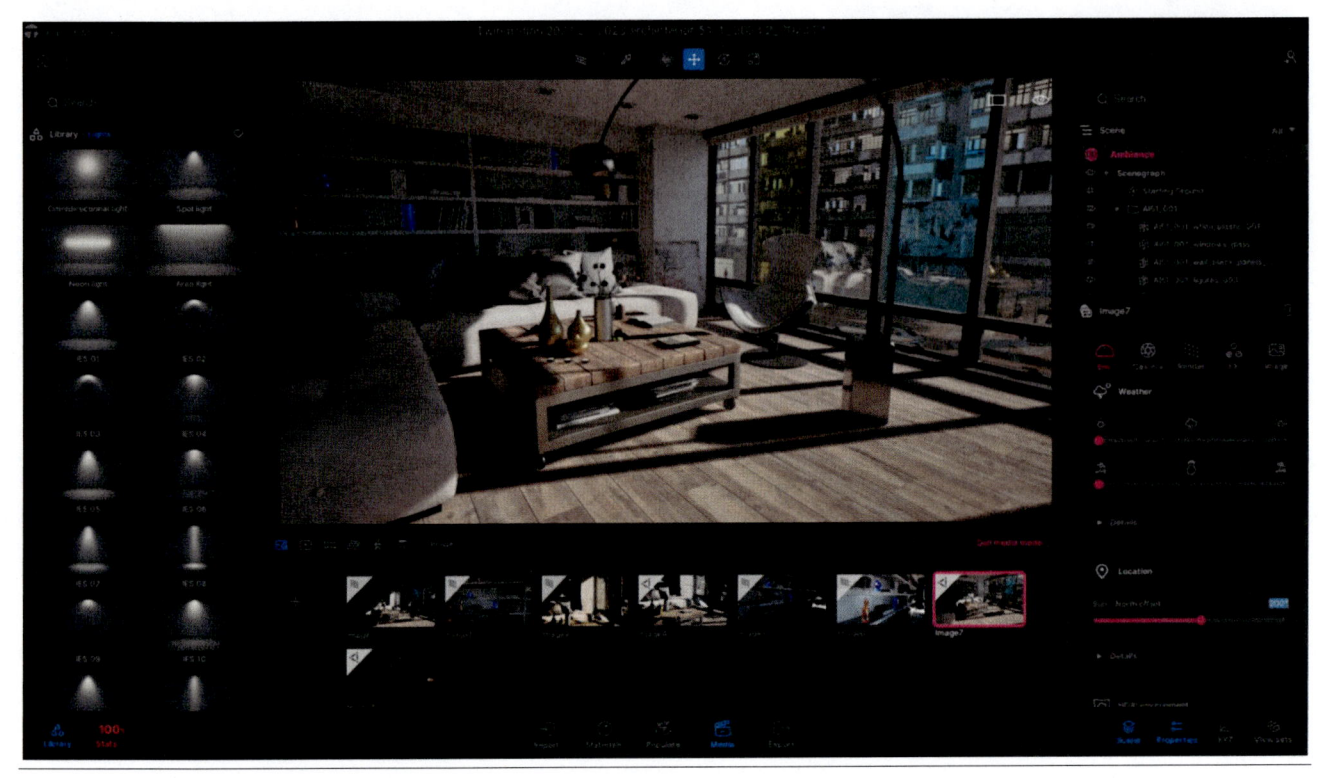

As you'll notice, there are two colored glass panels in the scene. Lumen doesn't account for these translucent materials, so to achieve true photorealism with Lumen, you have two options:

1. Make the colored glass transparent. This is a simplistic approach but could work if colored glass isn't crucial for your scene.
2. Use lights to simulate the color effect of the glass.

Be aware that you won't achieve the same quality as a Path Tracer, which I'm showing here for reference only.

In the image below, you'll see the blue and yellow hues of the glass noticeably affecting the scene. Note that here, too, I've only activated the Path Tracer without any special settings.

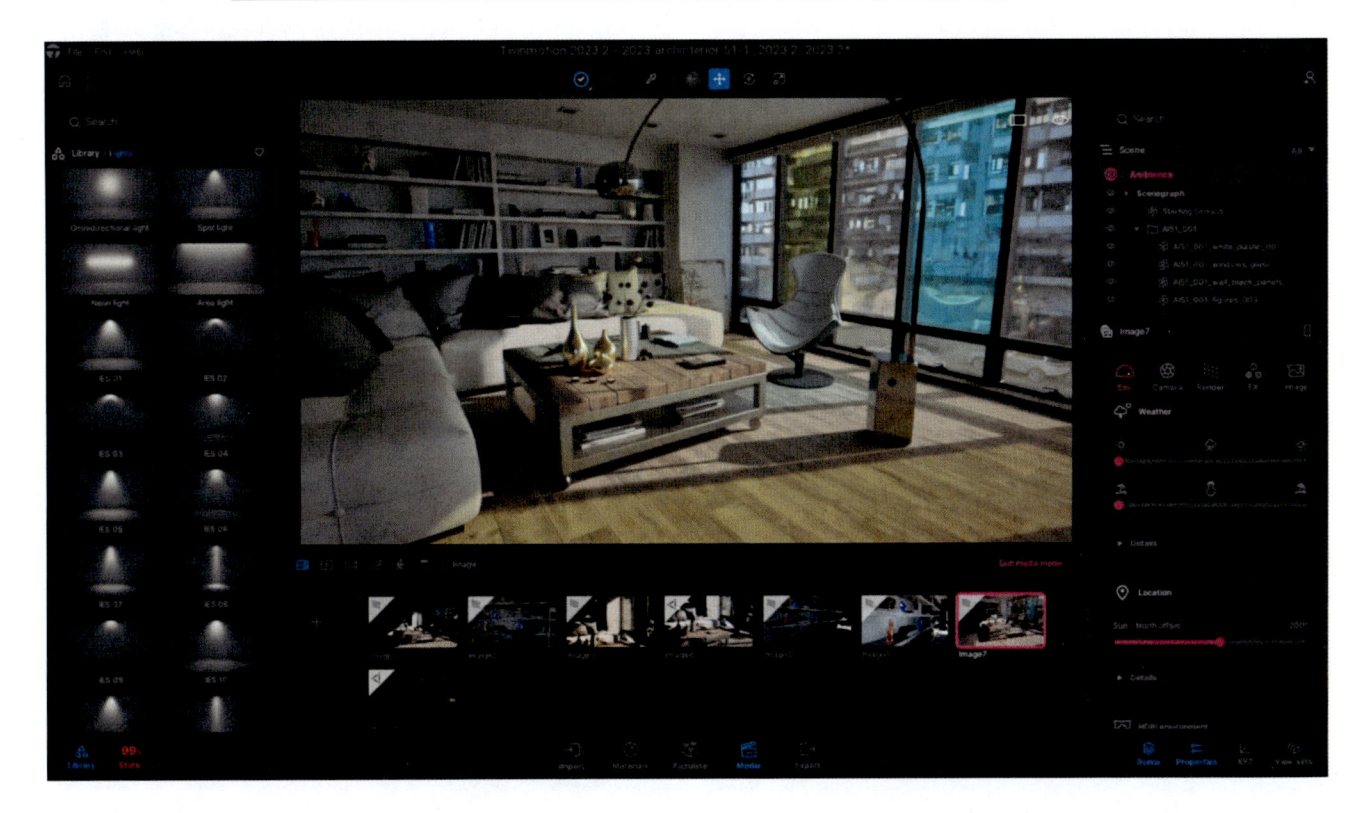

If you opt for the second approach, because you can't forgo the colored glass but still want a photorealistic rendering that accounts for these materials, you can use three distinct "area lights"—two yellow and one blue. Think of an area light as a cube that emits light. You can modify its dimensions to turn it into a rectangular shape that can be placed and rotated within the scene to mimic the colored shadow created by light passing through the glass.

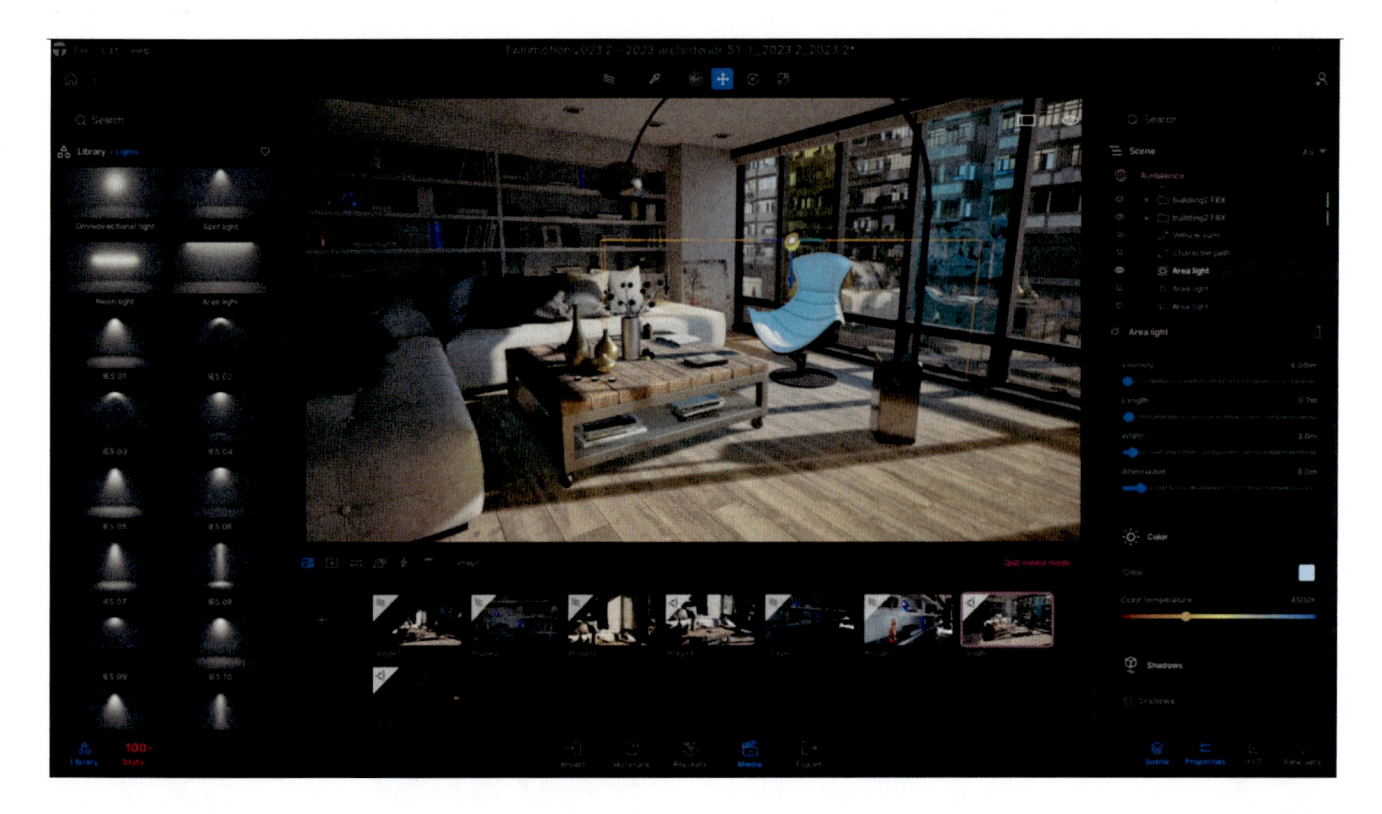

In the image generated with Lumen above, I've left the cyan light selected so you can see its position relative to the window and the colored shadow.

Above are two images created with Lumen. The one on the left lacks colored lights to simulate the shadow from the windows.

At this point, similar to the Path Tracer, we can identify an area to place the camera's focus by activating FOV (Field of View) and DOF (Depth of Field). A setup like this, typical in the archviz interior world, allows for the creation of high-quality photorealistic videos and offers the flexibility for various photographic shots under diverse lighting conditions and angles.

Below are some final images rendered with Lumen, along with details on the settings used for the rendering.

Luca Rodolfi - Photorealism with Twinmotion – Raster – Path Tracer - Lumen

77

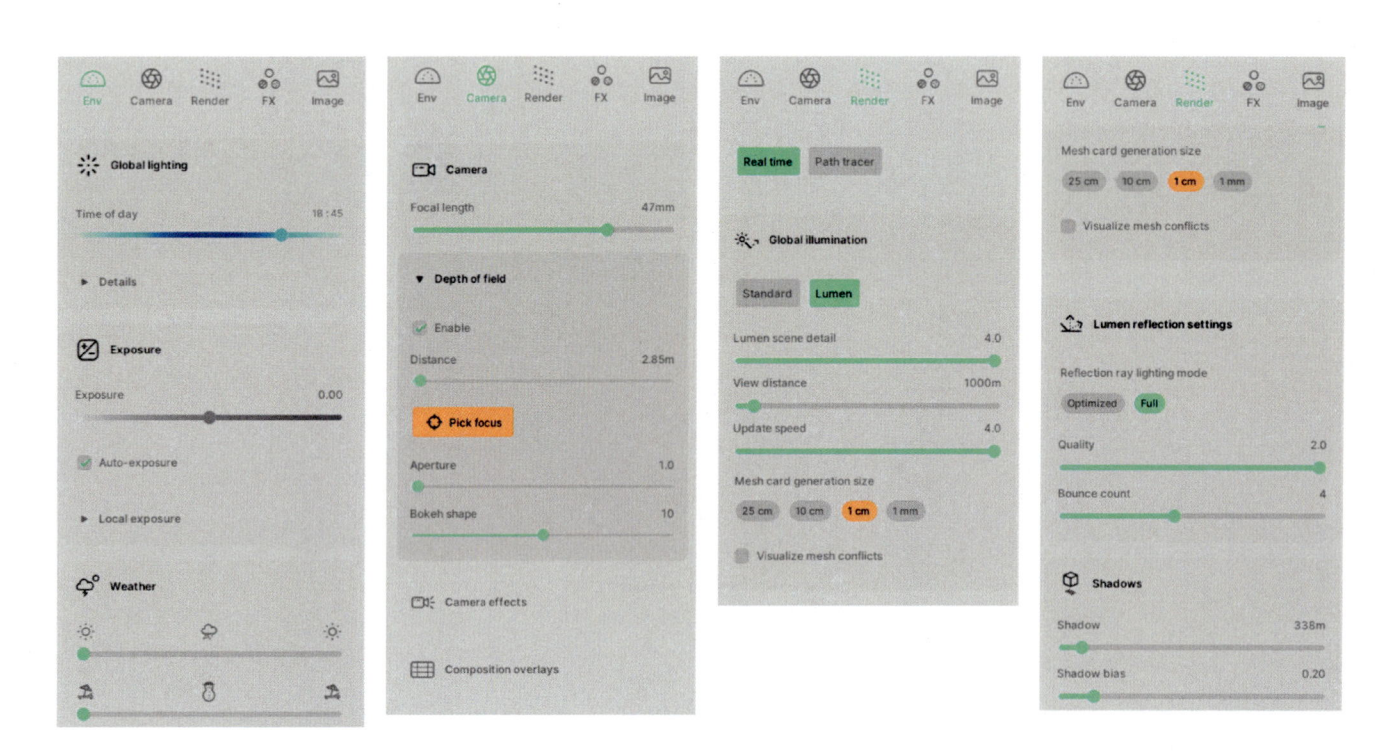

I'd like to present another test scenario: an evening setting in a city. This will allow us to explore optimal configurations for managing artificial lights in Lumen.

Photorealism here, too, hinges on your scene setup: models and materials, again. Lumen excels in low-light scenes with artificial lighting.

Using lights during nighttime differs somewhat from settings in the Path Tracer. You'll notice that when you switch from the Path Tracer to Lumen, the scene's color tends to become "warmer." In such cases, you may find it essential to work with the slider that adjusts the color temperature, making it either warmer or cooler.

I'll show you how to capture a clear city evening and then also take a photo with a more pronounced FOV (40mm) and the presence of heavy fog. You'll be amazed at how Lumen can deliver quality on par with that of a Path Tracer.

For the models in this scene, I relied on an intriguing KitBash3D package called "Art Nouveau." It features buildings in a distinctly Parisian style.

I built the scene by assembling some of these buildings, defining a street, and setting up the materials to utilize all available shaders (specifically color, normal, glossiness, and metallic). In some cases, I replaced KitBash3D's original textures with my personal textures, particularly for the glossiness shader. This was done to introduce some "imperfections," enhancing the material's realistic appearance.

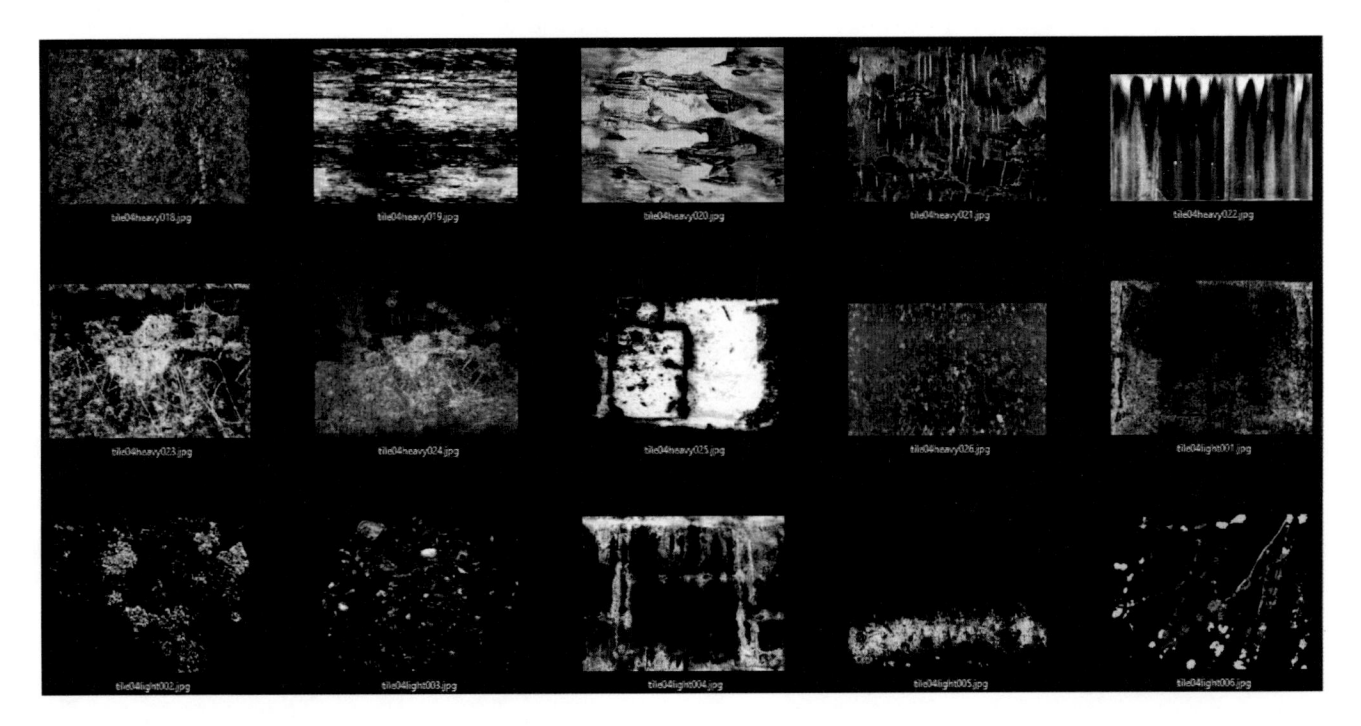

Above are some of the textures (from my old collection) that I've used for the glossiness shader.

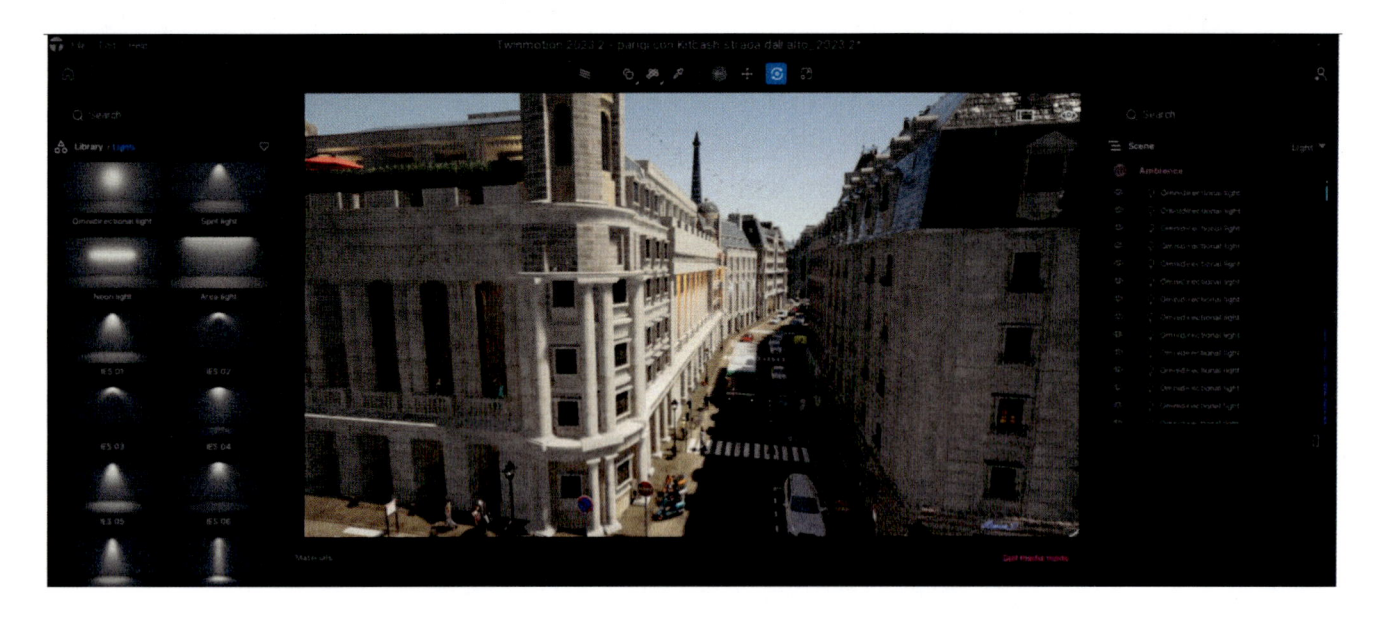

Above is the raw image from Twinmotion showing the positioned models. As you can see, there are numerous details and assets strategically placed to "bring the image to life": people, cars, a bus, scooters, signs, and road markings. Each detail enhances the scene's compatibility with photorealistic rendering.

I can't emphasize enough that achieving photorealistic rendering primarily depends on the details you can harmoniously incorporate into your scene. In the thumbnails above, you can see the multitude of assets used for this setting.

For an evening view of the city, I've placed a large number of lights in various buildings. Some lights are "cool," typical of street lamps or illuminated storefronts, while others are warmer and yellowish. This mix enhances the global illumination effect.

For the sky, I used a Twinmotion HDRI map called LowSun Overcast 29, which creates a moody sky filled with clouds, perfect for our evening setting.

I position the camera as if it were on the third or fourth floor of a building facing the street we aim to capture. I could have framed the shot at eye level, but that would limit the broader view that is the goal for this scene.

The magic of Lumen is almost instantaneous upon activation, offering a notable level of photorealism with minimal adjustments. On the right, you can see some of the numerous lights present in the scene.

Lastly, by tweaking exposure, contrast, and saturation settings, you can achieve the specific photorealistic look you're aiming for.

As you can see, the framing doesn't allow us to use features like FOV and DOF that would make the image more cinematic. However, this scene is well-suited for other shots where I will activate DOF and adjust the FOV, as well as change weather conditions. As always, I'll provide the parameters to achieve these specific results.

Twinmotion offers a wide variety of filters that can be applied to renderings in post-production. In the example above, I applied the "color gradient" MTX filter, which enhances the green hue of the film.

Below are the parameters used for setting up Lumen.

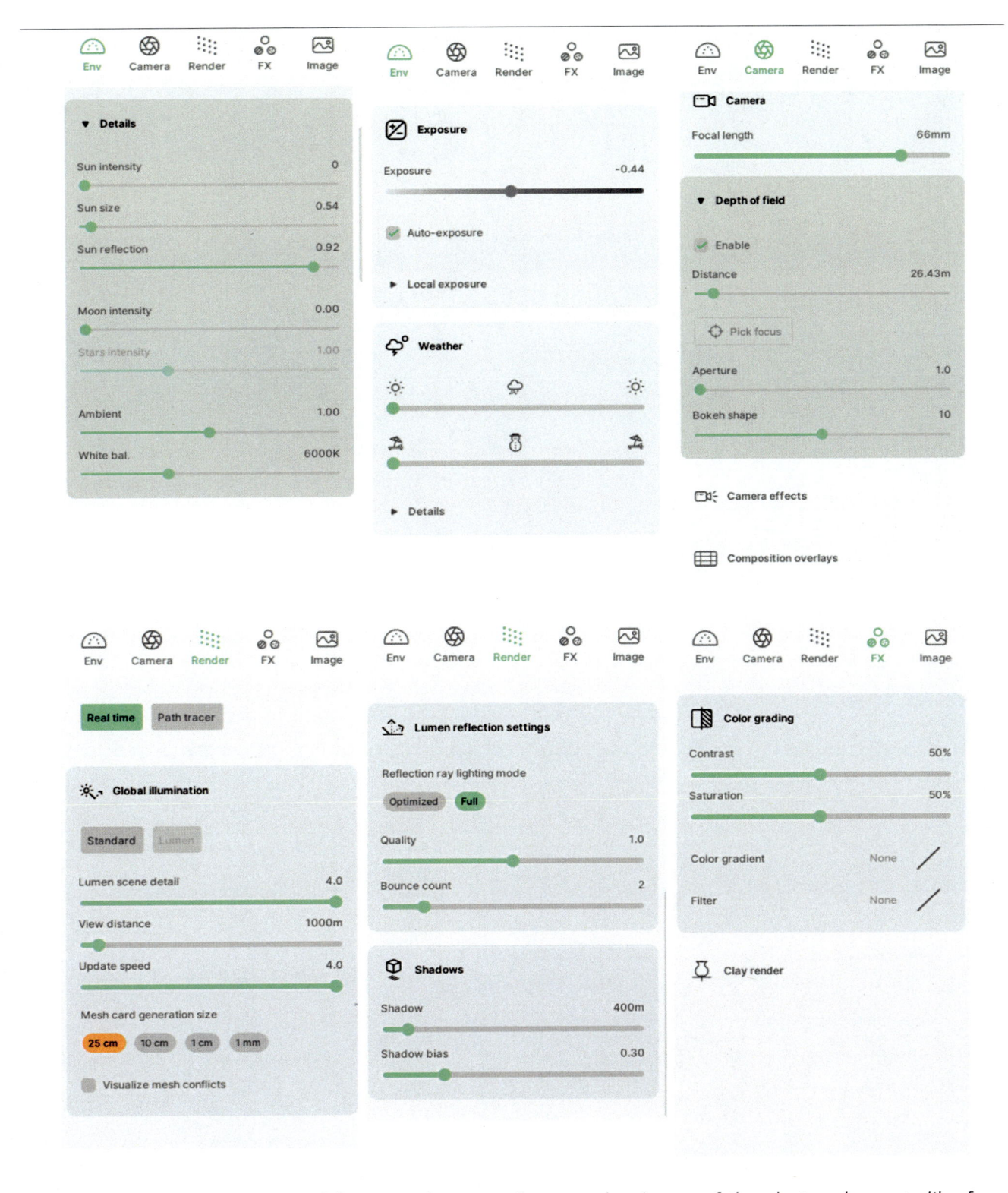

I now add some environmental features that contribute to the drama of the photo: elements like fog, rain, and dramatic camera zoom often make for extremely convincing photorealistic renderings.

All settings are the same as mentioned above except for the fog (set to 100%), rain (activated in the corresponding slider under the Env tab), and the FOV adjusted to 40mm.

As you may have gathered, the key points for achieving photorealistic renderings with Lumen particularly concern environmental and light parameters. By adjusting these parameters, you can see in real-time how Lumen responds to changes. The rendering engine parameters, such as level of detail and shadows, are also important but perhaps not as much as one might assume. Below, I list the parameters that, in my opinion, best contribute to the optimal configuration of Lumen (as per the current state of the art).

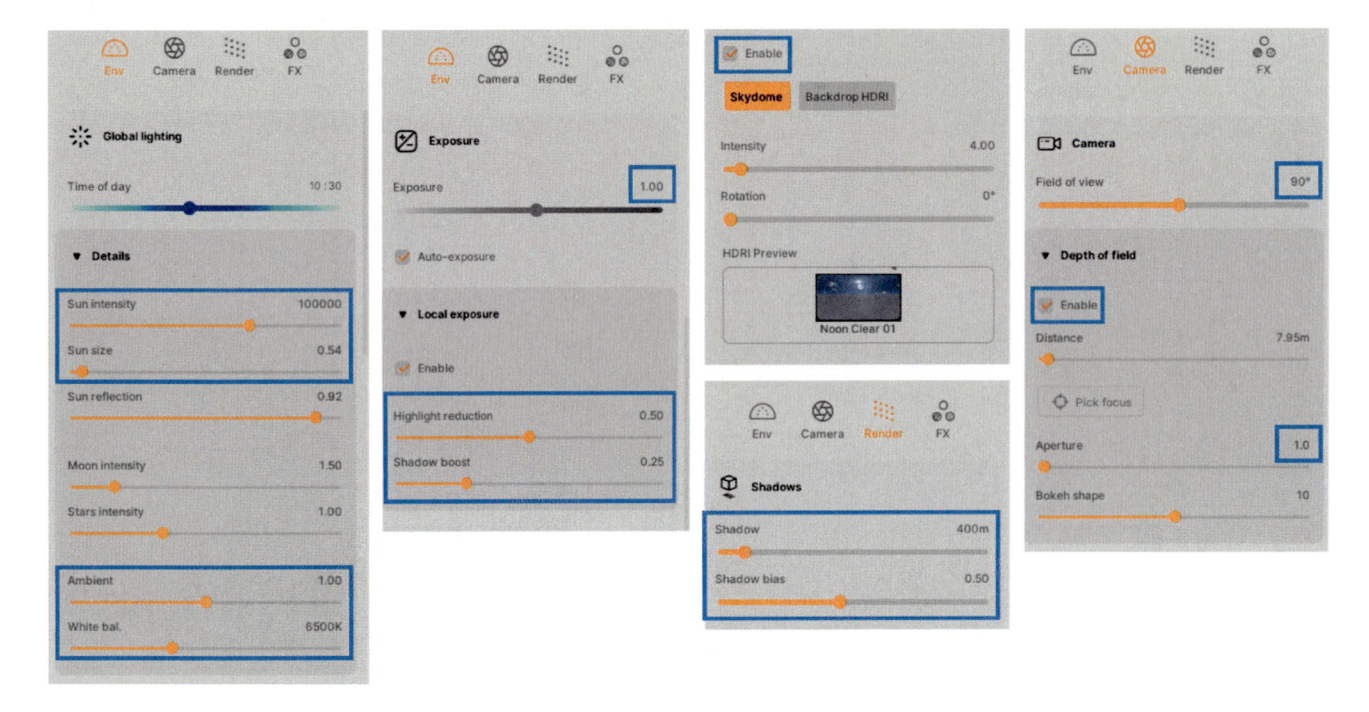

Mastering Urban Environments

The creation of urban environments in 3D rendering applications is a specialized challenge that particularly attracts architects and 3D artists. The rising interest in architectural visualization, or ArchViz, has led to a demand for tools that are powerful, efficient, and easily integrated into existing architectural workflows. Twinmotion stands out as a perfect solution for these multifaceted needs.

Architects engaged in ArchViz continually seek the most effective and quickest tools for rendering their projects. Efficiency is often as valuable as the quality of the final render, especially in an industry where time is of the essence. Twinmotion's strength lies in its incredibly fast workflow, allowing for real-time visualization and substantially speeding up the rendering process. What traditionally took hours can now be done in mere minutes, all without sacrificing quality.

Another strong point in Twinmotion's favor is its seamless integration with popular architectural software like SketchUp, Revit, and ArchiCAD. This compatibility ensures architects can easily import their existing models into Twinmotion and begin rendering without the need for cumbersome conversions or loss of detail.

As demonstrated in the preceding chapters, Twinmotion also excels in delivering photorealistic outputs. Equipped with powerful engines like RASTER, Path Tracer, and Lumen, the software captures even the most intricate details. From the reflections in glass skyscrapers to the subtle shades of the evening sky, Twinmotion offers an unparalleled level of realism.

In the competitive world of ArchViz, Twinmotion has become the go-to choice for architects searching for the perfect balance between speed, ease of use, and exceptional quality. Whether you're a seasoned architect or just stepping into the fascinating realm of ArchViz, Twinmotion provides the ideal combination of tools, speed, and photorealistic capabilities to bring your architectural visions to life.

In the following sections, we will delve into best practices for optimizing your urban environment renders. You'll learn how to get the best results with the various rendering engines when dealing with cityscapes and other urban settings.

Architectural Excellence: Rendering Cities and Buildings

Rendering urban scenes always presents a challenge, not only because you often need to introduce a high number of models into the scene—buildings, roads, cars, buses, people, vegetation, etc.—that directly affect your workstation's performance, but also because focusing attention on a specific structure isn't always straightforward.

Imagine wanting to showcase a series of renders of a building you've designed within an urban context, aiming for photorealistic qualities. You'll need to build a detailed scene around your main structure so that from various camera viewpoints, the scene remains plausible in terms of photorealism. Essentially, this equates to the need for considerable time and work, as well as access to an extensive model library to complement your scene. Thankfully, numerous resources are available both within Twinmotion— thanks to Sketchfab and Quixel bridges—and externally through marketplaces that offer thousands of quality models of various types and shapes.

However, crafting such a scene shouldn't distract from the main building that you want to feature. Simply placing it in the center of the image won't suffice to draw the viewer's attention. Your main structure should possess unique characteristics that naturally make it the focal point of the scene.

Another key consideration is the level of photorealism you aim to achieve. As discussed in earlier parts of this book, the real world is inherently imperfect. When rendering a building you want to sell to clients, you often aim to depict it in its utmost glory, free of imperfections. On the one hand, this showcases the building's beauty and harmony, meeting a primary objective. On the other hand, the quest for photorealistic rendering could be compromised by the model's perfection.

Once you've decided which elements to include in the render and what kind of image you wish to generate, it becomes crucial to determine the scope of the scene. Rendering a close-up of a building that takes up 80% of the image is far less complex than situating it within a broader urban landscape. In the latter scenario, I prefer to add supporting buildings to the image first, followed by the road network. This allows me to quickly establish the desired proportions. This process can be further streamlined if these elements are already defined in your modeling software; all you'll need to do is include them in the scene while enhancing materials and appearance later.

By following these guidelines, you'll be better equipped to manage the complexities of rendering urban environments, allowing you to effectively feature your main architectural subject while maintaining the desired level of photorealism. In the following sections, best practices for achieving optimal results with various engines when dealing with urban settings will be highlighted.

If your rendering involves a large portion of a cityscape, you'll likely need to manage low-poly models with low-resolution textures. Generally speaking, this allows you to populate your scene with dozens or even hundreds of models without overwhelming your computer. Rendering such a scene strikes a good balance between detail and quality. A tip I can offer is to focus on adding detail to the portions of the scene closest to the camera.

The image below, rendered with Lumen, contains nearly 30 million polygons, even though the building models are low-poly. Imagine how resource-intensive a similar scene would be with high-poly models. Making the right choices in terms of model detail and polygon count, as well as texture resolution, can mean the difference between being able to create and manage a scene, and reducing your computer to a 1 FPS crawl.

As you can see in the image, the lower portion closest to the camera features various details like graffiti and objects that enrich the scene. The buildings in the background, on the other hand, are low-poly versions with 512x512 resolution textures.

Speaking of details you can add to the scene, in the image below you'll notice the difference between the original, raw model devoid of details—which is not well-suited for high-quality rendering—and the same model enriched with numerous details that I've sourced from Sketchfab and Quixel, directly within Twinmotion.

Above is a raw model from Evermotion's Archmodel 234 collection, rendered with Path Tracer. You can see that the model has a reduced polygon count and the textures are low-resolution. The area with the 'Grocery' sign is pixelated, the stairs aren't actual steps but rather an inclined plane with a texture simulating steps, among various other limitations in the model. This is the same model used in the previous image, which appears much more realistic when viewed from a distance.

Above is the same model, but enriched with details sourced from Sketchfab and Quixel: decals, stairs, and assets placed over the low-definition ones to make the scene more realistic.

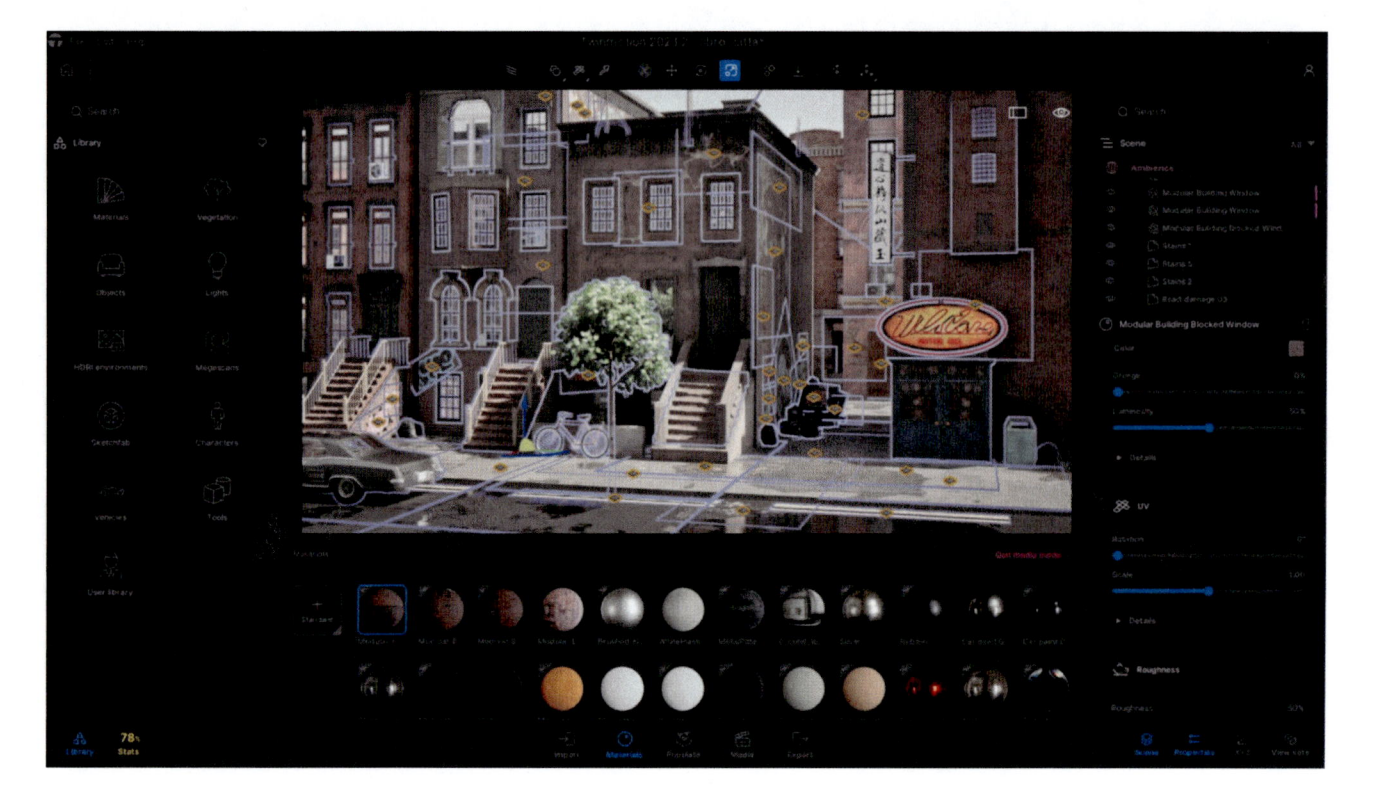

In the viewport above, you can see all the objects that I've added to the original model. The changes were extensive: I not only added glass planes to simulate windows but also sourced window frames, doors, a tree, a bicycle, a car, roof antennas, trash, doors, and decals featuring graffiti and wall imperfections, among other things.

Take this rule to heart, applicable across all contexts: Photorealistic images are not just about good lighting and framing; they also require high-quality models, detailed features, and PBR materials.

The upcoming images will showcase the rendering of a classic archviz project, where the integrity of the model to be rendered and photorealism often have to reach a compromise.

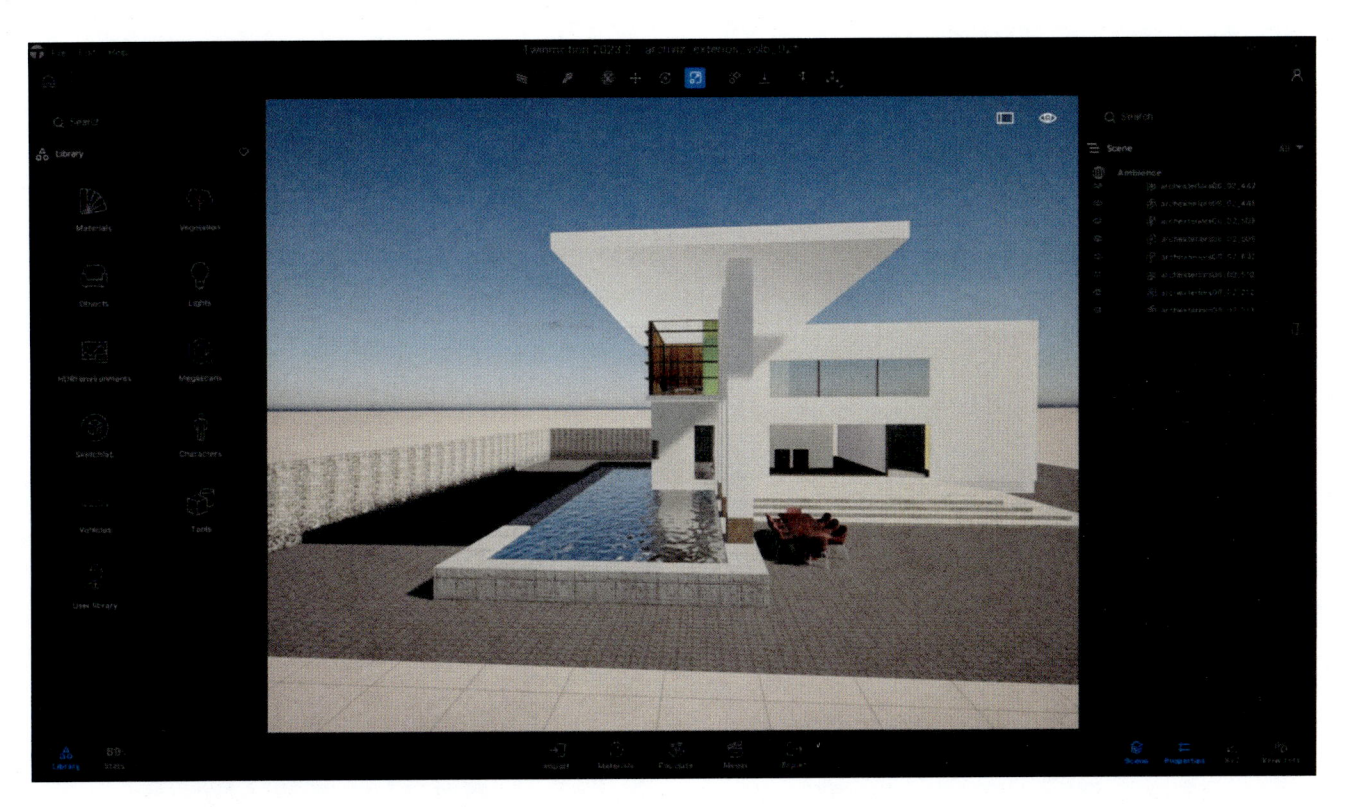

Above is the typical appearance of a model imported into Twinmotion from a 3D modeling software—in this case, the project was created in 3D Studio Max. The scene is basic, the materials are very simple, and there is a complete lack of any specific elements that might suggest photorealism.

The first thing we'll do is work on the materials to use realistic and high-quality ones. The scene from the Evermotion ArchExteriors vol 6 package offers materials with only two shaders: color and normal.

Let's redefine the materials in Twinmotion by taking advantage of available textures and also employing other shaders where possible, such as glossiness, which allows for better control over the reflection of certain materials (like marble, for example). We'll use the original rendering done with 3D Studio and V-Ray as a reference to recreate the rendering using Path Tracer and Lumen.

3D Studio Max and Vray | Twionmotion 2023.2 Beta4 and Path Tracer | Twionmotion 2023.2 Beta4 and Lumen

In these images, you can see that the focus of the rendering is the building in the foreground. Adding too many details, imperfections, or decals, as we did in previous examples to achieve the best possible photorealism, would be counterproductive in this type of archviz rendering.

Above is the rendering done with Path Tracer, and below are the settings used in Path Tracer and Lumen for this type of rendering.

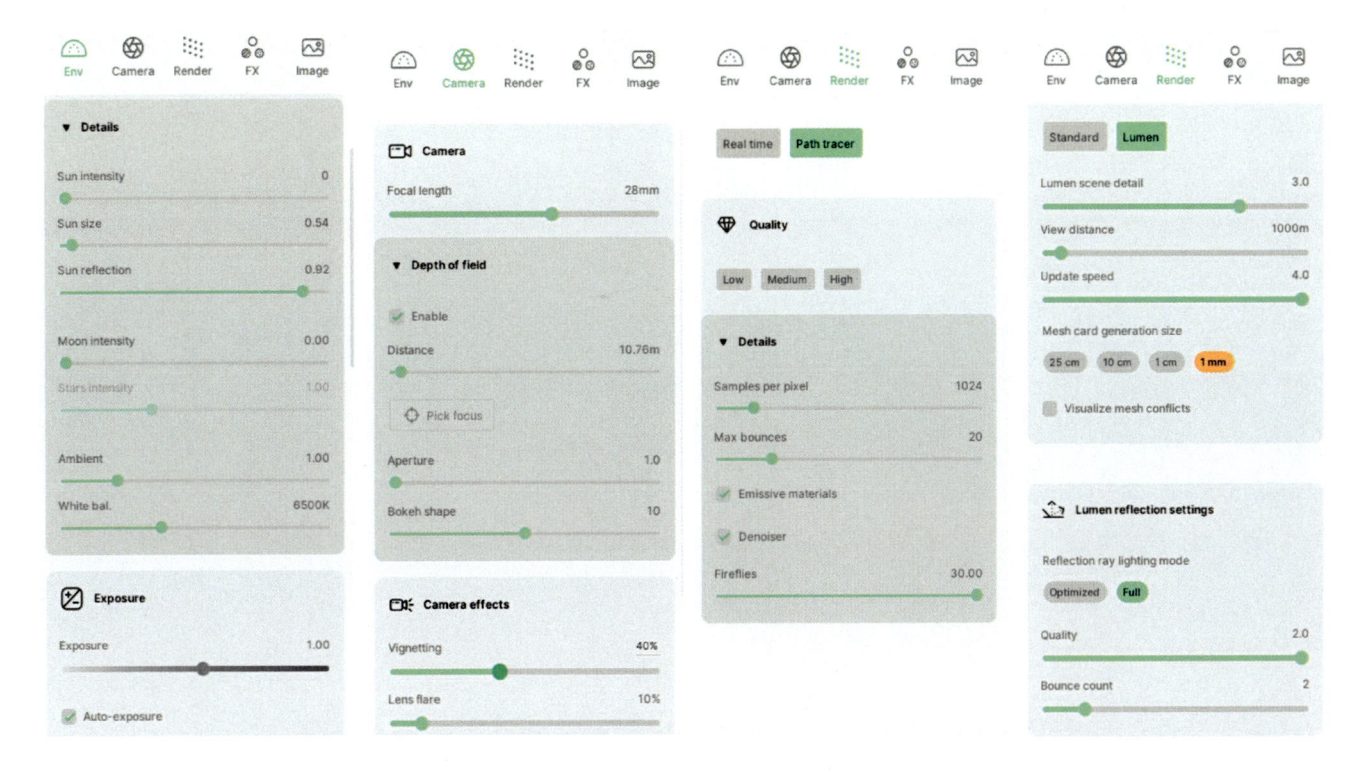

Another example of models and scenes used in archviz rendering, freshly imported from 3D Studio Max into Twinmotion. This one also comes from the Evermotion ArchExteriors vol 6 pack.

The workflow is always the same: start with setting up the materials, and then find the best lighting and point of view (POV) for a photorealistic rendering. Importing from 3D Studio Max using the Datasmith bridge may result in the loss of some textures. This is primarily due to the fact that some materials in 3D Studio Max are composite materials, which are not all compatible with Datasmith export. Additionally, it's often not advisable to adjust models like trees and bushes in Twinmotion, unless they are crucial elements to keep in the scene. It's usually better to remove them and simplify the scene, to which you can then add, for example, native Twinmotion trees.

Above is the scene with the materials properly set up and all superfluous, low-quality, or hard-to-manage elements removed. At this point, you can work on the lighting and settings, and then add any missing elements such as vegetation.

Above, you can see how I've added vegetation using the paint vegetation tools. As you'll notice, the model is surrounded by trees and bushes. Some of these trees will be behind the camera's point of view (POV), but it's important that they are there. This is because the house model has several glass panels that will reflect the surrounding environment, including the area behind the camera. Ensuring that trees and vegetation exist behind the POV will lead to more realistic reflections in the glass panels.

Creating a convincing ArchViz rendering can be a challenging task. In my opinion, the theme of lighting is crucial. Below, you can see the same scene at three different times of the day. Twinmotion offers a 'Dusk to Dawn' function for lights, allowing you to have lights automatically turn on during the evening hours. This way, you can experiment with different times of the day without worrying about having to manually turn on the lights as sunset approaches.

And here are the settings for the three renderings done with Path Tracer.

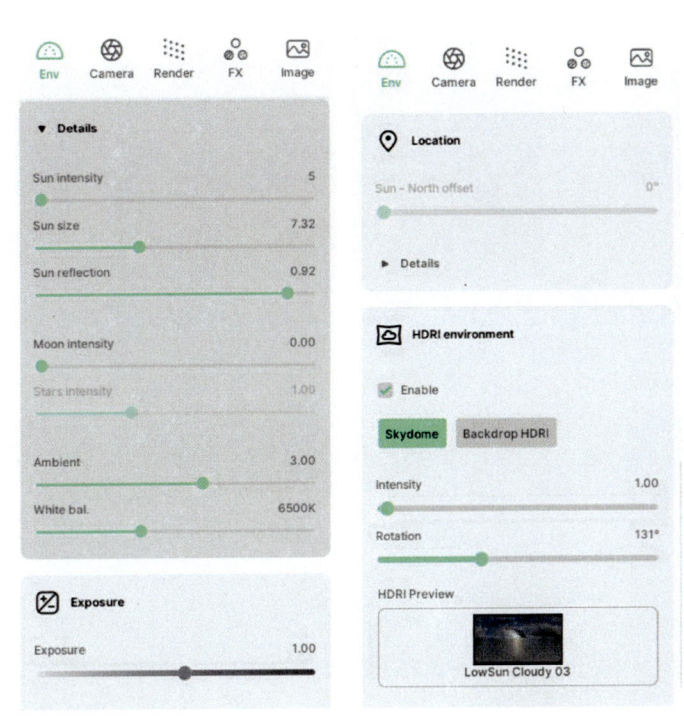

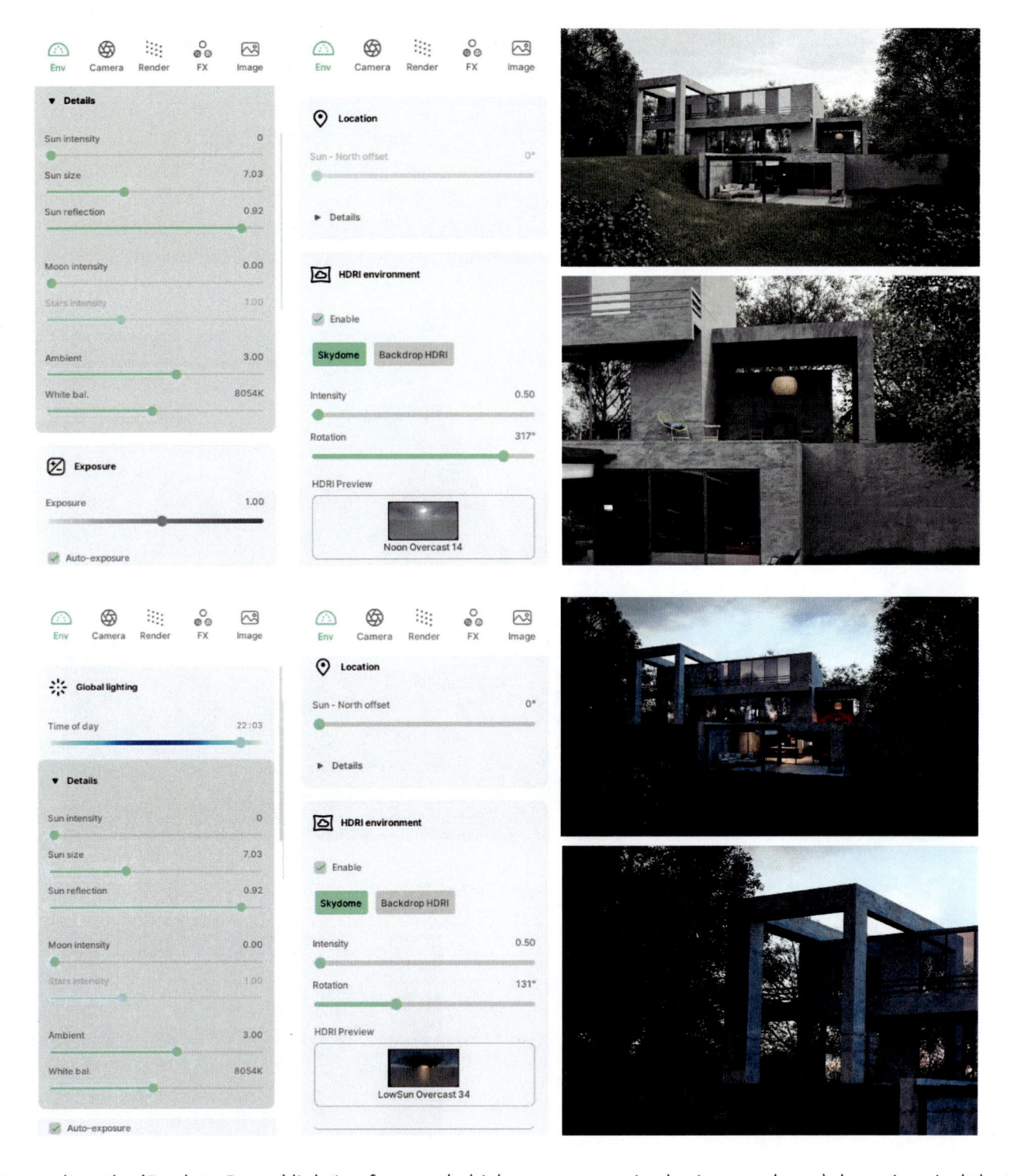

Regarding the 'Dusk to Dawn' lighting feature (which you can see in the image above), keep in mind that when you use a Skydome, the time of day is locked and cannot be changed. If the Skydome is not set to nighttime, your lights will remain off. To resolve this issue, simply go to the Skydome control panel and uncheck the 'Lock Sun to HDRI' checkbox. This will allow you to adjust the time of day while still using the Skydome.

On the Move: Crafting Realistic Cars in Urban Spaces

In 3D graphics, a modern urban scene often feels incomplete without the inclusion of vehicles like cars and buses. Twinmotion offers functionalities specifically designed to populate your scenes with realistic vehicle paths. You can easily sketch out routes on your map and adjust the traffic level with a simple slider, adding a layer of dynamism and realism.

Beyond mere traffic, several small tricks can elevate your scene's photorealism. In a nighttime setting, for instance, consider how city and vehicle lights can interact to create a visually compelling and realistic environment. Proper use of lighting settings, like diffuse and direct light, can profoundly influence the overall atmosphere.

During daylight scenes, leveraging cinematic techniques such as Field of View (FOV) and Depth of Field (DOF) can add another layer of realism. A wider FOV can provide a sense of open space, whereas a narrower DOF can highlight a specific element like a car, subtly blurring the rest of the scene.

So, when working with Twinmotion to create urban scenes, never underestimate the role of vehicles. From lighting configurations to traffic paths, these elements can act as potent tools to bring your artistic vision to life.

The image above illustrates a rendering I've created to emphasize the photorealism of an urban scene where the main focus is car traffic. The setting is during the evening hours when car lights are turned on. The scene is further enriched with extra elements like parked cars, pedestrians, and buses—all of which are readily available in Twinmotion's libraries.

For this rendering, I've used path tracing and strategically positioned low-poly buildings with low-resolution textures, as I've discussed in earlier chapters. In the background, you can see the red tail lights reflected in the building windows, an effect achieved using 2D planes and the "glass" material setting.

What you'll notice immediately is that the only light sources in the scene are the car headlights. I've deliberately avoided adding distractions like billboards or street lamps. The aim was to capture a snapshot of evening urban traffic in a setting that resembles Brooklyn.

To achieve this specific look, I used particular settings, which you can observe here. Notably, in this instance, the Depth of Field (DOF) is turned off. Keeping DOF disabled allows the viewer to focus on the entire scene rather than isolating specific elements, aligning with the goal of representing a busy urban environment.

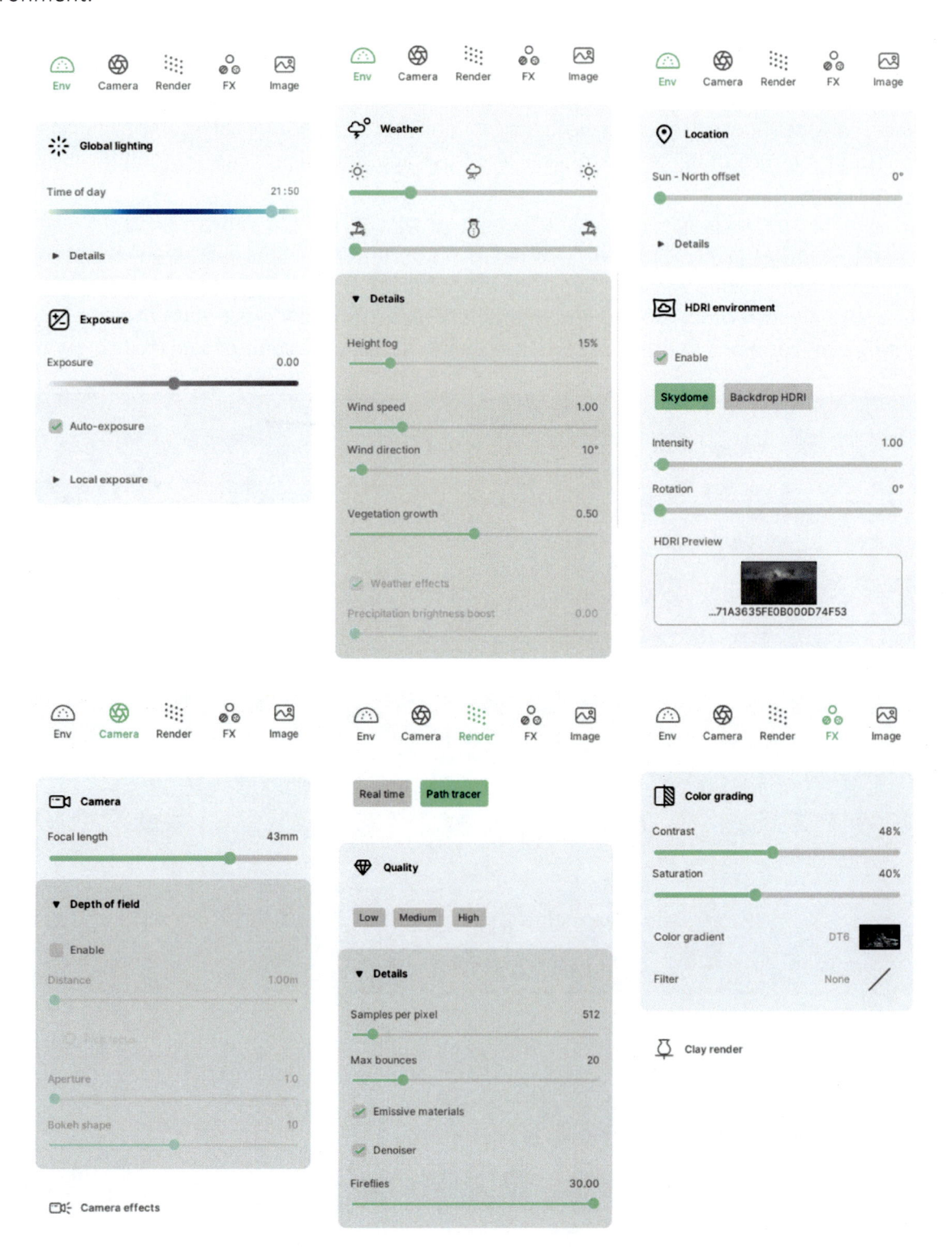

Switching settings, let's produce another rendering, but this time we'll use Lumen and set the scene to a bright morning environment. However, the majority of the scene will be in the shadow. If you recall what I've written in previous chapters, areas that are too brightly lit by the sun can actually hinder achieving flawless photorealism.

To enhance the "morning" ambiance, adding some fog can create a beautiful haze effect, allowing the sun rays to filter over the buildings. This helps to produce that ethereal quality often seen in morning urban landscapes, balancing out the lighting and adding depth to the scene.

Using these settings, Lumen's real-time global illumination technology will do the heavy lifting, filling in the shadows with soft, bounced light while keeping the overall scene bright and morning-like. You'll see that the combination of these elements—soft morning light, haze, and predominantly shadowed areas—contributes to a more convincing and photorealistic rendering.

One challenge you might encounter with Lumen is in rendering soft shadows. While using a Path Tracer, softening shadows is straightforward—simply adjust the 'Sun Size' for natural light or increase the 'Radius' for artificial lights. However, Lumen is less effective in this aspect. You'll often find that modifying the 'Shadow' and 'Shadow Bias' settings doesn't produce the same level of softness you might achieve with other rendering methods.

In the image above, on the left is a rendering using Lumen and on the right is one using Path Tracer with a 'Sun Size' value set to 4.
Below, you'll find the settings used for the Lumen-rendered image.

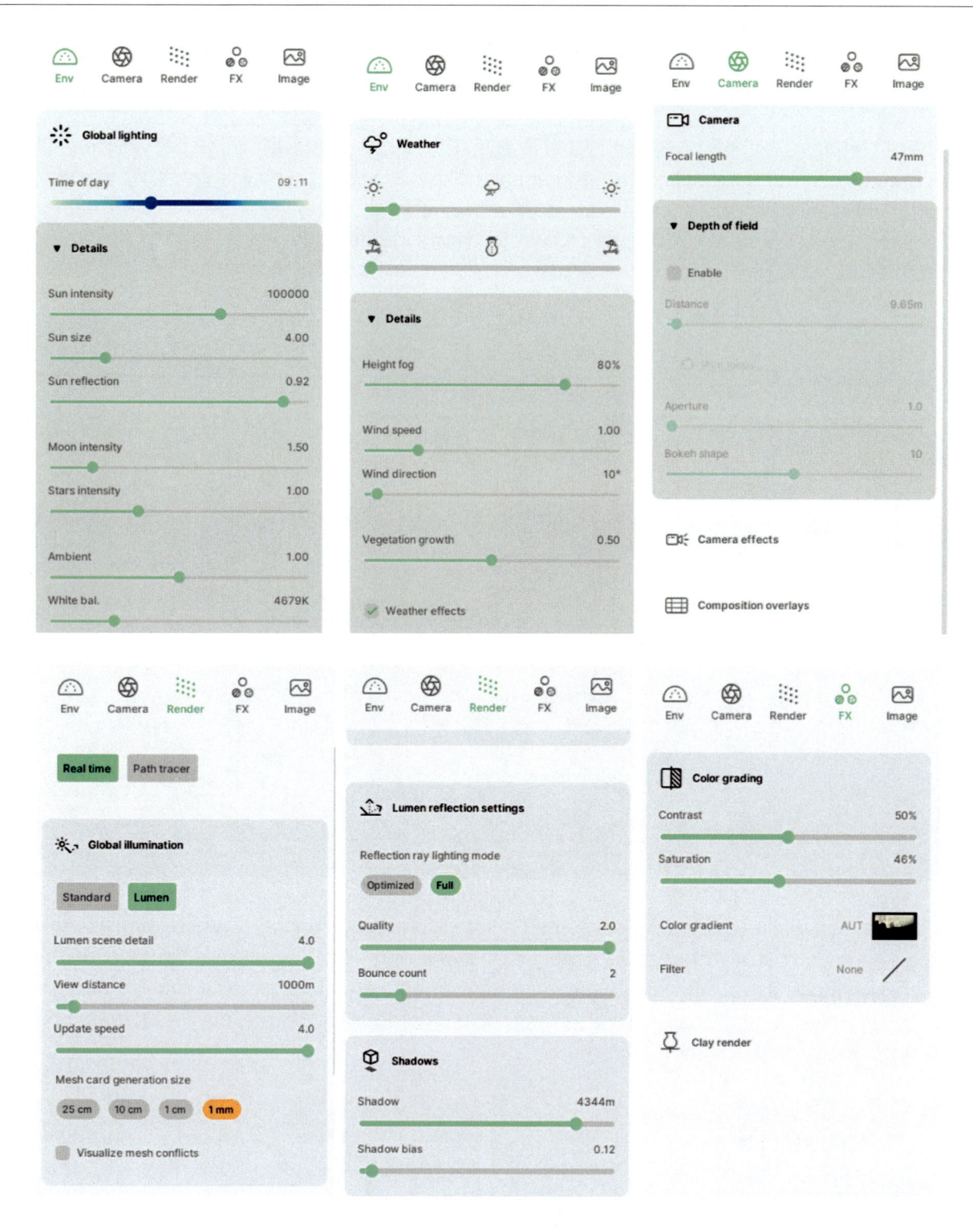

It's unfortunate that I can't show you the quality of Lumen in animations. Urban settings with moving car traffic, convincing atmospheric effects like rain or snow managed by Twinmotion, and the camera's cinematic framing capabilities, thanks to FOV and DOF parameters, can result in highly engaging videos.

In the image above, you can see the effect of rain, while the image below showcases snowfall, both achieved using Twinmotion's built-in "weather" features.

The settings for these renderings are identical to those previously detailed for the Lumen "morning" render. The only changes made were setting the time of day to 22:25 and activating the weather effects for rain and then snow. In the snow image, I've also added a Quixel "modular Snow Road" asset in the foreground.

Mastering Archviz: Interior Rendering

Lighting, one of the most transformative elements in interior rendering, can be approached in multiple ways depending on your chosen rendering engine. Whether you're using Lumen or Path Tracer, the settings you'll need to navigate are distinct. For example, in Lumen, you'll find a focus on real-time results, enabling quick iterations that are particularly useful during the design phase. The engine adapts to changes in light sources, both natural and artificial, offering you a dynamic playground to experiment in. On the other hand, as you will have now learned, when you opt for Path Tracer, you'll venture into a deeper level of calculation. While path tracing may require more time and computing power, it provides you with a hyper-realistic representation of how light photons travel and interact with surfaces. In this chapter, we'll walk you through the specific settings, techniques, and considerations you should keep in mind for each engine.

Material selection is the next pillar that we'll thoroughly explore. Every surface in your scene—from the gleam of marble countertops to the texture of wooden floors—impacts how light interacts within the space. Here, too, you'll find that the optimal settings can differ between Lumen and Path Tracer. For instance, high-gloss finishes might require different settings in Path Tracer to capture the nuanced reflections, compared to what you'd typically use in Lumen. We'll guide you through the complexities, offering tips and tricks on how to tailor each material to your selected rendering engine for maximum impact.

The art of camera placement is our final, but no less critical, focus point. The camera is your narrative tool; it's the eye through which your audience experiences the world you've constructed. Whether you're framing a wide-angle shot to reveal the grandeur of a hall, or choosing a tighter frame to showcase design details, your camera settings can be fine-tuned differently in each rendering engine. For example, Lumen's real-time capabilities allow you to experiment with camera angles dynamically, while Path Tracer's more calculated approach might require you to be more deliberate in setting up your shots. You'll find a comprehensive guide on how to make the most of each engine's unique camera settings in this chapter.

The Role of Lighting: Natural vs. Artificial Sources

The Role of Lighting: Natural vs. Artificial Sources is an essential sub-chapter that digs deep into the nuances of setting up lighting for interior architectural visualization (Archviz). Whether you're working with real-time Lumen or aiming for cinematic photorealism with Path Tracer, understanding the balance between natural and artificial lighting sources can be a game-changer for your projects.

Natural Lighting
When you think of natural light in Archviz, you think of sunlight and how it streams through windows, dances on the walls, and casts soft or hard shadows, depending on the time of day. Natural lighting tends to make spaces appear larger and livelier.
Best Practices for Natural Lighting: Window Placement: Consider the architectural design, including the position and size of windows, to take full advantage of incoming sunlight.

Time of Day: Twinmotion allows you to change the time of day dynamically. This feature is especially useful in Lumen, where you can see real-time changes. For Path Tracer, while it may take longer to render, playing with this setting can yield dramatic differences in your final output.
HDRI Sky: Often underestimated, a High-Dynamic Range Image for the sky can significantly affect the quality of natural lighting in your scene.

Artificial Lighting

Artificial lights, like spotlights, point lights, and ambient lights, play a crucial role in setting the mood of an interior. Whether you aim for a cozy, warm atmosphere or a bright, vibrant office space, your choice of artificial lights will be pivotal.
Best Practices for Artificial Lighting: Intensity and Color: Varying the intensity and color temperature of your artificial lights can make or break your render. Lumen excels in providing real-time feedback, while Path Tracer offers unparalleled quality in terms of light dispersion and color accuracy.
Light Positioning: The positioning of artificial lights should complement natural sources. Place your lights in a way that eliminates harsh shadows or overly bright spots. This is especially critical for Path Tracer, where each render could be time-consuming.
Use of IES Lights: IES light profiles can add a layer of realism to your renders by mimicking real-world light behaviors. Both Lumen and Path Tracer engines in Twinmotion support IES lights, but the settings might differ slightly to achieve the best results.

Let's take a closer look at the following rendering to understand the critical role of lighting in an interior Archviz context. You'll also see the differences in settings between Path Tracer and Lumen. Interestingly, the disparities are less significant than one might assume, but Path Tracer's superiority in delivering photorealistic interiors is evident.

The first set of images (Archinterior vol 52 - 10 model) features indirect natural light. In this case, the only light source is the sun, but its rays are directed away from the windows. The light illuminating the interiors is, therefore, indirect ambient light. As you can see, the initial renderings with the active Path Tracer, without any settings optimization, produce an image that is too dark.

By tweaking contrast, exposure, ambient light, and saturation, you can quickly find a balance that yields a photorealistic rendering. However, these options often result in a rather dark image. In such cases, people usually opt to manipulate parameters like indirect lighting and exposure further. While this is good practice, for lighting conditions like the ones in this example, it might not be sufficient. You may need to directly adjust the sun's light intensity.

Be cautious—having a darker image with the default sun intensity settings is not inherently wrong. You've likely seen several photographs of interiors with dark, indirect light, while the environment outside the window seems exceptionally bright. However, this type of photorealism may be less useful when creating an Archviz interior rendering.

A scene so rich in details and assets lends itself well to various types of rendering. Focusing specifically on natural light, you can run tests by adjusting the time of day and light direction. For instance, you might aim for a golden sunset with rays dramatically streaming through the window. Another option is positioning the camera and utilizing Depth of Field (DOF) to create images that are both cinematic and photorealistic. In the following thumbnails, you'll find a few examples of these possibilities: from left to right, a close-up detail using DOF, a scene with direct sunlight coming through the window, and a 7:00 PM scene featuring a touch of fog to simulate a bit of haze.

Here are the settings used with Path Tracer to achieve the final image:

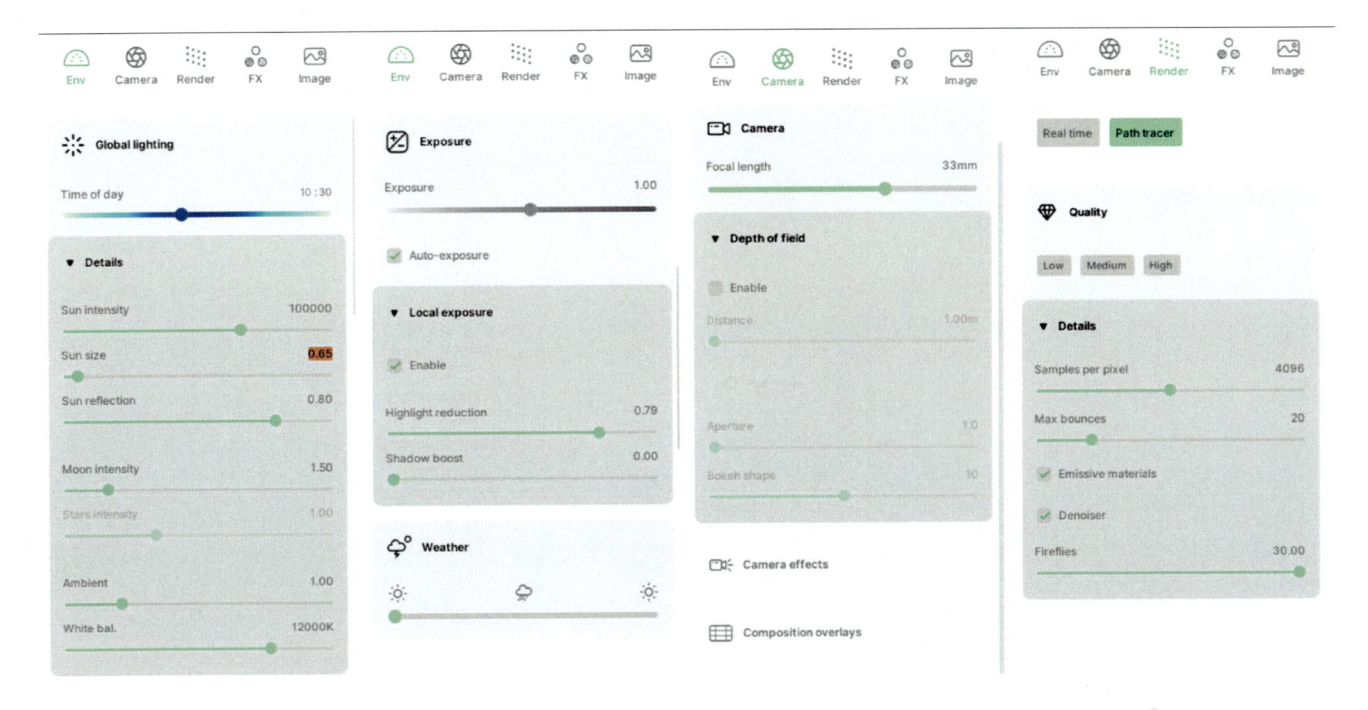

Now let's shift our focus to the same scene rendered using Lumen. For Lumen, this type of rendering is challenging due to the numerous reflections and presence of glass, which don't play well with real-time engines. Therefore, it's crucial to carefully choose the type of glass material to use. Colored glass, which is perfect for Path Tracer, may not be the best option for Lumen (or raster engines, for that matter). To capture the best glassy effect typically seen in glassware, I opted to use "item glass" in the standard version rather than the colored one.

Unfortunately, activating Lumen with this scene produces some unpleasant surprises. Let's delve into the issues and discuss potential solutions we can implement.

The most evident issues can be grouped into three main categories:

1. Light arches appear between the ceiling and the wall, an artifact that is independent of the lighting setup and related to the imported model.
2. The metal material of the chairs appears much darker compared to the version rendered with Path Tracer.
3. The sofa material seems to have lost its roughness, appearing too smooth.

Let's start by addressing the most critical issue, which is the first one: the wall and ceiling are part of a single mesh, and this is not compatible with the Lumen engine. As outlined in previous sections, when importing a model to use with Lumen, it's crucial to have it divided into different meshes. In this specific model, the wall is a single piece, and Lumen fails to generate the necessary card meshes for accurate rendering.

The best way to solve this issue is to separate the various models. I typically use 3D Studio Max.

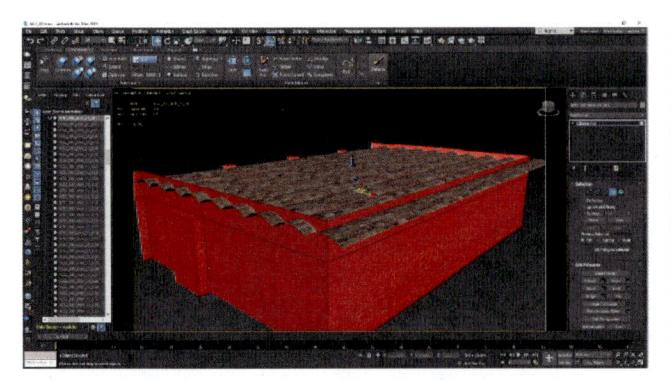

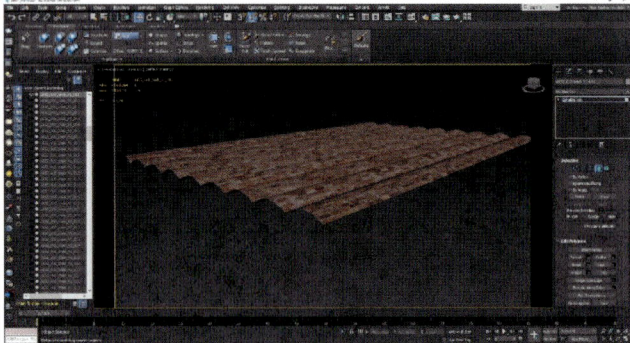

Above, I identified the problematic mesh, selected the wall, and deleted it, leaving only the ceiling. In reality, to ensure that Lumen correctly generates the card meshes, I should also subdivide the ceiling into smaller components.

I addressed issues 2 and 3 by making direct adjustments to the materials. I lightened the color of the metal to make it appear more in line with the Path Tracer rendering, and I reduced the roughness of the sofa material.

Modifying materials to get the desired results with Lumen is not a best practice, especially if your project requires both still images and videos, necessitating the use of both Path Tracer and Lumen engines. Changing materials can lead to inconsistencies and a more complicated workflow to manage. In such cases, it's better to find a balanced approach that works well with both engines, or to commit to using just one for both stills and animations, accepting the limitations on quality and performance.

And what about the good old Raster Engine? Well, these are not scenes suited for a raster engine. You can refer to the guidelines in the previous chapters for building a render and conducting the appropriate post-processing to achieve a satisfactory result. However, the lighting and glass-like materials in these scenes create significant challenges for the raster engine.

Below are the settings used for the Lumen engine.

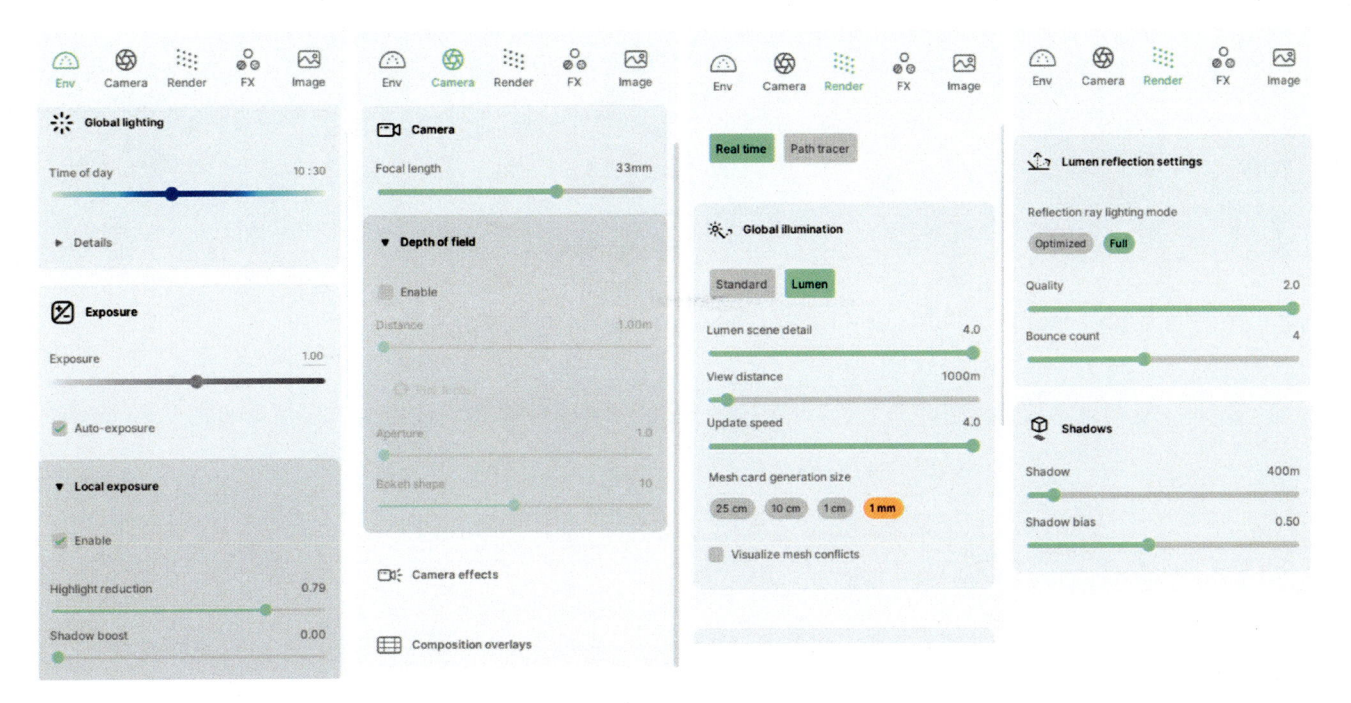

In the following exercise, we will delve into the intricacies of rendering a complex architectural interior using two distinct rendering engines: Path Tracer and Lumen. A pivotal element in this experiment will be the utilization of artificial lighting, adding a layer of complexity to the already detailed scene.

In this context, multiple light sources will be employed to illuminate various aspects of the space. Specifically, each lamp within the architectural setup will be lit using an 'omnidirectional light' setting. Additionally, shadowing will be enabled for these light sources to contribute to the overall realism and depth of the final render.

For those opting to use Path Tracer for this exercise, it's advised to configure the 'radius' parameter to a value of 8. This adjustment serves to soften the edges of the shadows, effectively imbuing the scene with a more natural and photorealistic lighting ambiance.

Here are the parameters for lights and rendering with the Path Tracer.

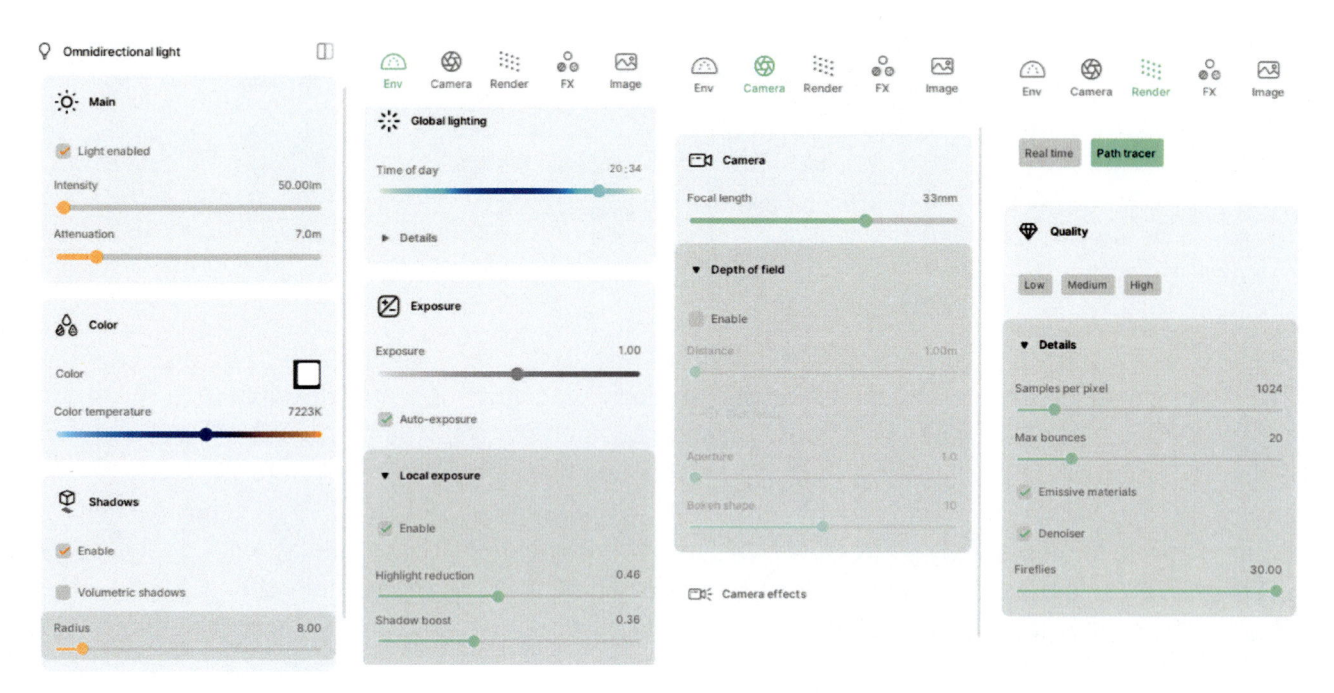

Let's also take a look at the same rendering done with Lumen; in this case, the artificial lights perform well, though I wasn't able to soften the shadows they cast. This is because the shadow approximation and its resulting softness work particularly with sunlight and not with artificial lights.

And here are the parameters used.

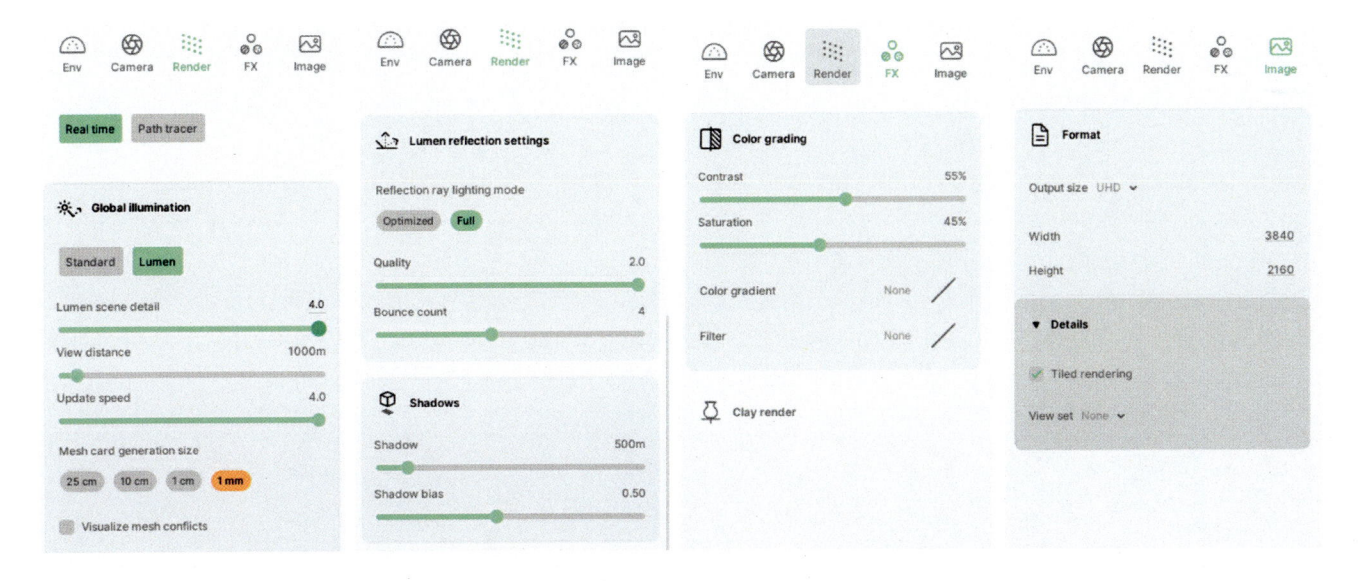

I should note in the parameters that I had to use tiled rendering, because with my computer, this scene was too demanding with Lumen, leading to GPU memory exhaustion and subsequent Twinmotion crash.

Material Matters: How to Choose and Apply Textures

In architectural visualization, especially for interiors, materials are not just aesthetic choices; they are the cornerstones that can either make or break the photorealism of your scene. One of the most potent ways to achieve realism is to utilize Physically-Based Rendering (PBR) materials, a more advanced technique that accurately simulates how light interacts with various surfaces.

Let's delve into some key shaders that are commonly used, while recognizing that these are merely a subset of the vast array of shader options available. Diffuse serves as your base color and is the fundamental shader that determines how a material will appear under neutral lighting. Roughness controls the surface's tactile quality, ranging from mirror-like smoothness to the coarseness of sandpaper. The Metallic shader adjusts the reflective qualities, dictating whether the material appears metallic or non-metallic. Normal maps are used for adding smaller, more intricate details by simulating bumps or wrinkles on the surface.

Adding to this list, the Displacement shader offers an even greater level of detail by physically altering the geometry of the material's surface. This shader is particularly useful for replicating textured materials like stone or brick, providing an extra layer of realism that goes beyond what Normal maps can achieve.

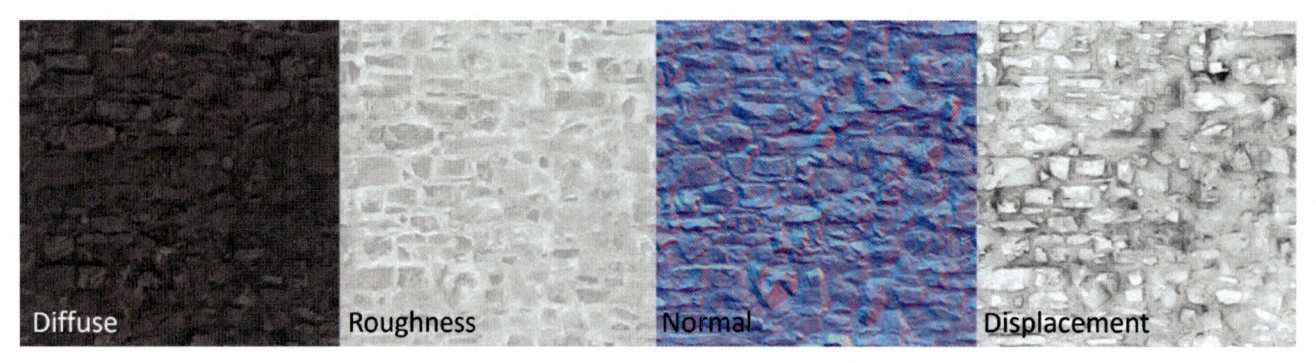

Image from Artstation

Now, how do these shaders translate in an enclosed environment like an indoor setting? The quality and choice of materials are especially critical here, as light behaves differently based on the surfaces it interacts with. For example, a rough surface may scatter light diffusely, while a smooth metallic surface may produce sharp, focused reflections. Understanding these interactions is key to achieving a photorealistic result in your interior archviz scenes.

Here's how two materials used in the scene of this chapter change when the values of the different shaders are modified (rendered with Lumen).

Choosing the right materials and shaders for your scene requires a strategic approach. Consider the narrative elements of your scene: Is it day or night? Is the weather sunny or rainy? These conditions will influence your choice of materials and their properties like Diffuse and Roughness.

Additionally, camera placement plays a significant role in how these materials are perceived. The Depth of Field (DOF) and Field of View (FOV) settings can greatly influence the viewer's focus and perspective, further underscoring the material's importance in indoor archviz.

Camera Placement: Finding the Best Angles

Camera placement is both a technical skill and an artistic endeavor in architectural visualization. The position, angle, and lens choice can significantly impact the narrative, visual flow, and emotional resonance of a scene. Poor camera placement can turn even a meticulously designed interior into a visually unappealing space.

Starting with the basics, maintaining straight vertical and horizontal lines is essential, especially in interior architectural visualization. A camera tilt can distort perspectives and affect the spatial relationships within your render. To maintain natural verticals, position the camera at eye level, typically around 1.6 meters from the ground.

When it comes to lens choice, understanding the trade-offs between wide-angle and narrow lenses is critical. A wide-angle lens allows you to capture more of the space but can also distort the proportions. On the other hand, a narrow lens provides a more natural perspective but limits the extent of the area captured in the frame.

Depth of Field (DOF) plays a pivotal role in focusing the viewer's attention within the scene. A shallow DOF can make certain elements pop, adding a cinematic quality, whereas a deep DOF will keep everything from foreground to background in sharp focus. The use of DOF can create different moods and emphasize particular design details, making it a powerful tool in your visualization arsenal.

Field of View (FOV) is another parameter that affects how much of the scene is visible in the final render. A high FOV can capture more of the environment but may result in distortions at the edges of the frame. A lower FOV will constrain the view but can offer a more realistic representation of space.

The interplay between camera placement and lighting should not be overlooked. Different angles interact uniquely with the lighting setup, creating a range of shadow and brightness patterns. This is especially crucial in interior scenes, where light can bounce and interact with walls, furniture, and fixtures in complex ways.

Lastly, consider compositional frameworks like the Rule of Thirds or the Golden Ratio to achieve a balanced and visually satisfying image. But remember, once you've mastered these rules, don't hesitate to break them creatively to serve your scene's unique needs.

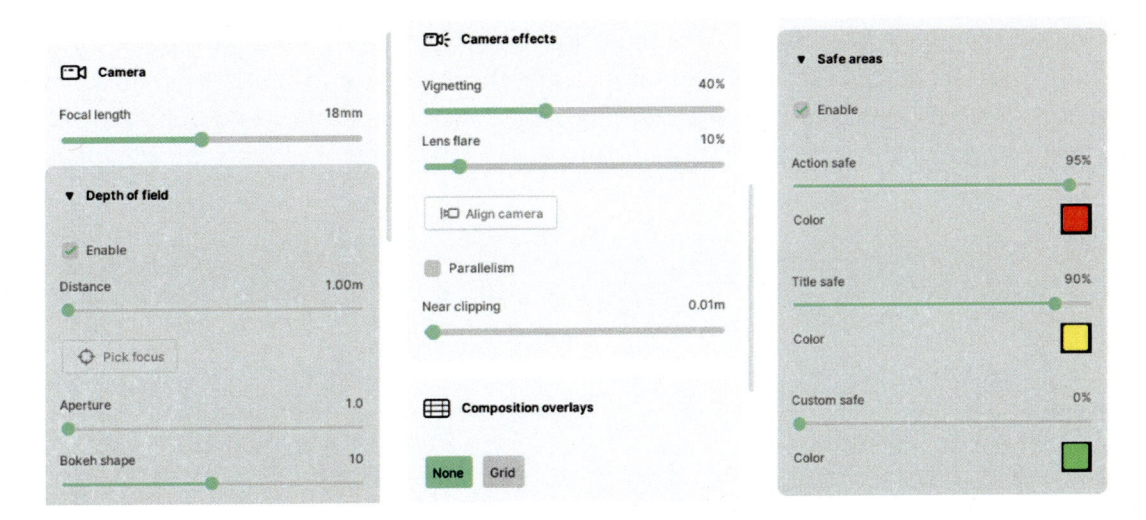

Unlocking the Beauty of Natural Environments

Twinmotion is a game changer in rendering natural environments as well. Its quick workflow and capability for photorealistic outputs lend themselves remarkably to landscape design and outdoor visualization.
Picture this: a mountainous setting rendered with striking fidelity, where sunlight filters through tree leaves and reflects off the surfaces of lakes and rivers. Twinmotion makes this possible, offering a toolkit specifically designed for modeling natural elements. From conifers to aquatic plants, you can populate your scene with a diverse range of flora, even adding atmospheric effects like mist or rain to elevate the realism.
Another significant feature is the software's sophisticated handling of textures and materials. For instance, you can deploy high-definition textures for ground surfaces, making mountains and trails seem tactile. And let's not overlook the available water simulations, from the placid lake surfaces to rushing river rapids, which you can customize in detail concerning optical and dynamic properties.

However, the real magic happens when you combine these elements with Twinmotion's powerful rendering capabilities. Whether you're utilizing engines like Path Tracer or Lumen, you can capture the visual essence of a natural environment with unprecedented accuracy. Elements such as lighting, shadows, and reflections are managed with a level of finesse that can mean the difference between a flat render and a scene bursting with life.

Quality models are the backbone of any successful rendering, and this is particularly true when crafting natural environments. The realism of your scene is only as good as the 3D models you use, and Twinmotion offers a robust library of high-quality assets specifically geared for this purpose.
Using high-definition models for vegetation, rocks, and water surfaces adds another layer of credibility to your scene. Imagine the intricacy of leaf textures in high-resolution, or the granular details of rocks and soil that make you feel like you're standing right there in the midst of it all. Quality models offer you more than just visual delight; they provide you with physical attributes that interact with light, shadow, and reflections, thereby enriching the overall composition and feel of your rendering.
When working on complex natural settings, the need for quality models becomes even more pronounced. Their detailed geometry and textures engage synergistically with Twinmotion's powerful rendering engines, allowing you to depict everything from the rustling of leaves in a breeze to the ripple patterns on a lake's surface with unparalleled realism.

In the following sections, we'll explore how to optimize these elements to craft natural environments that are not just lifelike but genuinely communicate the beauty and complexity of nature. From atmospheric effects to techniques for photorealistic rendering of vegetation and bodies of water, you'll have all the tools you need to transport your audience into a natural world that's indistinguishable from reality.

Lush and Alive: Rendering Rocks and Vegetation

The photorealistic rendering of natural environments presents unique challenges that we haven't yet encountered. Some natural elements are not always easy to render convincingly, with water serving as a prime example. In addition to large bodies of water like lakes and oceans, there are streams and rivers that pose their own sets of challenges. Some of these can be overcome, while others are more stubborn in nature.

Water is particularly complex due to its transparency, reflective properties, and the way it interacts with other natural elements like light and vegetation. Twinmotion, however, offers specialized tools to handle these challenges. For instance, water shaders can be customized to emulate various types of water bodies—from calm lakes to rushing rivers. Yet, despite these capabilities, achieving the perfect rendition of fast-flowing water or intricate waterfalls may still pose a challenge.

In the following sections, we'll explore strategies to navigate these hurdles, discussing when to push the software's built-in capabilities and when it might be better to integrate external assets for that extra layer of realism. Whether it's mastering the art of rippling lake surfaces or understanding how to portray the light-dappled bottom of a shallow stream, Twinmotion offers an array of options to get you closer to your vision of a perfect natural environment.

In the image above, you'll see two of my renderings created using Path Tracer. While light elements and the video camera always play pivotal roles, capturing the "soul" of these natural scenes is not always straightforward. Unlike architectural or urban environments, where geometry and structure guide the viewer's eyes, natural settings demand a different sort of attention. The mood can be defined by the interplay of light with the leaves, or how shadows dance across a body of water.

Each natural element contributes to the overall atmosphere of the scene. The texture of rocks, the translucency of leaves under sunlight, or the way water reflects the sky all work together to create a living tableau that speaks to the viewer. Capturing this essence demands not just technical prowess but also a deep understanding of natural aesthetics. In the upcoming sections, we'll delve deeper into how to evoke this "soul" in your natural environment renders. We will also touch upon the importance of utilizing high-quality models to ensure your natural scenes are as photorealistic as possible.

I recommend taking a look at this video on Twinmotion's official channel where I show you how to create a natural setting from scratch. You'll notice in the video a small trick to simulate a fog effect with the Path Tracer. In fact, the version of Twinmotion used in this video did not yet have compatibility with fog. The current version would not require such a workaround to create a fog effect; it would simply be a matter of activating it through the weather option.

https://www.youtube.com/watch?v=IMQR69K7zWs

Creating a photorealistic rendering of a natural environment raises the bar of difficulty: indeed, having access to quality models of natural objects is mandatory, otherwise the result will not be satisfactory.

Fortunately, Twinmotion's library is a valuable source of natural assets. In particular, the Quixel library and Twinmotion's native library offer thousands of assets.

The Quixel Megascans library

In the world of 3D graphics, Quixel Megascans has carved out a special place for itself as a go-to resource for natural elements like rocks, trees, and vegetation. What sets it apart is the photorealistic quality of its assets. Each 3D model in the Megascans library is rooted in real-world scans, which means the textures and details are virtually unparalleled. But Megascans doesn't stop at 3D models; it also provides a wide range of 2D assets, such as surface scans and decals. This makes it incredibly versatile, useful for a variety of project types beyond 3D rendering.
One of the most compelling aspects of Megascans is its optimized workflow. The library's assets are designed for ease of use across multiple rendering software platforms, including industry staples like Unreal Engine and Unity. This streamlines the creative process, allowing designers to focus more on the artistry and less on technical troubleshooting.

When it comes to rendering natural environments in 3D, the significance of Megascans cannot be overstated. The sheer quality and diversity of assets on offer make it an invaluable tool for professionals. The lifelike detail of each 3D asset contributes to creating natural scenes that are almost indistinguishable from reality. In essence, Megascans is a powerhouse resource for anyone looking to elevate their environmental designs to a professional level.

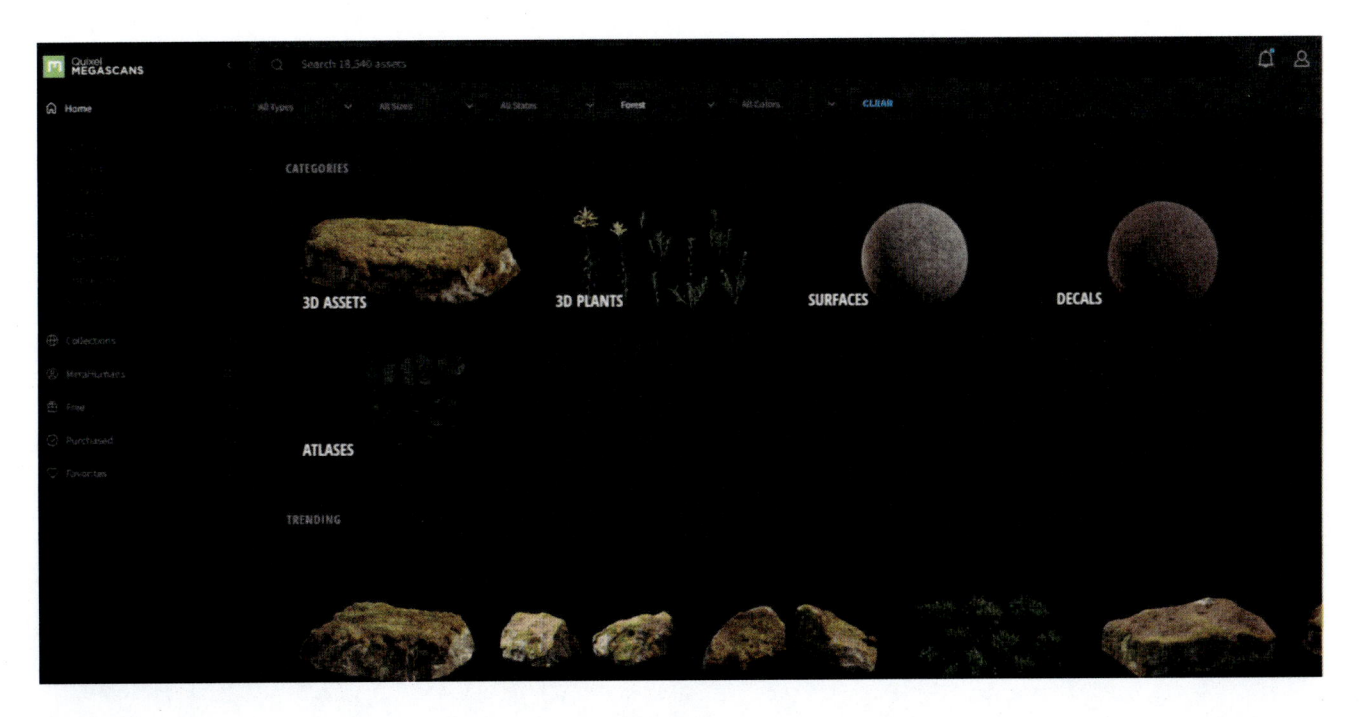

The Megascans library is natively integrated into Twinmotion. This allows users to search for and insert resources directly into their scenes through the Twinmotion interface. This integration provides a level of convenience and speed that simplifies the workflow significantly.

However, it's worth noting that downloading assets directly from the Quixel website offers some distinct advantages that shouldn't be overlooked when choosing how to utilize these resources.

While Twinmotion will automatically download assets with a 2K (2048x2048) texture resolution, this might not always meet the needs of every project. This resolution provides good model quality for most use-cases but could show limitations when the rendering involves close-up details. For those cases, the Quixel website offers a solution by allowing users to download the same model but with higher texture resolutions such as 4K (4096x4096) and 8K (8192x8192). When deciding on the resolution to use, it's crucial to weigh the impact on your computer's performance against the level of detail you aim to achieve.

In the accompanying image, you can observe a side-by-side comparison of the same Quixel asset. On the left, the asset is downloaded directly through Twinmotion's integrated library at a 2K (2048x2048) resolution. On the right, the same asset is downloaded from Quixel's website with an 8K (8192x8192) texture resolution and imported as an FBX file into Twinmotion. As is evident, the level of detail on the right is significantly higher.

I frequently use Quixel assets, either directly through Twinmotion or from the Quixel website. With thousands of assets available, creating a convincing, photorealistic natural scene can often be accomplished quickly using Quixel's resources. In the example image below, there are only two models: a ship and a Quixel asset labeled "Gigantic Tundra".

You can clearly see how the material quality and the 8K texture details combine to create a single, perfect model for naturalistic scenes. In this case, simply positioning the model in the scene was enough to achieve an incredibly lifelike rendering.

The Details of the Natural World

The importance of asset quality is particularly significant when the elements in question are trees and vegetation. Twinmotion's native library provides a plethora of options in this regard. However, it's worth noting that several tree types may not offer adequate resolution for close-up shots, thereby revealing the limitations of some models. Personally, I augment my workflow with third-party libraries, especially when I need high-quality trees or flowers in the foreground.

It's crucial to remember that Twinmotion's native trees and vegetation come with the added benefit of being responsive to environmental factors like seasons and wind. You can alter a tree's appearance by adjusting parameters such as size, age, and reference season. Changing from spring to autumn to winter, for instance, will see some trees transition from green leaves to yellow, and finally to a barren winter state. This feature is naturally unavailable if you import third-party models.

Consider that the wind effect, though theoretically useful for videos, is actually somewhat limited. The wind-induced movement is confined to leaves, leaving the branches static. If you're aiming for a scene with strong wind, you'll likely be disappointed. I'll revisit this topic later to share some tips for achieving more realistic wind effects on external models.

In the image below, you can see the advantage offered by Twinmotion's native trees. Being able to modify the age and season of trees significantly speeds up your scene creation workflow. When you find yourself managing numerous trees, and if these trees aren't the focal point, you can achieve photorealistic scenes with some tips that I will share later.

In the following images, I compare the details of a native Twinmotion tree with a third-party model, specifically from an Archmodel collection.

Numerous specialized marketplaces offer high-quality vegetation models. However, always consider the computational cost of using highly detailed trees with high-definition textures. This could negatively impact your computer's performance. The general rule applies here, as I've mentioned before: elements that are far from the camera can have lower definitions.

In the image below, on the left, you'll see a native Twinmotion tree model, and on the right, a more detailed model from Archmodel by Evermotion.

In Twinmotion's development roadmap, a series of improvements are planned in both the quality and quantity of assets related to trees, grass, bushes, etc.

If the focus of your image is on a landscape or natural area, you need to consider, even more so than in architectural visualization (archviz), the importance of details. A scene that features a mountain trail with rocks, stones, grass, and flowers will be characterized by a high number of different details, of both small and large natural objects like dead leaves, pine cones, and scattered branches. Capturing this essence allows you to create the photorealism you are aiming for; lighting and camera settings come after setting up a natural scene rich in details.

Quixel offers numerous assets to meet these types of needs as well. Here's an example of the rich variety of elements that you can use with Twinmotion for natural environments:

Look at the image below (created with Path Tracer). Let's try to analyze the details and assets that have been inserted to create the illusion of a believable image from a photorealistic standpoint.

1 – Strategically positioned Quixel assets such as pine cones, stones, and branches.
2 – Specific flowers and plants resized to fit the scene.
3 – Natural debris; in this image, almost a thousand small Quixel debris have been placed using the gravity tool to simulate material dispersal on the ground.
4 – Native Twinmotion grass tufts.
5 – In areas where the model might show imperfections, you can place natural elements that will cover the critical point.

Below is the version with Lumen, where you can notice that the blue light of the sky has less influence compared to the Path Tracer.

And here are the settings for the Path Tracer and Lumen for the renderings of the images above.

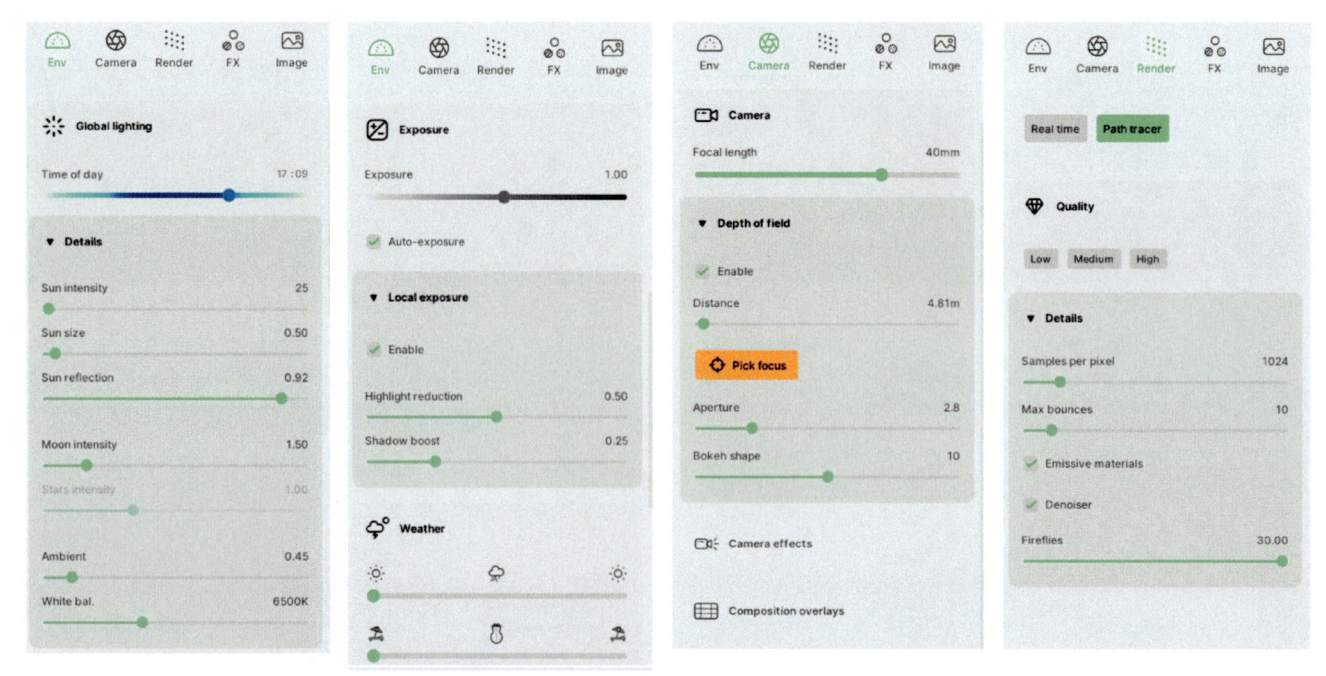

Above are the settings for the Path Tracer, and below are those for Lumen.

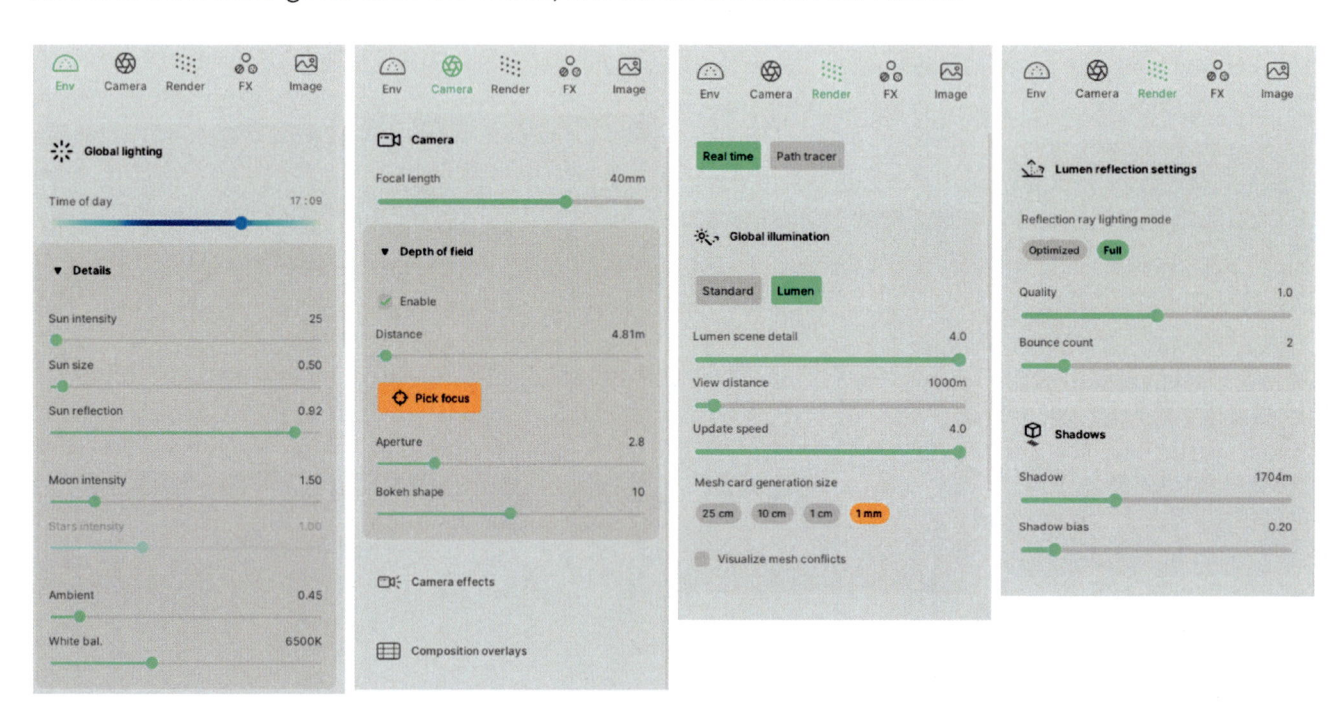

An interesting thing about Lumen's settings concerns the shadows in the rendering panel. As I've already highlighted in previous pages, creating soft shadows with Lumen is challenging. However, with the parameters you see here (shadows at 1704 meters and shadow bias at 0.20), the result is commendable.

The image shows the difference in shadow softness with Lumen by working on the shadow settings in the rendering tab. On the left is the default value with shadows set at 400 meters and shadow bias at 0.50, while on the right is a softer shadow with the modified parameters set at 1704 meters and 0.20.

Below are two more examples (Path Tracer and Lumen) with the same settings as previously mentioned, but with a saturation set almost to 60% to make the image more vivid.

The model of the girl comes from 3Dpeople, and the trees are from Archmodel – Evermotion.

In the final rendering of this chapter, I'll show you how to handle some artifacts that may occur in Quixel models, even when using 8K textures. Specifically, lighting can create shadows that reveal the low-poly nature of the Quixel asset, even when you're using LOD0 models, which have the highest polygon count. As you can see from the image below, the standalone asset produces unnatural, sharp-edged shadows that don't look photorealistic. You can resolve this issue by adding more assets and details, strategically placing them to conceal the shadow imperfections. Of course, this should be done after establishing the correct lighting setup. Refer to the second image for the improved result.

The Power of Water: Simulating Oceans and Rivers

Water is one of the most captivating yet challenging elements to render in any 3D environment. This isn't solely because of its intrinsic material properties like translucency, reflection, and refraction. The real challenge comes in when you consider the environmental context. Whether it's a stormy ocean or a tranquil lake, water is never truly still. Waves, ripples, and other forms of movement add layers of complexity that can be daunting when you're aiming for photorealistic results in Twinmotion.

Now, let's tackle this head-on. You might think that rendering water is an uphill battle, and you wouldn't be entirely wrong. But don't worry; in this chapter, I'll guide you through the best practices to get the most photorealistic results possible when working with water.

When dealing with water, you have to consider how light interacts with its properties under different environmental conditions. Is it a sunny day, casting sharp reflections on the water surface, or a cloudy atmosphere that creates diffused lighting? These factors will influence your rendering settings, and understanding them is crucial for achieving realism.
One of the first things to do is to experiment with Twinmotion's native assets. Both Quixel and Twinmotion's native libraries offer a range of water assets that can be manipulated to fit various scenarios. Start by choosing an asset that closely matches the body of water you're trying to simulate.

Water is always in motion, even when it looks calm. For a lake, subtle ripples might suffice, while for an ocean, more significant wave patterns would be necessary. Twinmotion provides tools to adjust these properties, so play around until you find what works best for your scene.
Remember, water isn't just blue; its color can vary based on depth, time of day, and surrounding landscape. Play around with color settings to make sure your water blends seamlessly with the environment. Adjust the translucency and refraction indices to give it a natural look.

Finally, let's talk about the all-important subject of lighting. How you illuminate your water scene will make or break the photorealism you're striving for. Since you've already tackled lighting in other contexts, use those skills here but adapt them to water's unique properties. Given the different types of light interaction on water, including reflection and absorption, you'll need to experiment with light sources and settings to get it just right.

So there you have it. By understanding the complexities of rendering water and how to manipulate Twinmotion's features to your advantage, you'll be well on your way to achieving photorealistic water scenes.

An important tip to keep in mind, especially when you're using the Path Tracer, is the technique of simulating water through colored glass. Although this concept has been discussed in a previous section of the book, it's worth revisiting. Colored glass can be an excellent stand-in for water when you're striving for high levels of photorealism. Given the unique ways in which light interacts with glass—much like water—this can sometimes yield more controllable and realistic results. Make sure to adjust the color, opacity, and refraction indices to best mimic the water conditions you're aiming to recreate. It's one more tool in your arsenal, and understanding when and how to use it can make all the difference in your final render.

To summarize, you can create the effect of water in four different ways:

1. Using the "Ocean" feature
2. Using the Water asset (either cubic or cylindrical), although this is rarely practical
3. Using one of the "water" type materials (ideal for Raster and Lumen engines, as well as animations)
4. Using colored glass material (ideal for Path Tracer and still images)

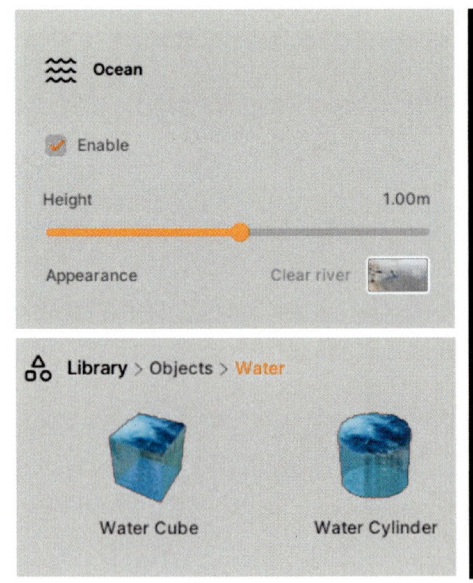

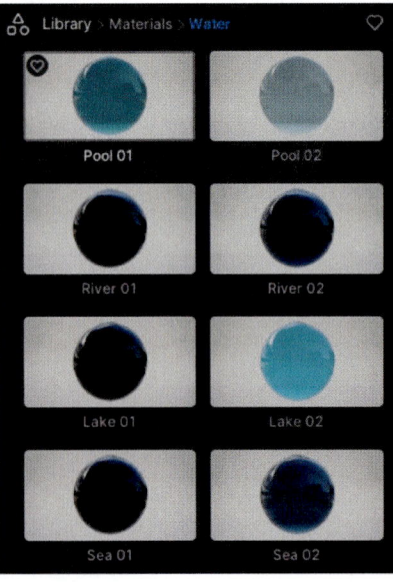

For animations, the best functionality is certainly option 1, the Ocean feature. This option allows you to create a body of water with relatively realistic waves and movements, using some reference templates. This choice responds quite accurately to the environment and lighting conditions.

In the image below, you can see how the ocean parameter is influenced by light and the template used. In the first four smaller images, we see three of the available templates and a nighttime shot. The two larger images show the difference between Lumen on the left and Path Tracer on the right. As you can notice, the Path Tracer has an extra edge in terms of photorealism.

Many Twinmotion users confuse the real-time viewport (which loses its real-time capability when the Path Tracer is activated) with the quality of rendering produced by the Path Tracer. It's important to pay attention to this point: if you want to render a video using the Path Tracer, you cannot gauge the final result by looking at the viewport with the Path Tracer activated. However, I can assure you that the final video effect in Path Tracer will have a perfectly rendered ocean.

What happens if we replace the Ocean function with water material applied to a surface? The first observation concerns the presence of a certain repetitiveness in the water's texture. While the Ocean feature shows foam and areas with different wave patterns, the water material is much more uniform. Personally, for large expanses of water like seas and oceans, I find the most realistic solution to be the Ocean option.

On the other hand, the water material has numerous settings and is well-suited for specific cases like lakes and pools (though remember the limitations with Path Tracer that prevent effective use of water material in some situations).

Below, you can see some settings in action. By adjusting the turbidity and caustics, you can achieve various convincing effects.

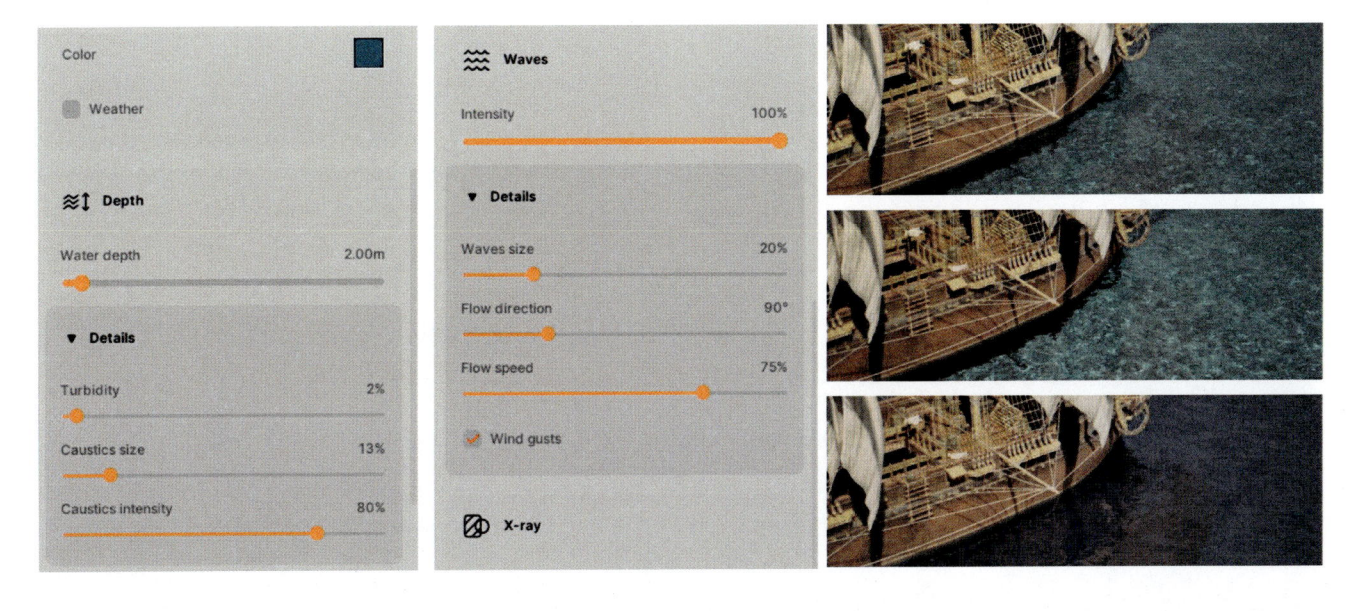

Remember that water material, like colored glass, can be applied to any type of model. This opens up an interesting possibility when you're faced with a flowing body of water, like a stream, where the water isn't a flat expanse like the ocean. In such scenarios, I prefer to use colored glass. This offers greater control over transparency, translucency, and reflectivity compared to water material, which has fewer options.

Indeed, while the water cube and water cylinder objects are virtually useless for our purposes, the option for colored glass makes a significant difference.

The next image, rendered with the Lumen engine, is a frame from a rather convincing animation all done within Twinmotion. I'll explain how I achieved this immediately afterward.

The presence of Depth of Field (DOF) slightly blurring the water is a small trick that serves multiple purposes. It not only makes the rendering more photorealistic and cinematic but also helps to mask some minor flaws that the assets representing the water flow might have.

The effect of flowing water is achieved using ring-shaped models that rotate beneath the terrain. Thanks to a number of rotators turning at different speeds, a small part of these rings emerges from the ground, creating the sensation of flowing water.

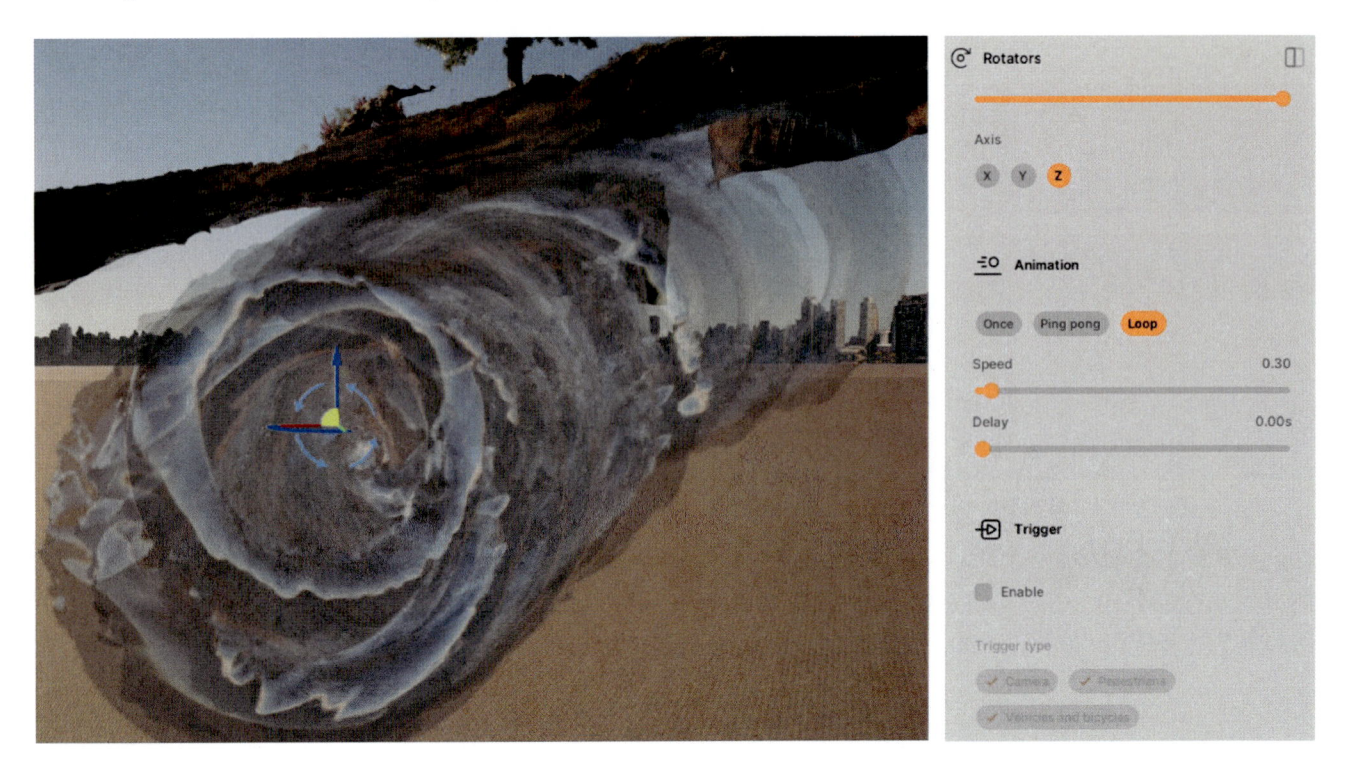

I modeled the rings in 3D Studio Max, applying a "noise" function to them, and then imported them as FBX files into Twinmotion.

This gave me the ability to precisely control the form and behavior of the water surface, making it more dynamic and realistic.

Peaks and Valleys: Capturing Mountains

Capturing the grandeur of mountainous terrains in Twinmotion requires a nuanced approach to deal with the unique challenges of 3D rendering expansive landscapes. The first step toward achieving photorealistic outcomes is to address scale and proportion accurately. Unlike smaller scenes, where approximations might suffice, the monumental scale of mountain ranges demands precise adjustments, achievable through Twinmotion's 'Scale' tool.

Texture is another critical aspect of rendering mountains convincingly. Mountains in the real world offer a rich tapestry of materials like rock, snow, and grass. Twinmotion's built-in texture library allows for layering and blending to emulate this complexity. It's essential to focus on how different textures interact at various elevations, with snow caps at higher altitudes, rocky outcrops in the middle, and grassy plains at the base.

Lighting can make or break your mountain rendering. Real-world mountains are subject to a variety of lighting conditions depending on time and weather. Twinmotion's 'Physical Sky' settings offer a way to simulate these varying conditions, and sliders for 'Sun' and 'Clouds' provide control for specific lighting effects, such as the golden hour or overcast conditions.

Atmospheric conditions like mist and fog can also add another layer of realism. Twinmotion provides various weather effects, and the key here is subtlety. Overdoing these effects can result in an unrealistic scene.

Balancing realism and computational performance is also crucial. The preview feature in Twinmotion can help validate your scene's realism without excessively taxing your computer's resources. Lastly, seamless integration of your mountain scene with other elements like buildings or roads is crucial for a coherent final rendering, facilitated by Twinmotion's 'Asset Placement' tools.

The first thing to consider in your scene is whether the mountains will serve as a mere backdrop or if they will be the main focus of your rendering. If the mountains are secondary and the focus is on other elements like a building, house, or city, you may opt for simpler solutions. For instance, you can import low-poly models from platforms like Sketchfab through Twinmotion and place them appropriately in your scene. If you maintain realistic proportions and distances—placing large models far away as in the real world—you can achieve photorealistic effects, particularly from atmospheric conditions like mist or haze that often contribute to realism.

The issue of proportions is crucial in achieving photorealism. You can strategically place a mountain model so that it appears to be the correct size and at an appropriate distance. However, this effect may be achieved because the mountain model is actually much smaller than it should be and is merely positioned close to the scene. While this approach can work, it opens up risks in terms of photorealism. Lighting or weather effects that influence the mountain could disrupt the realism, something that wouldn't happen if the mountain were at the correct distance.

Therefore, paying close attention to scale and proportion is critical when aiming for photorealistic rendering in Twinmotion, especially when dealing with expansive elements like mountain ranges.

In the image above, the focus is on the entire landscape, with hills in the foreground and mountains in the background. As previously explained, the proportions in this image are "realistic." The mountain model, downloaded from Sketchfab, measures 5x5 kilometers and has a height of 500 meters.

By using the Paint Vegetation tool, I've added three types of trees and two types of bushes, distributed across two different vegetation layers. This creates a multi-layered, nuanced environment that adds to the realism and complexity of the scene.

The model downloaded from Sketchfab, labeled as "grassy mountains geo," is ideal for a scene requiring a mountainous setting. The topography, including the hills and riverbed, offers extensive creative possibilities. However, it's important to note the details of the model: a model like this will not yield high-quality results if you zoom in too closely with the camera. It's designed for wide-angle views.

Here are the rendering settings for the aforementioned scene:

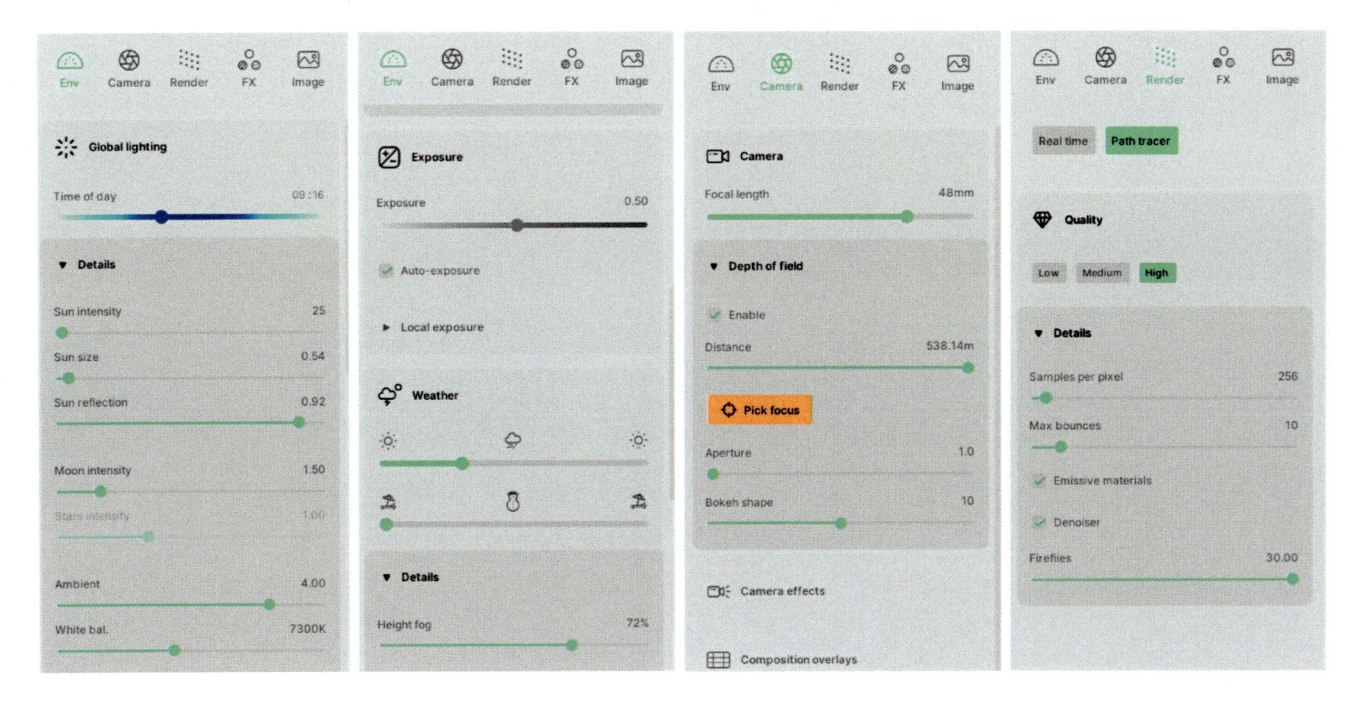

Twinmotion also has specific tools for sculpting natural environments. You can create landscapes and then sculpt them as you please to form valleys and elevations. To be honest, I'm not a huge fan of this feature. Perhaps I lack the skills to use it effectively, but I greatly prefer importing ready-made models or sculpting them with other tools like ZBrush or 3D Studio Max.

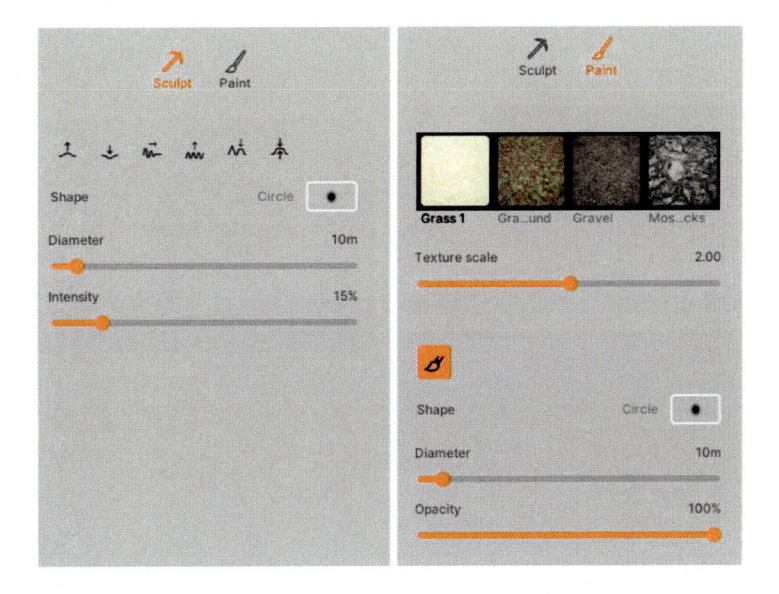

Starting from this rendering, I added some details like planes with mirror material to simulate ponds and lakes, along with some additional structures like a small church and a castle. The scene featuring the mountain and hills thus comes to life, thanks to the painted vegetation and added models that make it more captivating.

Rendering landscapes in Twinmotion opens up a wide array of expressive possibilities. Some renderings are not just photorealistic but also carry a strong artistic sensibility. Take for example the image below, depicting perhaps a sunrise over the hills of Tuscany in Italy. Created using the standard vegetation tool for the fields, convincing mist achieved by setting the fog almost to 100%, and a slight Depth of Field (DOF) with a cinematic Field of View (FOV)—all rendered using path tracing—the result is stunning.

Exploring Fantasy Environments

In this and the upcoming chapters, I'll guide you through the process of constructing distinct and compelling environments. I'll provide you with targeted guidance and appropriate settings, focusing not only on how to use Twinmotion's rendering engines for photorealistic results, but also on sharing my personal creative journey. My hope is that my experience will serve as an inspiration for you to explore your own creative boundaries. By incorporating elements beyond technical specifications, such as design philosophy and artistic vision, we'll move beyond mere realism to create truly captivating and imaginative spaces.

In the world of 3D graphics, imagination is your only limitation. With cutting-edge tools like Twinmotion and Unreal Engine at your fingertips, the possibilities for crafting stunning, immersive fantasy environments are virtually limitless. These software platforms serve as powerful conduits for translating your wildest creative visions into palpable virtual realities.

As we journey through this chapter titled "Exploring Fantasy Environments," we delve into the art and science of constructing intricate, otherworldly landscapes. These aren't mere backdrops but dynamic spaces where storytelling and atmosphere unite, transforming digital polygons into enchanted forests, mythical cities, or futuristic landscapes.

While traditional architectural visualization aims for photorealism, fantasy environments challenge us to think beyond the confines of the real world. Here, the laws of physics can be bent and your creative whims take precedence. These tools offer advanced features such as dynamic lighting, high-fidelity textures, and complex geometries, giving you the freedom to craft scenes as detailed, expansive, or fantastical as you can imagine.

So fasten your seatbelt and prepare for a thrilling odyssey into the realm of fantasy visualization. By the end of this chapter, you'll have a comprehensive understanding of how to leverage the immense potential of 3D graphics software to bring your most imaginative environments to life.

Sci-fi Realms: Crafting Futuristic Landscapes

As a massive fan of science fiction, franchises like Star Wars have always fueled my imagination and creativity. Crafting technological and futuristic settings is one of my favorite activities. The wealth of incredible resources available online makes setting up these sci-fi environments significantly easier.

Kitbash3D serves as an excellent marketplace that offers professionally designed, theme-specific model packages. These kits seamlessly integrate into Twinmotion, making it convenient to populate your sci-fi landscapes with highly detailed and realistic elements.

In this chapter we take a turn away from the traditional and the realistic, steering into the limitless possibilities of imagination and future-oriented design. This chapter offers a comprehensive guide to envisioning, conceptualizing, and rendering fantastical, otherworldly environments. When it comes to science fiction, the canvas is vast and uncharted, allowing for the exploration of advanced civilizations, post-apocalyptic wastelands, or even alternate dimensions.

The sci-fi genre offers a unique opportunity to break free from conventional design constraints. Whether you're envisioning a cybernetic cityscape, an abandoned space colony, or a network of subterranean tunnels on Mars, the goal is to immerse the viewer into an unfamiliar yet captivating realm. While our focus will be primarily on the architecture and layout of these settings, we'll also delve into the smaller, nuanced elements that contribute to the overall atmosphere—think neon signs in an alien script, futuristic transportation systems, or even artificial weather conditions.

The importance of story and context also comes to the forefront in sci-fi settings. What is the history of this space? Is it a utopia or a dystopia? Has technology been the savior or the downfall of this society? These questions not only influence your design choices but also engage your audience, offering them more than just a visual feast—they get a storyline, a world, a universe to immerse themselves in.

In a genre where the improbable becomes the norm, the key to crafting compelling futuristic landscapes lies in the details. Everything from the scale and proportion of buildings to the way light interacts with different surfaces can make or break the illusion of an otherworldly environment. It's the cohesion of these elements that will make your Sci-fi realm not just a collection of cool designs, but a believable, immersive world.

By the end of this chapter, you will have the tools and insights needed to create breathtaking, realistic-yet-futuristic landscapes. Your understanding of sci-fi tropes, combined with the powerful capabilities of tools like Twinmotion and Unreal Engine, will help you transform the visions in your head into tangible, awe-inspiring scenes.

In this first image, we are presented with a panoramic view of an alien city, created using the Outpost pack from Kitbash3D and rendered with Path Tracer.

In this view, a variety of assets and techniques come together to create a cohesive scene. The bird's-eye perspective was chosen deliberately to give a broad overview of the city, emphasizing its vitality through the presence of multiple buildings, people, and evenly spaced vegetation. Various modes of transport and other enriching details are also visible, enhancing the overall composition.

The terrain and mountains are Quixel Megascans assets, adding another layer of realism to the scene. Specifically, the ground is rendered in 8K, downloaded directly from Quixel's website. This detail contributes significantly to the scene's depth and realism.

As I've mentioned in other parts of this book, the placement of the sun and lighting is strategic. The partial shadows in the scene make the image appear more realistic. Direct sunlight on the buildings would have washed out several details and made the image look flatter.

For the technicalities, the environment settings for the rendering were achieved using a Path Tracer. In the "render" tab, I set it to 1024 samples and 10 bounces, while all other settings were left at their default values. This balances quality and computational load, ensuring a compelling yet efficient render.

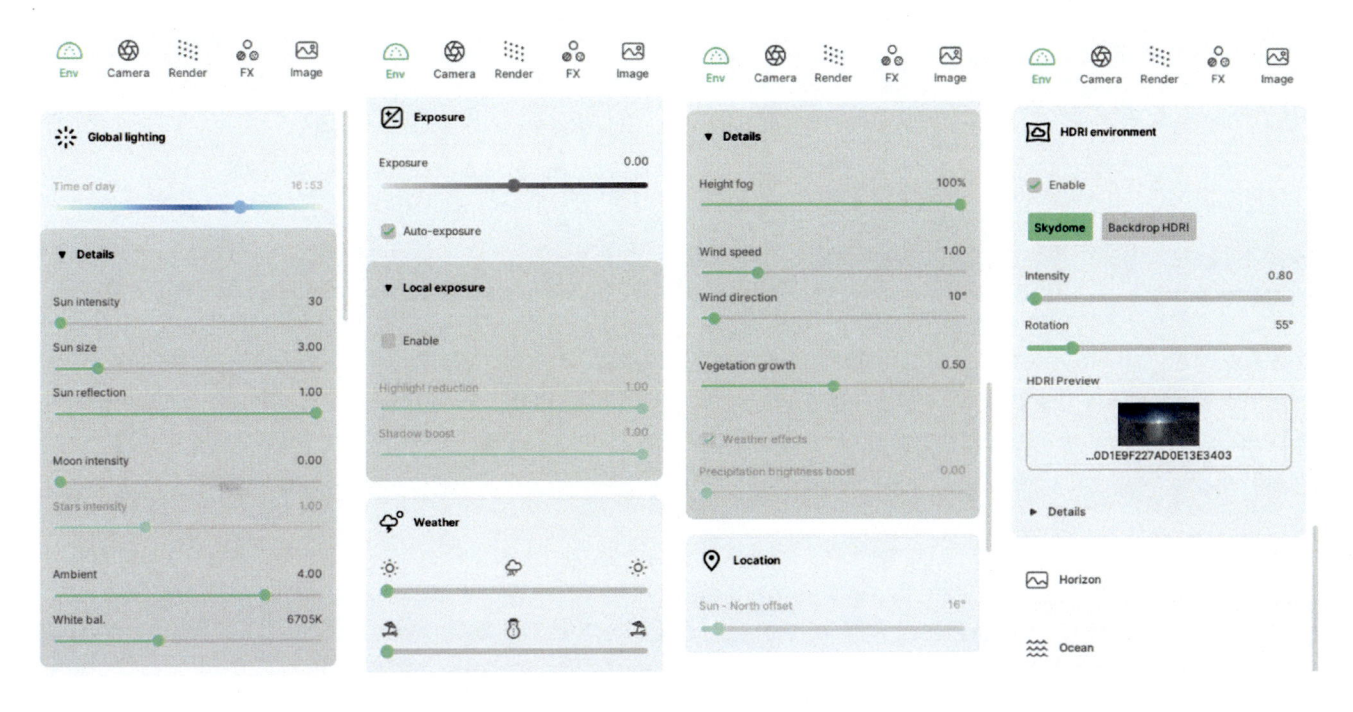

In renders covering extensive areas—on the scale of thousands of square meters—atmospheric elements can behave quite differently depending on whether you're using a Path Tracer engine or Lumen. It's worth noting that raster engines behave similarly to Lumen but lack advanced features like global illumination and realistic reflection.

Simply switching to the Lumen engine can produce markedly different results compared to using a Path Tracer. Environment settings have a far greater impact in this mode. For instance, setting the fog level to 100% can create a striking volumetric lighting effect across the scene. Particle-based objects like fog banks also become much more visible with Lumen. If you're aiming for similar outputs between the two engines, you may need to reduce the fog intensity and perhaps even shift the ambient color toward a cooler tone.

Achieving this effect is more challenging with a Path Tracer, which offers fewer customization options for certain elements, fog being a prominent example. The intricacies of these engines make them suitable for different kinds of scenes, and understanding their strengths and weaknesses is key for optimal rendering.

I've touched on this before, but I often turn to Pinterest for references and inspiration. My creative process frequently starts with exploring images on themes like Sci-Fi and fantasy through this platform. A simple search immediately opens up a world of high-quality suggestions. It provides a rich tapestry of visual cues, lighting effects, and thematic elements that can serve as the building blocks for my own designs.

Leveraging such a resource effectively can be a game-changer in the ideation phase, offering a diverse range of concepts to explore and refine. Whether you're looking to emulate a particular style or fuse multiple influences into something uniquely yours, Pinterest can be an invaluable tool for sparking creativity.

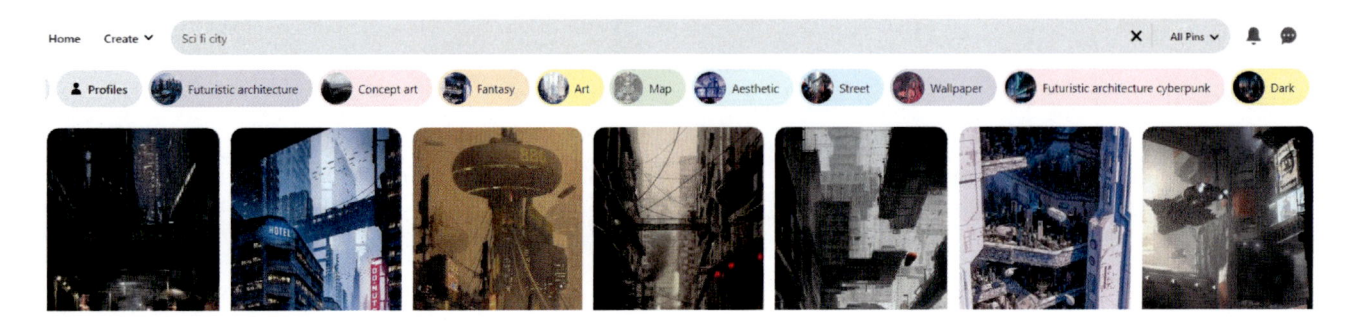

The next image, rendered with Path Tracer, conceals significant complexity. While the room framing the shot may seem straightforward and can be interpreted in various ways—perhaps even suggesting a story through its details—the window offers a glimpse into a futuristic city brimming with buildings and skyscrapers. What you see through that window is not a mere backdrop; it's an actual city composed of hundreds of building and skyscraper models.

This juxtaposition between the apparent simplicity of the room and the intricate cityscape outside creates a compelling narrative tension. It opens the door to multiple interpretations and thematic explorations, making the render not just visually stunning but also rich in storytelling potential.

The main challenge was the city setup. I had to use certain techniques to prevent the sheer number of models from overwhelming my computer. Decimating polygons and using textures with resolutions of 1024x1024 and 512x512 played a crucial role. Always remember that a model located hundreds of meters away from the camera doesn't need to be high-definition and consume valuable computing resources.
The models in the room come from Sketchfab and Quixel. The larger and more detailed skyscrapers are from Kitbash3D. The city's outskirts feature a model I created a few years ago, specifically designed for renders of this nature. The process of creating such supporting models is enlightening. It reaffirms what I've mentioned multiple times: low-poly models placed far from the camera can still be impactful elements without posing performance issues due to their polygon count.
So, while setting up scenes of this complexity may seem daunting, intelligent resource management and strategic model placement can allow you to achieve impressive results without sacrificing performance.

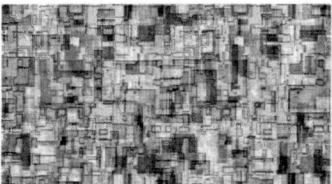

I created the model in 3ds Max and sourced a typical sci-fi suburbs texture to apply to it. As you can see in the image on the right, some artifacts resulting from the texture orientation led to various inaccuracies in the model. Texture alignment is a subtle yet significant aspect of 3D modeling; if not done correctly, it can disrupt the visual coherence of the scene.

I then worked on the textures to give them a cylindrical appearance, making them suitable for application on the final model, which you can see in the image at the top left.

This adjusted model can be seen below in the Twinmotion viewport, set up within the scene featuring the room and the window overlooking the city.

The configuration for rendering with the Path Tracer is outlined below.

I certainly can't capture the vast world of sci-fi in this book; that would require a volume dedicated to the theme!

Twinmotion provides you with all the tools needed to unleash your imagination and build science fiction worlds of every kind. And when I say "every kind," I mean it in the broadest sense. I demonstrate this with the following render. Photorealism here heavily relies on the quality of the character model. The model, available on Sketchfab, is of good quality, but a more accurate model with higher-definition materials would have further enhanced the render. However, my objective in this case is to showcase Twinmotion's versatility, even in renders like this one.

Rendering a character like Grogu from the Star Wars™ universe underscores the unique challenges involved in achieving photorealism for characters. The complexity is significantly heightened by the unique characteristics of living beings, such as skin, hair, and eyes.

Skin, for example, has subsurface scattering properties, meaning light doesn't just bounce off the surface but also penetrates the skin and scatters internally. This creates a particular glow that is difficult to replicate accurately.
Hair and fur present another set of challenges. Each strand interacts with light differently, and the sheer number of strands can make rendering computationally intensive. You'll also need to consider how hair or fur moves and changes shape, adding to the complexity.

Then there's the clothing, which can include various materials, each with its own set of properties when it comes to reflection, absorption, and texture.

All these factors need to be meticulously accounted for to produce a convincing, photorealistic character. Even with advanced tools and features in software like Twinmotion, the task demands a deep understanding of both the software and the physical properties you're trying to emulate.

Regarding the Path Tracer settings, most are default values. Important for rendering are:

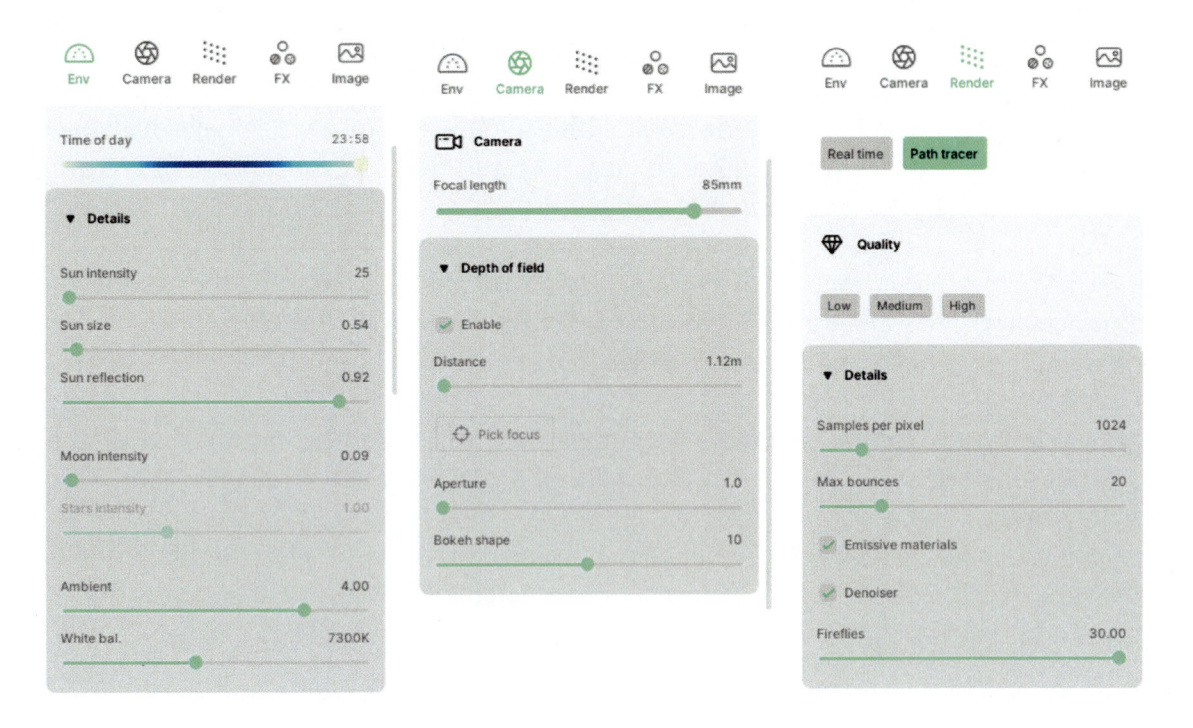

In this rendering, it's interesting to examine the material characteristics of the character's skin. First and foremost, the material type is 'subsurface,' which allows for the partial penetration of light through the ear, creating a more realistic effect. The material also employs normal and glossiness shaders to further enhance its realistic appearance.

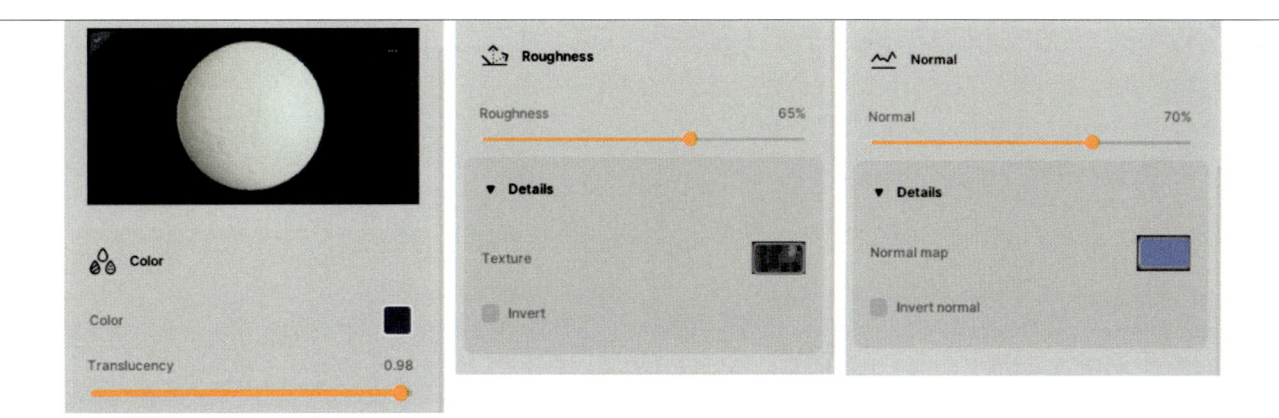

When using Lumen with a "biological" model where skin, hair, and fur materials are often critical, the resulting image can be noticeably different. Despite the high-quality output, there are two things you'll immediately notice about the skin material:

1. The normal shader is far more intense, resulting in much deeper facial wrinkles on the character.
2. The subsurface material properties don't function as we would expect. This is particularly evident when observing the ear, which appears completely opaque.

These observations underscore the importance of understanding how different rendering engines interact with complex materials like skin, especially when striving for photorealism.

It's noteworthy that the 4K rendering using the Path Tracer took 14 minutes and 30 seconds on my computer, while the Lumen rendering was completed in just 38 seconds. For this particular scene, Lumen was almost 23 times faster than the Path Tracer. Given this significant speed difference, it might be worth sacrificing subsurface details and accepting some extra wrinkles if time is a critical factor for you.

The Lumen settings for this rendering are identical to those used for the Path Tracer, with the difference being that the Lumen parameters were set to their maximum values. Specifically, 'Details' and 'Update Speed' were set to 4, and 'Reflection Quality' was set to 'Full' with 2 bounces. The default settings for 'Shadows' and 'Shadow Bias' were retained, which are 400m and 0.5, respectively. This configuration shows that even with maximized settings, Lumen offers a much faster rendering time while still delivering quality results, although with some trade-offs in material realism.

Stepping Back in Time: Creating Historical and Fantasy Scenes

Recreating history and diving into fantastical worlds isn't just an act of imagination; it's an art form that requires a mastery of technology, an understanding of human perception, and a knack for storytelling. When it comes to historical settings, details are crucial. From the cobbled streets to the period-accurate costumes, every element serves to transport the viewer back in time. The same is true for fantasy scenes, whether you're inspired by Tolkien's Middle Earth or your own original world teeming with magic, heroes, and mythical creatures.

In historical scenes, research is your best friend. The architecture, for instance, can say a lot about the period you're depicting. Whether it's the Victorian era, with its grand, ornate structures, or ancient Rome, with its colossal feats of engineering, the buildings should reflect the time. Using specialized software, you can access asset libraries filled with historical elements that can be customized to fit your scene.

In the realm of fantasy, the sky is the limit—or perhaps not even that. You might have dragons soaring above enchanted forests or underwater kingdoms that defy the laws of physics. Here, rather than being bound by historical accuracy, you're only limited by your imagination. However, it's essential to maintain internal consistency within your world. If a particular kind of magic or technology exists, it should follow rules that make sense within the context of that world.

Character creation varies significantly between historical and fantasy settings. While historical characters often require subtler, more realistic features—like wrinkles, scars, or specific styles of clothing—fantasy characters can be as extravagant as you wish. Orcs, elves, wizards, and warriors can sport features and costumes that have never been seen before, opening up a wealth of creative possibilities.

Subtle nuances can make a significant difference, especially in fantasy settings. If you're aiming for a 'Lord of the Rings' feel, pay attention to the texturing of surfaces like wood, stone, and metal to make them look aged, worn, or enchanted. Use lighting to create an atmosphere that complements the setting, be it the warm glow of a medieval tavern or the eerie, ethereal light of an enchanted forest.

I've always found abundant resources for such images; there's no shortage of objects and characters. Quixel and Sketchfab offer a plethora of assets. I'd also like to point out the website of the company "Big Medium Small" at https://www.bigmediumsmall.com/. Here, you can find quality assets and an exceptional medieval asset library.

In this rendering (done with Path Tracer), I used the Big Medium Small (BMS) library named "Medieval collection" for the characters, while the houses are from Kitbash3D.

For this scene, the creative concept was particularly important to me. I wanted to transport viewers to a chilly, winter environment that harkens back to medieval times. The returning army of crusaders forms the crux of the scene, met by a crowd of uncertain emotion—leaving it ambiguous whether the soldiers are returning as victors or the defeated. The soldiers carrying their banners high serve as the central focus.

From a technical standpoint, achieving this vision required careful planning and optimization. Each character model is low-poly, expertly designed by BMS, and precisely positioned within the environment. The decision to go with low-poly models serves a functional purpose; it enables the computer to render the scene without excessive computational overhead. High poly-counts are usually reserved for close-up shots where intricate details are necessary, as I've mentioned earlier in this book. The lighting and atmosphere were achieved through an HDRI skydome. This technique brings multiple benefits, including realistic natural lighting and a dynamic sky that can adjust according to the scene's needs. I set the intensity of the sun to 1, causing the scene to darken considerably. This created a challenge to balance out the lighting parameters so that the visual elements remain coherent and maintain the mood I aimed to evoke.

One thing to note is the impact of texture resolution on the overall scene quality. In prior sections of this book, I've stressed the importance of resource management. Overloading your scene with 8K textures can be a shortcut to a frustrating experience with laggy performance and slow render times. However, the flip side is that higher-resolution textures can add an incredible level of detail to models that are in the foreground of the scene.

So, what's the trade-off between using an 8K texture (or 4K) as opposed to a 1K or 2K one? In terms of visual fidelity, the difference can be night and day when the texture is applied to a model featured prominently in your rendering. While you'll be able to discern the general material and color properties with a lower-res texture, an 8K texture will give you that much more detail, potentially adding a new layer of realism to your work. This stark difference in quality will become evident in the subsequent illustrations.

Luca Rodolfi - Photorealism with Twinmotion– Raster – Path Tracer - Lumen

In a bid for photorealism, the texture quality of your models becomes a critical consideration.
Take, for example, the iron chainmail armor worn by the knight in the scene. On the left, we have a 1K texture, and on the right, a 4K texture.

Even to an untrained eye, the difference in resolution has a pronounced impact on the level of detail, particularly in close-up shots.

The 1K texture might suffice for models that occupy the background or are less critical to the overall narrative. However, when it comes to foreground elements that demand attention and detail, a higher-resolution texture is almost always preferable. In the case of the knight's chainmail, the 4K texture showcases the intricacies of each individual link, providing a level of realism that the 1K texture simply cannot achieve.

Using lower-resolution textures for important foreground elements can hamper the photorealism of your rendering. It's like putting a high-quality actor in a poorly designed costume; no matter how good the performance is, the audience will be distracted by the shortcomings in detail. Therefore, it's crucial to allocate higher-resolution textures where they are most needed, ensuring that your scene doesn't just look good, but looks 'real.'

And as usual, here are the parameters used for this rendering with Path Tracer.

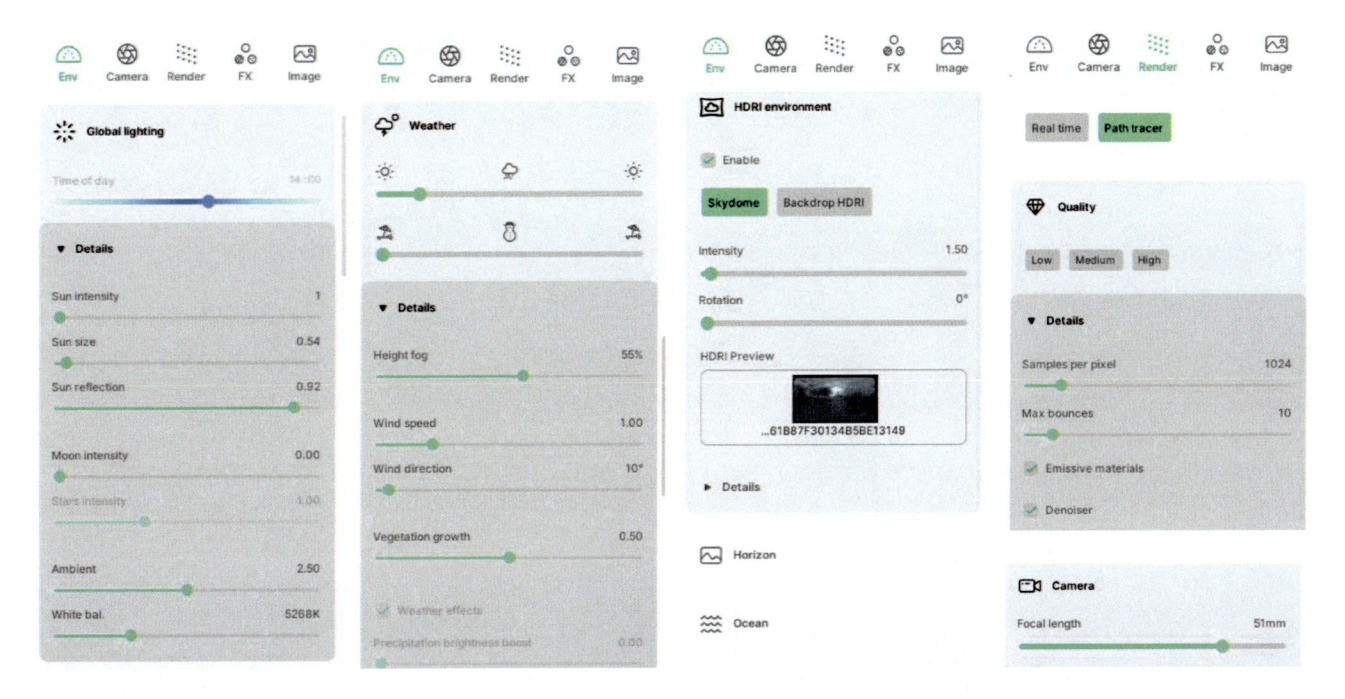

Switching to Lumen, the scene remains largely unchanged, although it does lose some overall brightness. As I've emphasized in previous sections, Lumen is quicker but may not capture all the nuances of global illumination that you'd get with Path Tracer.

Lumen's capabilities shine particularly bright when you're dealing with time-sensitive projects that require quick turnaround times, without severely compromising quality. It's often good enough for creating animations or drafts that can give your clients or team members a very accurate idea of what the final product will look like.
However, as mentioned before, the current Path Tracer technology has a broader range of features, especially when it comes to rendering atmospheric effects like rain and snow. These subtle touches can significantly enhance the realism and emotional impact of a scene. So, if your project demands a meticulously detailed environment with realistic weather conditions, the Path Tracer would generally be the better choice.

That said, not all scenes require such detailed atmospheric conditions. In cases where the weather elements are not a focal point—say, you're rendering an indoor scene or the emphasis is more on the characters rather than the environment—Lumen's speed can be a considerable advantage.

So, while Lumen might lose a bit of global brightness compared to Path Tracer and lacks some of the more intricate environmental effects, its rendering speed can often more than make up for these shortfalls. It's all about picking the right tool for your specific needs, and as you've seen in previous chapters, both Lumen and Path Tracer have their merits.

Below is the rendering comparison between Path Tracer and Lumen under the same environmental and camera conditions.

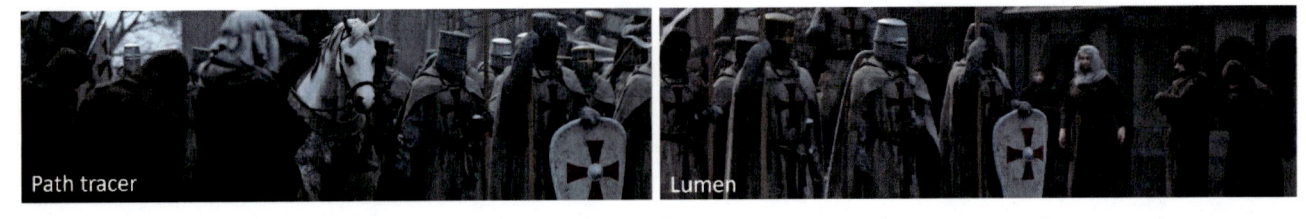

Below are the parameters for the Lumen rendering (Environment and camera settings are the same as those used for the Path Tracer).

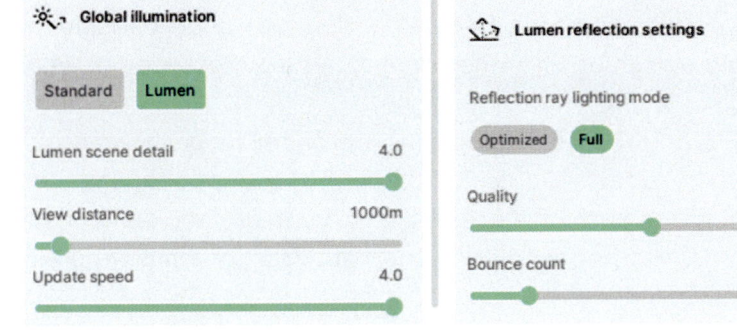

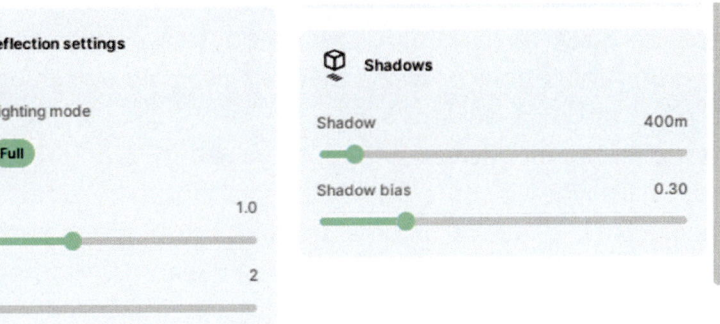

Let's take a leap forward in time and try to imagine a scene set in Victorian London.

In this rendering (made with Path Tracer), we immerse ourselves in the essence of Victorian London, capturing its cobbled streets, grand townhouses, and the signature London fog that adds a layer of mystery to the early morning scene. Contrary to what one might expect, the gas lamps are off, allowing the natural light of early morning to be the scene's sole light source.
Technically speaking, the Twinmotion rendering pays close attention to historical authenticity. The materials for the cobblestone roads and building facades are chosen for their period accuracy. Textures are high-resolution and can be scaled up to 4K to emulate the aged appearance of structures from this time. This high level of detail becomes especially important for foreground objects and surfaces, contributing significantly to the realism of the scene.

Natural morning light fills the atmosphere, its subtle luminance calibrated to reflect the actual lighting conditions one might expect at dawn in Victorian London. Since the gas lamps are turned off, the focus is entirely on how this natural light plays off the architecture and cobblestone streets, casting soft yet detailed shadows that add depth and texture to the rendering.

Camera settings are fine-tuned to offer an intimate perspective on this historical world. A narrower field of view enhances the sense of being 'in' the scene rather than merely observing it. Depth of field settings are also managed to draw focus to key architectural elements, with other elements slightly blurred to add a cinematic touch.

The assets used come from Kitbash3D, Sketchfab, Evermotion, 3Dpeople and Quixel.

Below is a detail of the image (rendered with Lumen) showing the detail of the assets present in the scene.

Sketchfab offers a wide range of characters, and I've found that the free online tool Mixamo is excellent for posing them correctly. When we use characters in our 3D renderings, we often need them to be in specific poses. Creating a skeleton within a 3D software like 3D Studio Max or Blender to then modify the original pose of the character can be both difficult and time-consuming.

Whenever possible, I use a simplified workflow that leverages Mixamo:

1. I find a suitable character on Sketchfab for posing.
2. I upload it to Mixamo.
3. I choose from one of the hundreds of predefined animations.
4. I export the animated model that Mixamo's artificial intelligence system has correctly posed.

For instance, you can select a model from Sketchfab like "Fuse Civilian 2," created by Leonardo Carvalho, to get started with this streamlined process.

Download the model and upload the FBX format to Mixamo (www.mixamo.com). Allow Mixamo to generate the model's skeleton. You also have the option to fine-tune it by indicating the different parts of the body joints. This makes the posing process not only more accurate but also saves you a significant amount of time compared to manual rigging.

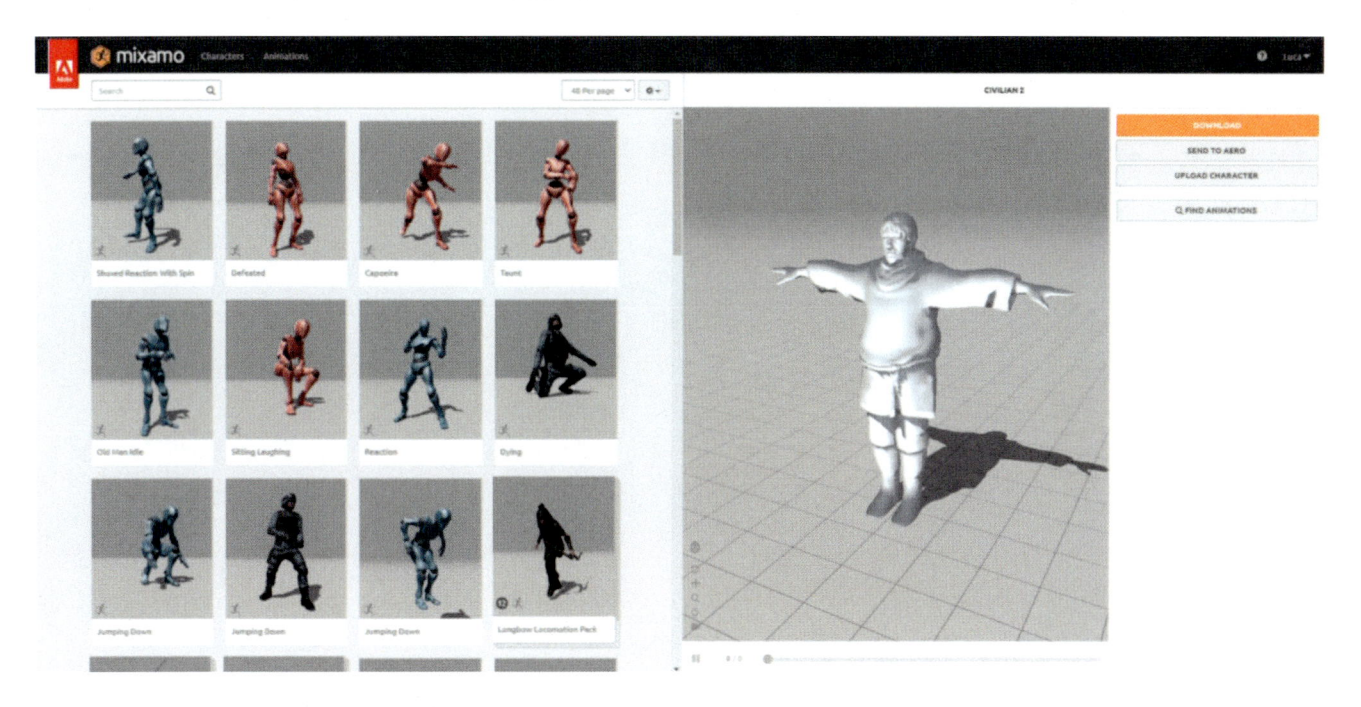

Choose an animation, such as "Looking Around," and export the frames that interest you by using the "Download" command. This feature is especially useful because it allows you to obtain specific poses without having to animate the character manually.

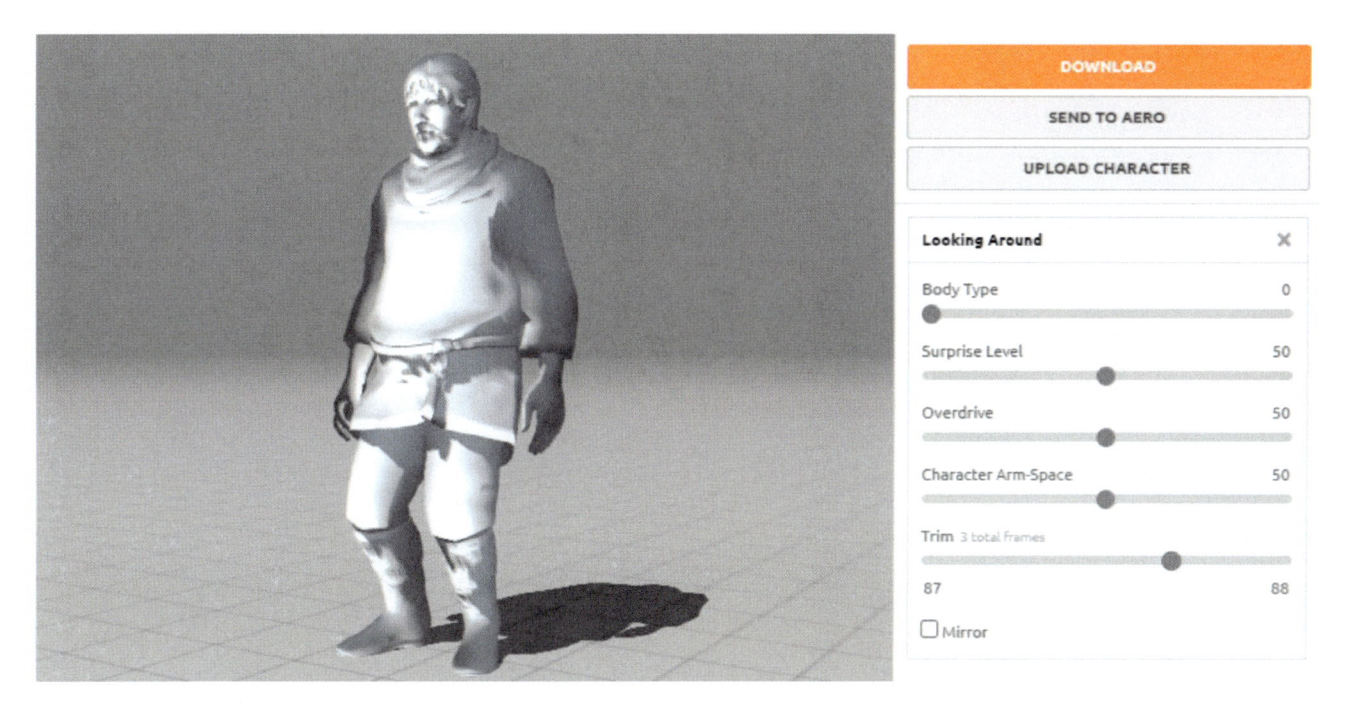

Note that Twinmotion's roadmap includes support for importing animated FBX files. However, in the version I'm currently using, this feature has not yet been released. As of now, this workflow is only useful for composing static scenes. It's reasonable to expect that once the animation functionality is available, you'll be able to save a complete FBX file with the entire animation directly from Mixamo.

If you import the Mixamo-created model directly, you might be unpleasantly surprised to find it not posed correctly in Twinmotion. The right approach in this case is to first import it into a 3D software compatible with animated FBX models. I use 3D Studio Max, but Blender, which is free, works well too.

Once you've imported the model into your chosen software, save it in a standard, non-animated format like OBJ. You can then import it into Twinmotion. Make sure to check that the materials and model dimensions are correct before integrating the asset into your scene.

The settings for rendering the scene using the Path Tracer are as follows:

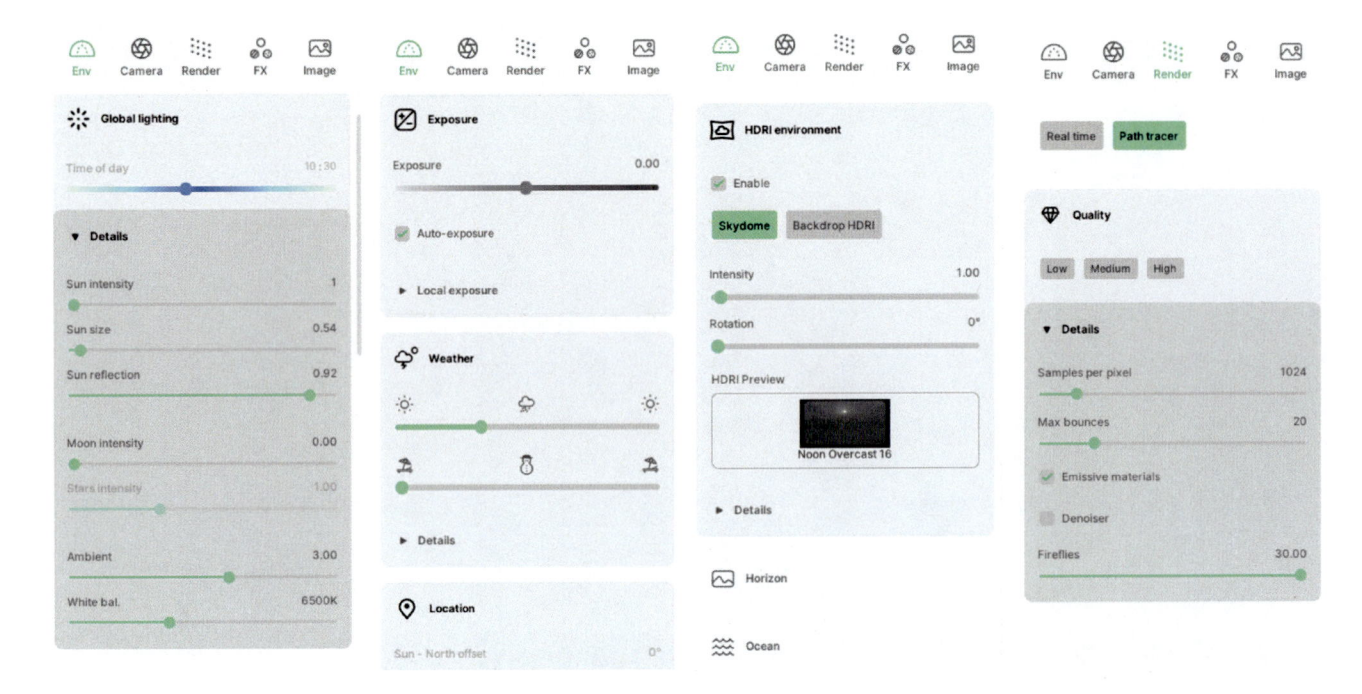

If you switch from Path Tracer to Lumen without changing any parameters, the first thing you'll notice is the reduced influence of the HDRI skydome light. The slightly greenish tint present in the Path Tracer mode disappears, but the quality of the rendering remains significant even without tweaking the environmental settings.

The Lumen engine parameters are set to default! I didn't have to do any optimization activities or particular settings. In this case, the difference is made by the environmental parameters, which are the same as those mentioned earlier for the Path Tracer.

I could show you dozens of examples of unique settings and demonstrate how Twinmotion can handle any kind of wild idea. I'll conclude this chapter with one final setting: a rendering with a typical fantasy appearance. Whether you're aiming for realism or exploring imaginative environments, Twinmotion offers the flexibility to realize your creative vision.

In the above rendering, we've incorporated assets from Sketchfab, Quixel, and BMS. The city is a commercial model that can be purchased on Sketchfab and is called Craco. The frozen sea is a texture sourced from the web and applied to the terrain.

The rock upon which the city rests had several visual flaws. To conceal them, I utilized the 'paint vegetation' feature, selected some rocks, and strategically positioned them over the less convincing parts of the composition.

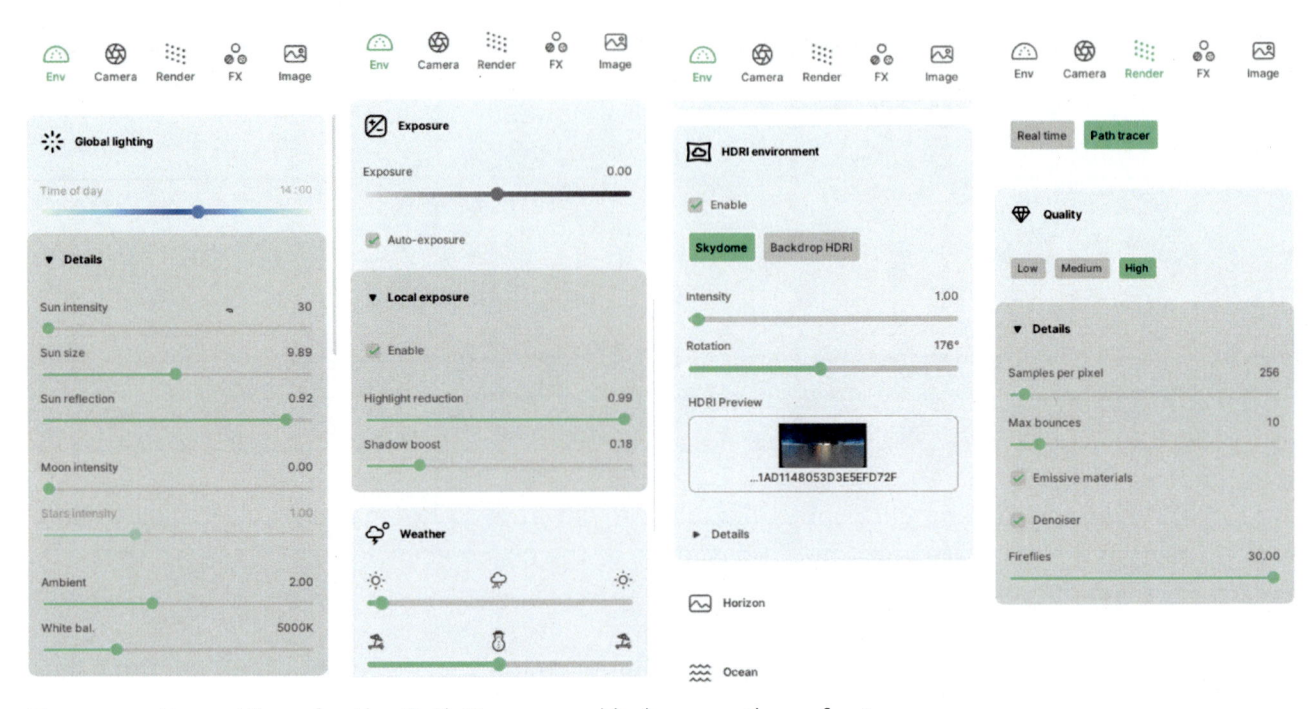

Above are the settings for the Path Tracer, and below are those for Lumen.

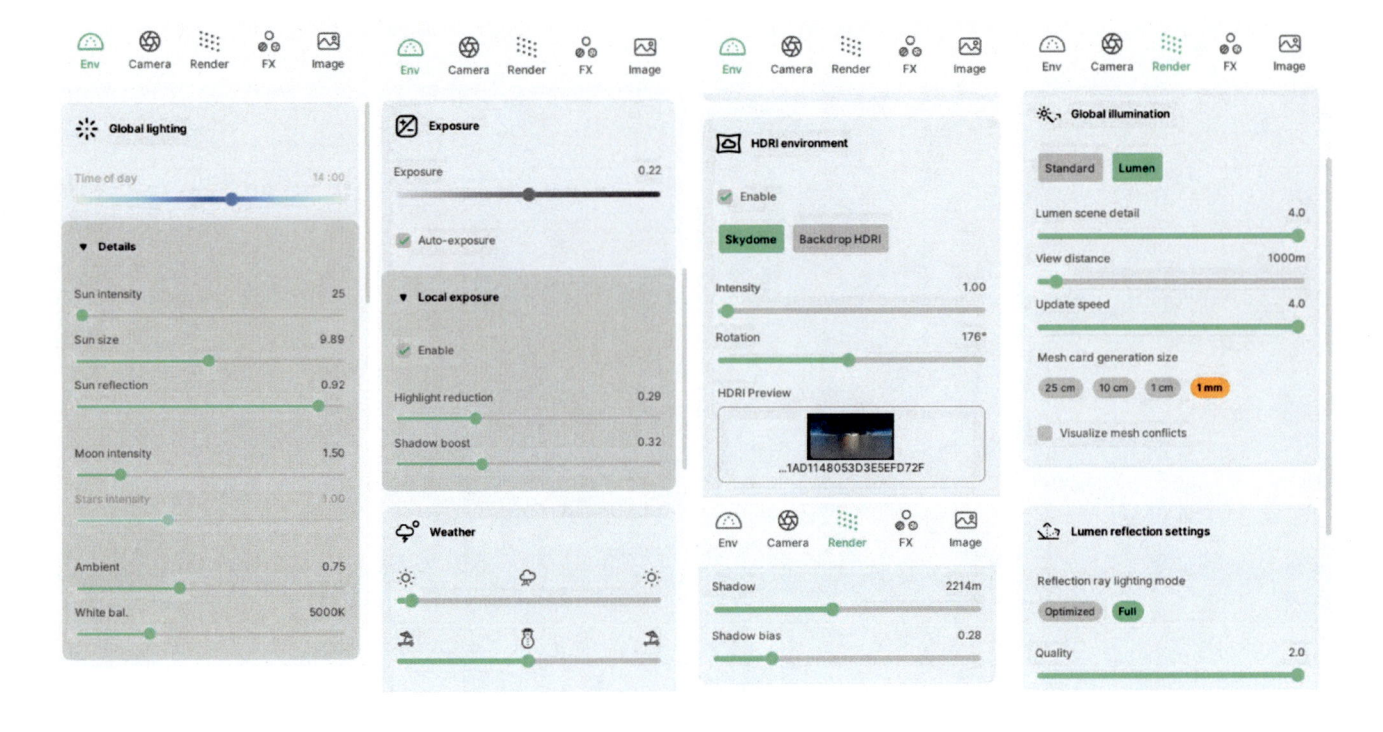

Enter the Matrix: A Look at Cyberpunk Environments

In the expansive world of 3D rendering, the cyberpunk genre stands out for its compelling, visually stimulating elements. Known for its neon-lit cityscapes and dystopian settings, creating a cyberpunk environment in Twinmotion offers a wide range of design possibilities. Setting the mood is a critical first step. Twinmotion comes equipped with various HDRIs and lighting settings, perfectly suited for achieving that signature neon-infused, rain-soaked look that's synonymous with cyberpunk.

Architecture also plays a significant role. The genre often juxtaposes futuristic high-rises with decaying older buildings, reflecting a world in which technological progress hasn't equally benefited everyone. Twinmotion offers a variety of assets that can help you capture this duality. From gleaming skyscrapers to crumbling facades, the software allows for a nuanced approach to building your cityscape.

Textures and materials also come into play. The grime and wear commonly found in cyberpunk settings can be effectively represented using Twinmotion's library of materials, which range from pristine to worn-out, allowing for dynamic contrasts.

Don't forget about the characters populating your scene. For a more authentic touch, consider importing character models that align with the cyberpunk aesthetic. As mentioned in previous chapters, tools like Mixamo can be invaluable for posing and animating these characters to fit naturally into your environment.

Let's start with a classic dystopian image that reveals its photorealism through the type of framing with the use of Depth of Field (DOF), but most importantly, through its richness in details.

The details become more evident in this wider framing.

The shelves feature some models rich with objects; the boxes of screws are composed of several hundred screw models placed inside a plastic container. The use of appropriate materials then made a substantial difference. In 3D rendering, it's these minute details that add layers of realism to a scene.

The images above pertain to the Path Tracer engine. To create the boxes, I had to use software like 3D Studio Max. I sourced an empty box from Sketchfab and, within 3D Studio Max, created some bolts and screws. I then used the scattering function to fill the box, which I subsequently imported as an FBX into Twinmotion. This was fairly time-consuming, but one of the most crucial elements for photorealism is attention to detail.

This meticulous process of modeling and scattering objects in 3D Studio Max before importing them into Twinmotion for the final render allows for a high degree of control over those minute details that contribute significantly to photorealism. While it's an investment of time and effort, the end result speaks for itself, providing a scene rich in complexity and texture.

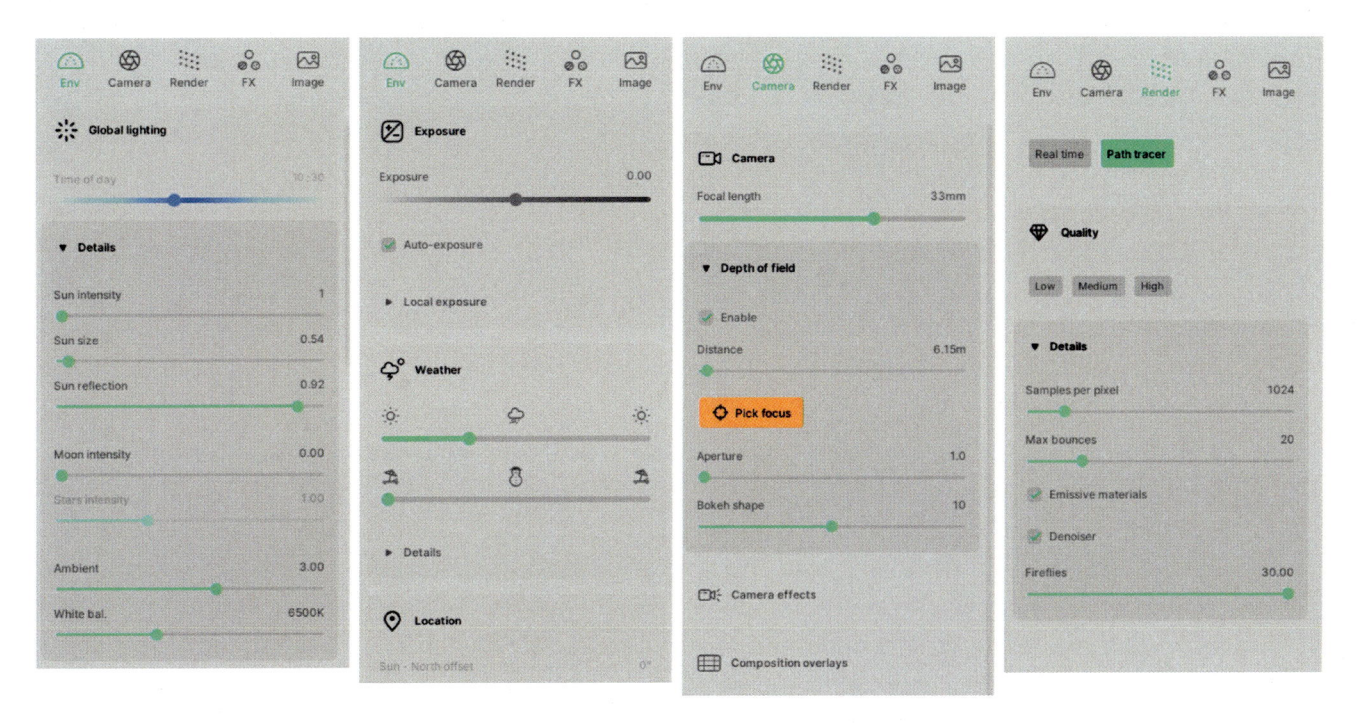

An urban cyberpunk environment paints a vivid picture, saturated with high-tech aesthetics in contrast to a backdrop of societal breakdown. Within this setting, light becomes a crucial storytelling element, cutting through thick layers of fog or illuminating the rain-slick streets of a sprawling metropolis.

Central to the cyberpunk visual style is the artful and deliberate use of colored lighting. Neon signs and holographic displays shimmer with intense colors, casting the streets and alleys in their surreal glow. These colors are not random but chosen for their ability to evoke specific feelings and atmospheres.

Combining lights of specific hues creates an atmospheric tension typical of cyberpunk visuals:

- Cyan and Magenta: This combination feels otherworldly, with the cold blue of cyan contrasting against the warm pink of magenta. It's evocative of the juxtaposition between the digital and the organic, the cold machine versus the warmth of human life.
- Yellow and Blue: Yellow, reminiscent of dirty, artificial light, contrasts starkly against the cool, ambient blue. This pairing encapsulates the dynamic between the grimy, lived-in world and the sleek, advanced technology that permeates it.
- Red and Green: Although less common, when red meets green, it's a direct nod to the coding systems of old computers. It also brings forth a feeling of being in between – not quite here, not quite there, much like the genre itself.

In a cyberpunk setting, these color combinations are not merely aesthetic choices but narrative tools. They tell a story of a world where technology is as much a part of the environment as the air inhabitants breathe. The play of lights against dark, smoke-filled skies, the reflection of neon on wet pavements, and the juxtaposition of deep shadows with vibrant colors are emblematic of a future that is at once familiar and entirely alien.

In any urban setting, the interplay of lights can profoundly alter the mood and ambiance, instantly transforming familiar surroundings into something straight out of a science fiction novel. The cyberpunk aesthetic, characterized by its neon-soaked, contrasting hues, finds its roots not just in fiction but in real urban landscapes that possess a futuristic yet decayed aesthetic.

For example, Hong Kong, with its densely packed skyline, labyrinthine alleys, and bustling streets, provides a perfect example. As darkness descends on the city, it comes alive with a kaleidoscope of lights:

- Neon Signs: Dangling over narrow streets, neon signs in characters and symbols bathe areas like Kowloon in rich shades of green, red, and blue. The inherent decay of some of these signs, flickering or partially burnt out, underscores the cyberpunk feel of a high-tech world in decline.
- Street Food Stalls: Illuminated by bright fluorescent bulbs or LEDs, these bustling hubs emit a stark, usually yellow or white light, creating sharp contrasts with the cooler tones of neighboring neon.
- Billboards and Screens: Giant electronic displays in districts like Causeway Bay or Mong Kok flash advertisements in a myriad of colors, reminiscent of the massive holograms and digital ads often depicted in cyberpunk media.
- Back Alleys: Veins of the city where shadows and light mix in imperfect harmony. A blue neon sign here, a red lantern there, combined with the steam rising from underground vents or food stalls, can create the atmospheric tension emblematic of the genre.
- Reflections: After a rain shower, puddles form on the streets, acting as mirrors for the neon cacophony above. This shimmering reflection is a trademark of the cyberpunk aesthetic, amplifying the interplay of lights and adding depth to the cityscape.

These real-life visuals are what inspired many of the genre's most iconic scenes and show that you don't need a dystopian future to experience the cyberpunk aesthetic. All you need is the right combination of light, color, and urban decay. By understanding and harnessing these elements, even a contemporary city can feel like a portal to a neon-infused future.

The image you can see below is an outstanding testament to how modern rendering technology, such as that offered by Twinmotion, can capture the essence of a scene. This peripheral corner of Hong Kong, captured in the serene aftermath of rain, is bathed in cyan and magenta lights, creating a mesmerizing combination. The depiction pays homage to the true cyberpunk spirit, highlighting how the right color palette, coupled with environmental conditions and expert rendering techniques, can transform an ordinary moment into a scene brimming with atmosphere and emotion.

And here's the same image but with different lighting. The transformation brought about by the change in illumination underscores the profound impact lighting has on mood, ambiance, and perception. While the core elements remain unchanged, the shift in lighting nuances can evoke an entirely different emotion and narrative, showcasing the versatility and power of the visual medium.

Manipulating Environmental Conditions

Mastering the art of 3D rendering isn't just about understanding the software's interface or knowing which buttons to press. It's about capturing the essence of a scene, and a significant part of that involves manipulating environmental conditions. Here's how to play with some of the most common conditions to achieve a desired aesthetic. I will showcase both an indoor and an outdoor example for each environmental condition discussed.

In reference to the parameters outlined in this chapter, many remain directly applicable when employing Lumen. Yet, there's a distinctive difference to be observed concerning the color of the ambient light. Lumen tends to render this with a warmer shade when compared to the Path Tracer. It's crucial to be aware of this nuanced shift, as it can significantly impact the final look and authenticity of your interior scenes. To ensure consistency and realism, adjusting the ambient light color to suit the architectural details and mood becomes essential.

The Dark Side: Night-time Rendering

Night-time rendering is all about subtlety. While the world sleeps, lights from buildings, streets, and cars paint a unique portrait of urban life. To master night-time scenes, focus on contrast. Bright lights should starkly contrast with dark shadows, and reflections play a crucial role, especially in wet conditions. Use ambient lights judiciously, ensuring they don't overpower the primary light sources.

Creating a nighttime rendering of an interior architectural visualization often presents challenges in achieving photorealistic results. At times, the outcomes can appear somewhat cartoonish. Adjusting the saturation (by reducing it) and tweaking the contrast can enhance the realism. For foreground photographic images, activating some depth of field (DOF) can further improve the photorealistic effect.

When introducing artificial lights, I always aim to achieve soft shadows. As we've already explored with the Path Tracer, this is relatively straightforward since adjusting the "radius" parameter of the light softens the shadow. This action, however, is not as feasible with Lumen, or at least not without compromising shadow quality.

In the creation of nighttime renderings, I often overlook just how dark the world can be outside. If you examine photographs of exteriors at night, especially in areas away from the city center with all its neon lights and signs, you'll easily observe how the influence of artificial light diminishes rapidly. The depth of darkness is much more prevalent than we envision and often more pronounced than how we portray it in our renderings.

Below are three authentic examples of nighttime photography taken in places away from the bustling city lights. The sheer depth of darkness in each image is strikingly evident.

In nighttime photography of isolated areas, the impact of darkness is more pronounced than in well-lit cityscapes. Away from city lights, night scenes are dominated by deep shadows, with only a few sources of light piercing the gloom. This kind of setting offers a genuine feel of the night, where darkness prevails, and light sources are sparse. For 3D render artists, replicating this balance between light and dark is key to achieving a realistic depiction of such environments. It's a challenge, but it helps in conveying the true ambiance of nighttime in remote locations.

When aiming for photorealistic images during nighttime, the common approach involves the use of artificial lights. However, with the "moon intensity" parameter, it's feasible to create nighttime renderings lit purely by moonlight. This essentially acts, to some extent, like sunlight. I've never executed nighttime renderings using only the moon, but it's indeed possible to craft evocative, albeit not strictly photorealistic, visuals. Below is an example where moonlight takes center stage.

Let's look at the parameters used for rendering.

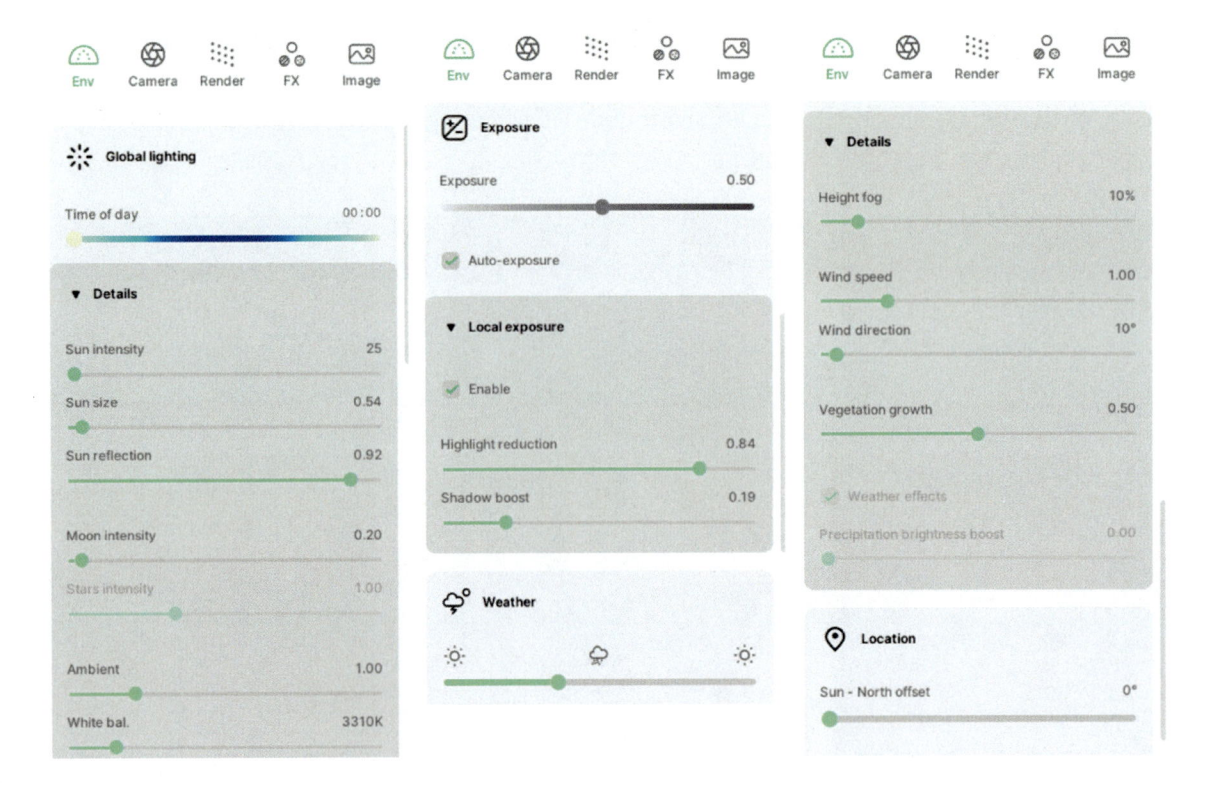

As you can see, I've used a relatively low setting for the Moon intensity. This ensures the moonlight isn't overwhelmingly bright, which would make the rendering appear too flat with an odd contrast.
The Path Tracer parameters are set to 1024 samples and 10 bounces.

Leaving the moonlit scene behind, let's delve into the three images below. They depict nighttime renderings in three distinct environments: an urban setting, an interior space, and a setting with natural elements like vegetation. We'll use these references in subsequent chapters addressing environmental conditions.

The parameters mentioned above are the same ones I employed for these nighttime renderings. The only distinction is found in the middle image of the interior rendering. To avoid artifacts and optimally manage the presence of glass, I adjusted the settings to 2048 samples and 20 bounces. For the third image, the Height Fog parameter is set at 60%.

A New Day: Cloudy Daylight Rendering

Overcast conditions can be some of the most challenging to render. The light is diffused, with soft shadows and a muted color palette. To effectively capture this, reduce the intensity of your primary light source, and lean into ambient lighting. This will help to reproduce the softness that's characteristic of a cloudy day.

In terms of photorealism, I must acknowledge that cloudy conditions produce a unique lighting atmosphere that is particularly conducive to achieving lifelike visuals. The magic behind this lies predominantly in the ambient and diffused lighting. Under cloud cover, the sky essentially acts as a vast diffuser, scattering sunlight evenly and reducing the formation of sharp shadows.

This ambient light, as it's known, is indirect and spreads uniformly, enveloping objects from all angles. This soft, encompassing illumination minimizes harsh contrasts, giving a more consistent and gentle tonality to the scene. Such evenly dispersed lighting emphasizes subtle details in textures and surfaces, enhancing the depth and realism of a render. When this naturally soft and balanced light interacts with the right materials and textures, the scene gains an unparalleled photorealistic quality that is both compelling and believable.

On cloudy days, interior rendering takes advantage of diffused ambient light that enters through windows and openings. Without the direct sunlight, you avoid sharp shadows and intense contrasts. Instead, you get an even, soft illumination inside, reminiscent of what you'd achieve with a softbox in a studio setup.

This even light emphasizes details—textures on walls, grains in fabrics, and the surfaces of furniture become more evident without overwhelming shadows. However, it's important not to let the scene become overly flat. Adding some contrasts, maybe with artificial lighting or reflective surfaces, can help add depth.

In short, using cloudy-day lighting in interior rendering can produce realistic and detailed visuals, making spaces appear calm and evenly lit.

For these renderings as well, I've detailed the environmental settings used.

Sun-Kissed: Rendering in Bright Summer Sunlight

Bright, sunny days, while offering vibrancy and sharp contrasts, come with their own set of challenges when aiming for photorealism in 3D rendering. The intense sunlight can naturally enhance the colors of a scene, leading to the risk of over-saturation where colors appear unnaturally vibrant, pushing the output towards a cartoonish appearance.

Moreover, while well-defined shadows are typical for bright days, they can be overly sharp in renders, making a scene appear more artificial, especially if the shadow edges are too crisp without a soft transition.

With the sun acting as a dominant light source, there's also the challenge of maintaining a balance in the scene. It's not uncommon for some elements to get washed out, with the direct sunlight and its bright reflections leading to areas of the render becoming overexposed, thereby losing essential details. Additionally, while adding a slight bloom effect can effectively capture the sun's brilliance, overusing it can give the scene a dreamy or ethereal appearance, which might not be the desired outcome.

To navigate these challenges, adjustments to parameters like saturation and contrast are crucial. By reducing the saturation, one can avoid overly vibrant colors, and fine-tuning the contrast ensures that the scene maintains its depth. Softening shadow edges and using effects like bloom judiciously can further aid in achieving a realistic sunny render.

Luca Rodolfi - Photorealism with Twinmotion – Raster – Path Tracer - Lumen

Below are the environmental parameters for the rendering shown in the three images above.

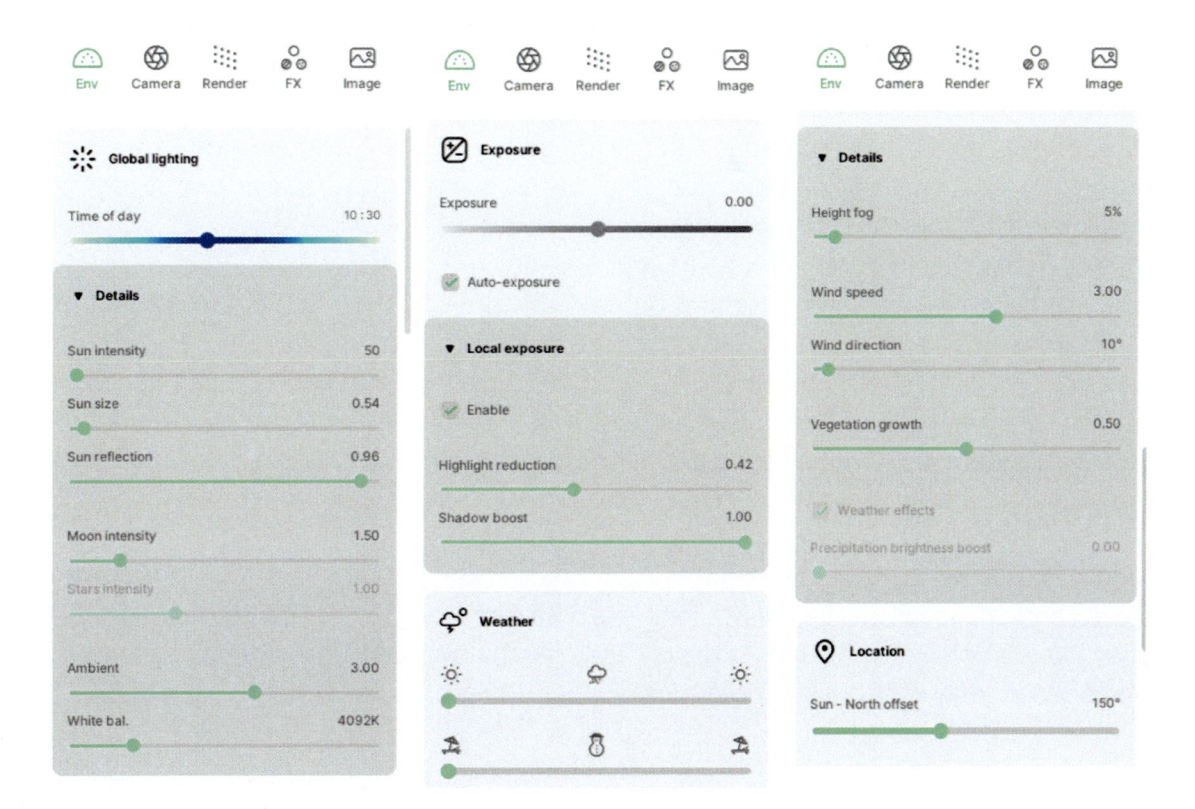

Conclusions

Reaching the culmination of this exploration into the art of 3D rendering and photorealistic graphics provides a moment of reflection. Having journeyed this far, you've not only absorbed vital techniques and methodologies to operate an array of software tools but also delved deep into the nuances of recreating diverse environmental conditions, harnessing the capabilities of rendering engines like Path Tracer, Lumen, and even the less commonly used Raster engine.

Throughout the chapters, you've navigated a spectrum of scenarios: moonlit exteriors, cloud-laden interiors, bustling urban scenes, and serene natural landscapes. Each presented its distinct challenges, but armed with the insights you've now gathered, you stand ready to master them all.

Diving back into chapters for a refresher can be incredibly rewarding. Remember, the path to mastering 3D rendering demands persistent practice. As you march ahead, consider these pivotal reminders:

- Engaging the Right Engine: Path Tracer and Lumen each bear their unique strengths, but understanding when to deploy each, depending on the scene and desired ambiance, is crucial. Additionally, while the Raster engine might not be your go-to choice, understanding its intricacies can offer deeper insight into the broader landscape of rendering.
- Mastering Light Play: As reiterated, light can be both an ally and an adversary. Ensuring the right balance, particularly on sun-drenched days, becomes imperative to sidestep results that veer into over-saturation or a cartoonish realm.
- Devil's in the Details: The minutiae of your scene can significantly sway its realism. Familiarity with settings—be it contrast, saturation, or light intensity—can transform your output from ordinary to outstanding.

In summation, the objective of this book was to arm you with an exhaustive toolkit, amplifying your prowess in 3D rendering. The knowledge and techniques unveiled serve as a launchpad into further graphic exploits, facilitating the crafting of ever more breathtaking and lifelike visuals.

As your journey unfolds, it's vital to remember that the domain of 3D graphics, akin to any art, remains in flux. Keep abreast of new advancements, innovate with fresh techniques, and most importantly, relish the journey. Your ardor and dedication to the craft will invariably radiate in every scene you craft. Here's to pushing boundaries and to brilliant renderings!

Remember, I've used and tested Lumen in Twinmotion using a Beta version of Twinmotion. Some changes might be introduced in the final version. This won't affect what you've learned in this book; you might simply have some additional features and improvements not available today.

Luca Rodolfi

Made in the USA
Las Vegas, NV
02 October 2023